EL Excellence Every Day

The Flip-To Guide for Differentiating Academic Literacy

First Edition

Tonya Ward Singer

Foreword by Jeff Zwiers

A Joint Publication

AT-A-GLANCE

Practical emphasis on mindsets helps teachers create powerful learning environments.

iStock.com/as

CHAPTER 2
ESSENTIAL MINDSETS

"How teachers perceive their students and themselves in relation to them, determine, to a large extent, what the educational experience of students will be."

—Noma LeMoine (2007, p. 6)

MINDSETS MATTER

I start this book with mindsets because they matter more than any strategy.

Seriously.

I can teach at a high level, actively engage students, and use awesome strategies, but none of this will make any difference if I do not value my English learner (EL) students and believe they will succeed.

Bold headings facilitate navigation from vision to reflection to action.

VALUE ENGLISH LEARNERS' ASSETS

VISION: Ensure ELs (and all students) feel affirmed and valued as members of the learning community. Build trusting relationships with ELs that foster safety and belonging, which are foundational to academic risk taking. Value students' home cultures, languages, and life experiences. Help students make intentional connections to their background experiences and home language(s) to deepen their learning.

WHY THIS MINDSET MATTERS

The purpose of this mindset is to ensure every student feels valued and a sense of belonging at school. A sense of belonging is a core psychological need (Maslow, 1943) and impacts student motivation and academic achievement (Goodenow, 1993; Walton & Cohen, 2007).

Without a sense of belonging, human brains go into fight-or-flight mode. Zaretta Hammond (2015) describes the impact of a perceived threat on the brain as an *amygdala hijack*: "When the amygdala sounds its alarm with cortisol, all other cognitive functions such as learning, problem solving or creative thinking stop" (p. 40).

In other words, a student's sense of belonging in a classroom physiologically makes or breaks the learning process. Valuing ELs to foster their sense of belonging in your classroom community is more important than any strategy in this book.

"We cannot downplay students' need to feel safe and valued in the classroom."

—Zaretta Hammond (2015, p. 47)

The symptoms of a student not feeling valued vary by individual—and are often internal. That a student doesn't feel a part of the classroom community can look to the teacher like lack of motivation or lack of initiative for learning. When a student is silent, opts to follow rather than lead, avoids challenge, or gives up quickly, there can be many reasons for such behaviors that are not about the individual student but about the climate we have created within our classroom for the student to thrive. When ELs exhibit such behaviors in an English-dominant classroom, reflect: Do my EL students feel a sense of safety and belonging in our community of scholars? Do they feel affirmation for who they are as individuals, for their unique life experiences, and for the cultural and linguistic assets they bring? What shifts will I make to ensure every EL feels a strong sense of belonging and value in my classroom learning culture?

WAYS WE MIGHT GET STUCK

Valuing EL assets often means valuing what we don't understand. This can be tough as it requires us to see beyond what we know and our own cultural sense of "normal" to value what is "normal" from others' point of view. This requires both humility to be aware of what we don't know and empathy to find value in how others experience and view the world. We can get stuck easily when we:

- MISS OUR OWN CULTURAL LENS: We all have cultural norms and values that are shaped by and shape our reality. These are the lens through which we interpret what is right, normal, just, unjust, important, unimportant, and more. To value students' diverse

3.3 SMALL-GROUP CONVERSATION STRUCTURES

WHAT AND WHY?

Small-group conversation structures are great for engaging a table group or any small group of students in a collaborative conversation. Unlike in a partner conversation, where the student listening will always be the next to talk, in a small-group conversation there are many possible dynamics for turn taking and building up ideas together. Use small-group conversations when you want to add variety or complexity to how students collaborate to discuss ideas.

STRUCTURES FOR SMALL-GROUP CONVERSATIONS

Numbered Heads: Have students at each table count up from one so that each student has a number (1, 2, 3, etc.). Ask a question to elicit discussion. When time is up, select a number and have the student with that number from each table report to the class. This is a go-to structure to give every student an accountable role while leaving conversation dynamics open-ended. A student can opt to be silent during the small-group conversation and still have an important role to listen and be prepared to report for the group.

EL Excellence Every Day

Flip-to engagement strategies help you increase academic conversations and active student participation in any lesson.

Numbered Heads in Context: After reading and annotating a text about ocean pollution, a teacher uses the numbered heads strategy to have students to discuss the effects of human pollution on the ocean environment. First, students discuss the effects in their small groups. Next, the teacher spins a projected spinner to randomly choose which number will report to the whole group. She calls on number 3, and has each student with that number show a silent thumbs-up or thumbs-down if ready to share. If any thumbs are down, she gives the table groups an extra minute to prepare the reporting student to share. Student number 3 from each table then reports an effect of ocean pollution to the group.

Talking Chips: Ask a question to elicit discussion. Each member receives the same number of chips (plastic markers, pennies, etc.). Each time a member contributes to the conversation, he or she tosses a chip into the center of the table. Once individuals have used up their chips, they no longer speak. Continue discussion until all members have exhausted their chips. This structure helps students build awareness about how often they speak in a group and gives them a tool to ensure everyone has a voice in the conversation. Try it occasionally for this purpose, then drop the structure to create room for the natural flow of authentic conversations fueled by engaging topics and texts.

Pass the Stick: At each table group, students pass a "talking stick" or other class-adopted object to designate the speaker. When holding the stick, each student takes a turn contributing to the conversation. This is the most structured approach for ensuring every student has a turn, and it's valuable for accountable participation. The flip side of this structure is it does not encourage students to respond to one another in a natural conversation.

Pass the Stick in Context: To build community, use the pass the stick strategy with getting-to-know-you questions like "What is one thing people may not know about you?" or "What is your favorite song?" Pass the talking stick and give all students an opportunity to share or pass when the stick comes to them. Start the year asking surface-level questions about favorites, and build toward deeper questions to check in with students' emotions, reactions to a current event, or priorities in the world. To review key concepts at the end of any lesson, use the pass the stick strategy to have students reflect in small groups, "What is one thing you want to remember from this lesson?" If you are reading this chapter with colleagues, try the pass the stick strategy to each reflect, "What is one strategy you want to try in your classroom?"

NOTES

_____

_____

Concise directions and relevant examples make research-informed strategies easy to integrate into everyday teaching.

Color-coded tabs and margins help you flip to what you want when you need it: Essentials (Blue), Engagement Strategies (Purple), Support Strategies (Orange) and Lesson-Ready Resources for Academic Literacy Goals (Green).

Flip-to support strategies help you build academic language with academic literacy.

Strong visuals model impactful strategies in relevant literacy contexts.

Emphasis on using (and losing) scaffolds strategically helps to accelerate high-level learning and foster student independence.

Differentiation charts show how to personalize supports to reach students across all levels of language proficiency and literacy learning.

6.1 LINGUISTIC FRAMES

WHAT AND WHY?

A linguistic frame, also known as a sentence frame or response frame, is a partially completed sentence or paragraph that students "fill in" in their oral or written responses to a task. A linguistic frame guides students to use a specific sentence structure and vocabulary when they converse with peers or write in response to a task.

EXAMPLES OF LINGUISTIC FRAMES

I disagree with the idea that _____ because _____.

That's an interesting point. However, you might consider _____.

I agree with your idea that _____. However, I propose _____.

In the article "_____," the author argues that _____.

The most important message in _____ by _____ is _____.

WHEN TO USE LINGUISTIC FRAMES

Use linguistic frames when they help students deepen their thinking and precision with language. Don't use frames when they limit student thinking or language use. Flip to Chapters 9–12 for specific examples of linguistic frames you can use to scaffold students' conversations before, during, and after reading academic texts.

EXAMPLES OF HOW TO DIFFERENTIATE USING LINGUISTIC FRAMES

	Steps to Use the Scaffold	Example
BRIDGING Light or No Support	Engage without linguistic frames. Listen closely to language choices. Only as needed, provide frames or word banks that elevate and extend students' use of academic language to express what they have already communicated in their own words.	In a language arts task to justify inferences with text evidence, a teacher listens to student conversations. She notices that students make claims and read text evidence but don't often explain the evidence. She provides frames and encourages this next-level skill: When the author wrote "_____," this shows that _____. The quote "_____" reveals that _____.
EXPANDING Moderate Support	1. Post *multiple* response frames that are appropriate for the communication task. 2. Introduce the frames and read them together. 3. Listen as students talk with peers, and provide modeling or feedback as needed. 4. When you hear students communicate effectively without using the frames, create new frames to validate and illuminate these additional possibilities for language use.	In a language arts task to justify inferences with text evidence, a teacher posts four frame options for students: One example from the text that demonstrates this is _____. Here on page ___ the author wrote "_____." This shows that _____. I know this because _____.
EMERGING Substantial Support	1. Write one linguistic frame. 2. Read it aloud while pointing to each word. 3. Model one correct response orally and write it under the linguistic frame. 4. Guide students in chorally reading the frame and the model. 5. Structure think-pair-share to have students each create and share their own sentence using the frame. 6. If needed, provide a word bank or bank of phrases students can use to complete the frame.	In an explicit language lesson with emerging ELs, the teacher says, "Today we are going to learn to ask permission in the classroom using the question frame 'May I please _____?' Let's read it together. One question we ask in the classroom [hold up a dull pencil] is 'May I please sharpen my pencil?' Let's read the question together." Students read and say chorally with the teacher, "May I please sharpen my pencil?" Then, the teacher says, "Now you make a request to a partner using the frame 'May I please _____?'"

11.2 JUSTIFY CLAIMS WITH TEXT EVIDENCE

PURPOSE: I support my claims with evidence to strengthen the power of my voice and help others understand my perspective. Justifying claims with evidence is a skill that helps me speak and write with influence in and beyond school.

EXPECT

What students will know and be able to do:

	LITERACY GOALS	LANGUAGE FOR SUCCESS
Support	I can **support** my thinking with evidence and explanation. I can quote or paraphrase relevant **text evidence**. I can **explain** how the text evidence supports my inference.	I can explain my ideas in conversations with peers and also ask questions to encourage peers to justify their ideas (e.g., "How do you know?"). I can write with expository organization to support my claims with evidence and explanation. I can use transitions and referents to connect ideas across sentences.

ENGAGE

What students do to learn and demonstrate current understandings about justifying a claim: Use this routine every time students reread a text to make inferences, draw conclusions, or respond to any open-ended task that requires students to make and justify claims. Watch students during these tasks as a formative assessment before, during, and beyond teaching the skill.

Use a three-step task to engage students:

1. *REREAD:* After reading a text (or excerpt) for literal comprehension, students reread it to make inferences or draw conclusions. This can be a broad task (e.g., making an inference) or a focused task guided by a specific question (e.g., "What is the theme?").
2. *ANNOTATE:* Write inferences in the margin or on a self-stick note. Underline clues in the text that support the ideas.

(246) EL Excellence Every Day

Literacy and language objectives align with college and career readiness standards.

High-level tasks help you put the goal into action to engage all students and gather formative data.

FOCUS	CONVERSATION PROMPTS	POSSIBLE LINGUISTIC FRAMES
Support With Text Evidence	How do you know? What evidence supports your idea? What clues gave you that idea?	One clue that shows me this is _____. I know this because I read _____. One detail that **shows** this is _____. The author **demonstrates this point** when (paraphrase text evidence).
Explain Your Thinking	What do you mean by that? Please explain how that evidence supports your idea.	This quote shows that _____. This means that _____. The quote "_____" **illustrates** that _____. It is **evident** that (repeat claim) when (describe a specific event or detail in text).

WORD BANKS

Nouns to Reference a Text	
text	poem
passage	stanza
story	line
paragraph	

SCAFFOLD EXTENDED CONVERSATIONS

To foster extended conversations and make supporting ideas central to your task, post questions partners can ask one another to elicit more information, such as "How do you know?" and "Tell me more." Flip to "Linguistic Frames for Conversations" (3.8, p. 70) for many examples of prompts and questions students can ask. Read these chorally with students and encourage them to use these in their conversations to ask one another for evidence and explanation to support their ideas.

More than 200 prompts and linguistic scaffolds facilitate academic conversations that deepen language and literacy learning.

Every literacy goal includes a rich menu of lesson-ready supports and a personalization guide to help you reach every unique learner every day.

FOR INFORMATION:

Corwin

A SAGE Company

2455 Teller Road

Thousand Oaks, California 91320

(800) 233-9936

www.corwin.com

SAGE Publications Ltd.

1 Oliver's Yard

55 City Road

London EC1Y 1SP

United Kingdom

SAGE Publications India Pvt. Ltd.

B 1/I 1 Mohan Cooperative Industrial Area

Mathura Road, New Delhi 110 044

India

SAGE Publications Asia-Pacific Pte. Ltd.

3 Church Street

#10-04 Samsung Hub

Singapore 049483

Program Director: Dan Alpert

Associate Editor: Lucas Schleicher

Editorial Assistant: Katie Crilley

Production Editor: Amy Schroller

Copy Editor: Melinda Masson

Typesetter: C&M Digitals (P) Ltd.

Proofreader: Theresa Kay

Indexer: Amy Murphy

Cover and Interior Designer: Scott Van Atta

Marketing Manager: Maura Sullivan

Printed in the United States of America

ISBN 978-1-5063-7787-2

This book is printed on acid-free paper.

SUSTAINABLE FORESTRY INITIATIVE

Certified Chain of Custody
Promoting Sustainable Forestry
www.sfiprogram.org
SFI-01268

SFI label applies to text stock

18 19 20 21 22 10 9 8 7 6 5 4 3 2

CONTENTS

FOREWORD

I spend a lot of time in schools with large numbers of English learners. The range and depth of learning in these settings can be enormous. And yet, as most teachers know all too well, the challenges can also be enormous. Teaching English learners who have widely varying collages of interests, backgrounds, and language proficiencies is the most challenging thing a person can do. We need resources that clearly and quickly help us to meet these diverse instructional needs every day in every classroom. *EL Excellence Every Day: The Flip-to Guide to Differentiate Academic Literacy* is such a resource.

This guide offers a suite of practices and strategies that help teachers to maximize the learning of language and content by English learners and the rest of the class. Powerful instruction, however, cannot thrive without a solid foundation of mindsets and principles, which are clearly described and connected throughout this guide. Mindsets include viewing students' differences as assets rather than liabilities, expecting excellence from every student, and continually reflecting on how students are learning as a result of instruction. Principles include engaging students to intrinsically motivate authentic learning, supporting the development of students' academic conversation skills, and strategically differentiating the scaffolding of language and content learning. While these ideas could fit into several books, *EL Excellence Every Day* adeptly weaves them together in this highly practical guide for real and busy teachers.

Many new content and language standards have entered the scene, all of which place extra high language and content demands on English learners. The increased emphasis on using more complex texts, for example, means that we must sharpen and strengthen our teaching practices for helping students understand and use the language in challenging texts for constructing meaning. Language develops when students engage in learning activities that encourage the transforming ideas and applying them in new ways, engage students in meaningful dialogue with one another, and ask them to be critical consumers of information. This guide provides clear ways for designing and supporting such activities, and it describes how to formatively assess student work in order to know where students are and where they need to go with respect to language and content.

When we attempt to address the complex challenges of teaching diverse English learners across a wide range of grade levels, content areas, and students, there are no simple solutions. But over time we can and must build up unique solutions for each of our settings, based on research, reflection, trial and error, and expert resources. Fortunately, *EL Excellence Every Day* is an expert resource that helps us to clarify the challenges and sculpt the solutions that are needed across a variety of classrooms.

—Jeff Zwiers

ACKNOWLEDGMENTS

"Where do you get such great ideas?" a teaching colleague once asked me. "In meetings like these," I said. "From teachers like you." Thousands of classroom teachers, administrators, students, parents, educational researchers, and authors make up the ecosystem that shapes my thinking and book. I am grateful to all of you for your influence and voices in this important conversation.

I especially want to thank systems leaders and teachers across the United States and Canada whom I am honored to serve in my consulting work, and my former colleagues and students in Houston, Redwood City, South San Francisco, and Roseland school districts. Our collective work has fueled both my sense of the urgency to write this guide and my clarity about how to shape the contents to realize our shared vision for EL students.

A humble thank you to the many authors and researchers I cite within this work. Keep researching and writing, as I love learning from you. Jeff Zwiers, thank you for influencing my work on conversations, and for your beautiful foreword. Thank you, Zaretta Hammond, for your insightful feedback and collaboration.

Bill Singer, Erin Earnshaw, and Kim Edwards, thank for opening your classroom doors to ongoing co-teaching and photo shoots. Thank you to Erin and her student Ariel Woodson for the exemplar in this text. To my friend Penny Hastings, thank you for helping create beautiful anchor charts.

To all reviewers named on the next pages, thank you for your valuable insights throughout the writing process. Thank you, also, to Venus Cenizal, Kim Nguyen, Ann DuBois, Dr. Marlene Bautista, and Cristina Huizar for your contributions to our focus group at the C.A.B.E. conference.

Thank you Goretti Barragan Hamlin and Angelica Salas, for your feedback on my Spanish dedication. Like many ELs, I especially appreciate peer feedback and encouragement before I take the risk to publish in a second language.

To my editor, Dan Alpert, I appreciate your editorial expertise and your heartfelt presence that always inspires me to be my best self. Thank you to my dream team at Corwin and SAGE: Maura Sullivan, Lucas Schleicher, Scott Van Atta, Mia Rodgriguez, Melinda Mason, and Amy Schroller, for collaborating to bring all the elements of design and content into synthesis. Betsy Lane, thank you for being my go-to copy editor and editing my book proposal, the catalyst for this work!

I appreciate Lisa Tamayo, Deborah Sandweiss, Caroline Hinkle, Taya Hall, Clare Venet, and my community of friends and family for fueling me and helping me find balance. Bill Singer, I am grateful for our shared adventures growing together as multilingual learners, teachers, and parents of our beautiful boys. Alec and Mateo, les amo muchisimo. Thank you for reminding me every day that each student in our schools is precious and unique.

PUBLISHER'S ACKNOWLEDGMENTS

Corwin gratefully acknowledges the contributions of the following reviewers:

Marlene Batista, EdD
Director of English Learners
Oxnard School District
Oxnard, CA

Michele R. Dean, EdD
University Field Placement Coordinator
and Lecturer
California Lutheran University
Thousand Oaks, CA

Elaine Ealy, EdD
Middle School Teacher and
Adjunct Professor
Crestwood Middle School—Palm Beach
County School District
Royal Palm Beach, FL

Erin Earnshaw
8th Grade ELA/History Teacher
Mark West Charter Middle School
Santa Rosa, CA

Terri Fradette
Assistant Superintendent Learning Services
Greater Saskatoon Catholic Schools
Saskatoon, SK, Canada

Carmen Gordillo, EdD
Literacy Specialist and Rutgers Part-Time
Lecturer
Liberty Middle School
West Orange, NJ

Zaretta Hammond
Owner/Senior Consultant
Transformative Learning Solutions
Pinole, CA

Kathy Harris
Instructional Coach
Piner-Olivet Union School District
Santa Rosa, CA

Yolandia Hodge
Middle School ELA Teacher
E.E. Jetter K–8 School
Millington, TN

Cristina Huizar
EL TOSA
Oxnard School District
Oxnard, CA

Wendy Hyshka
EAL Consultant
Greater Saskatoon Catholic Schools
Saskatoon, SK, Canada

Rebecca Irwin-Kennedy
Assistant Principal
Arlington Public Schools
Arlington, VA

Molly Lee
Second Grade Teacher
Highland Elementary School
Silver Spring, MD

Jennifer Martínez
Curriculum Specialist
Cali Calmécac Language Academy
Windsor, CA

Lynne McCune
Literacy Specialist
Colchester Public Schools
Colchester, CT

Alicia Nutall
Instructional Support Specialist
Shelby County Schools
Memphis, TN

Andrea Quintana, NBCT
Instructional Coach
Zuni Elementary School
Albuquerque, NM

Rebecca Cox Rocha
Principal
Cesar Chavez Language Academy
Santa Rosa, CA

Shaneena Rolfe
Early Literacy Consultant
Independent Consultant
Memphis, TN

Kulbir Sanhu
Second Grade Teacher
Meadow View Elementary
Santa Rosa, CA

Sara Stewart-Lediard
Teacher Librarian
Traner Middle School
Reno, NV

Katherine Strach
Literacy and Language Consultant
Independent Consultant
San Mateo, CA

Adrianne Sublett
Literacy Instructional Advisor
Shelby County Schools
Memphis, TN

Maureen Torrez, NBCT
Graduate Student MA Education Leadership
Harvard Graduate School of Education
Boston, MA

Para Humberto Ballesteros y Juana Cruz Pérez.
Cuando llegué a México de otro país y cultura,
su familia siempre me hizo sentir como en casa como parte de la familia.
Gracias por inspirar el trabajo que me ha apasionado.

For Humberto Ballesteros and Juana Cruz Pérez,
When I arrived in Mexico from another country and culture,
your family always made me feel at home like part of the family.
Thank you for inspiring my life's work.

ABOUT THE AUTHOR

Tonya Ward Singer is a language and literacy consultant who helps K–12 educators transform teaching for equity and EL achievement. Teachers and administrators describe her work as groundbreaking, dynamic, practical, relevant, and impactful.

Tonya's bestselling book, *Opening Doors to Equity: A Practical Guide to Observation-Based Professional Learning,* empowers teachers to engage in courageous, job-embedded professional learning. *Opening Doors to Equity* was a Learning Forward Book Club selection and recognized by the U.S. Department of Education via Teach to Lead's Leadership Lab.

Tonya has co-authored EL and literacy curricula for major publishers and publishes creative writing in literacy journals and performs on the spoken-word stage. With more than 20 years of experience in education, Tonya has taught at multiple grade levels and served districts as a reading specialist, an EL specialist, and a facilitator of transformative professional learning.

A parent, poet, and lover of the High Sierras, Tonya is fluent in Spanish and can negotiate the price of a tomato in Mandarin Chinese. Connect with Tonya on Twitter @TonyaWardSinger or via her website www.tonyasinger.com.

SECTION I
ESSENTIALS
FOR EL EXCELLENCE

iStock.com/kali9

CHAPTER 1

INTRODUCTION

"Every teacher is a language teacher . . . We need to bring all teachers to the table when it comes to designing curricula, assessments, and instruction for ELLs."

—Leslie Nabors Oláh (2008)

WHY THIS BOOK?

How do I reach every child? I am driven by this question, and have been since the very first day I became a teacher decades ago. I teach because I want to make a difference. I teach because I love the "aha" moments when a student suddenly understands or excels in a new way.

No matter what I teach or who is in my class, there is always a universal truth: Students are unique. Students come to me with a wide range of interests, abilities, strengths, and challenges. They learn in different ways. No one lesson or strategy is ever the perfect solution for every child.

This is what I love about teaching. It's also what can make me feel overwhelmed when I am the only teacher in a whole class of students trying to personalize teaching for every child. The need to differentiate teaching is real in any classroom, whether or not we have English learners (ELs) in our class.

For that reason, you will find the strategies in this book valuable for helping you reach *all* students.

That said, this book is about more than just good teaching. It specifically empowers you with the most effective, research-based instructional practices to help you ensure ELs thrive with rigorous academic language and literacy learning.

HELPING EVERY TEACHER EXCEL TEACHING ELS

Three in four U.S. classrooms have at least one student who is an English learner. Even in schools with EL specialists, ELs spend the majority of their instructional day with core teachers. EL excellence with rigorous content learning requires *every* teacher to be an effective teacher for ELs.

In my international work as a literacy specialist, EL specialist, and professional learning leader, I see a need for what I have created in this book. It is a breakthrough guide, unlike any EL strategy book to date. Here are four reasons why:

- PRACTICAL: Unlike other EL books that focus on theory, this book emphasizes daily action. The flip-to organization helps you apply research-based approaches to everyday teaching.
- RIGOROUS: Unlike EL resources that water down academic expectations, this book helps you raise expectations while personalizing teaching to ensure ELs (and all students) thrive.
- INTEGRATED: Unlike EL resources that emphasize EL strategies in isolation, this book helps you integrate EL strategies into core literacy routines to meet college and career readiness standards.
- STRATEGIC: Unlike EL resources that prescribe strategies as the solution, this book helps you use (and lose) strategies in a reflective process of inquiry about impact.

Based on your role, you will appreciate this book for different reasons.

CORE TEACHERS: You want to find the strategies you need, when you need them. I wrote this flip-to guide to make your job easier. It doesn't add to your plate but helps you amplify the impact of what you teach every day.

EL TEACHERS: This book helps you build academic language directly aligned to the types of listening, speaking, reading, and writing tasks that are often most challenging for ELs in core classrooms. If you co-teach and collaborate with core teachers, this book helps you get specific together about goals, where ELs are in relationship to those goals, and what specific strategies to use to ensure their success.

TEACHER LEADERS AND COACHES: You want to empower your colleagues with strategies and pedagogy to raise student achievement. Use Sections I–III to build teaching capacity in strategies to value, engage, and support ELs with rigorous learning. Use Section IV as a flip-to reference to address your highest-priority literacy goals.

ADMINISTRATORS: You want to prevent long-term ELs. You want to increase student engagement, raise literacy achievement, and ensure all learners thrive with collaboration, critical thinking, and other 21st century competencies. Engage teachers in using Chapters 2–7 to build essential mindsets and strategies to engage and support ELs. Use Section IV as a go-to resource to address high-priority goals for EL achievement through rigorous expectations, active engagement, data-driven differentiation, and reflection to refine teaching for impact.

TEACHER EDUCATORS IN HIGHER EDUCATION: You want to ensure every new educator is fully prepared to thrive teaching English learners and Standard English learners. Use this book to help preservice teachers translate theories of language acquisition into classroom-based mindsets and actions. Facilitate collaborative opportunities for teacher candidates to use this resource to co-plan, co-teach, co-observe, and co-reflect on impact to build both their acumen with strategies *and* their self-direction as lifelong learners to always use formative data to refine teaching.

WHO ARE ELS?

An English learner is a student who speaks another language besides English and has yet to demonstrate full proficiency in English on local measures of English proficiency. Students classified as "EL" are as diverse and different from one another as any students in your classroom. ELs come to school with a wide range of home languages, cultures, and proficiency levels in English. Some ELs speak no English; others have high levels of oral proficiency and only need support with academic language and literacy to thrive in schools. Other terms we often use to communicate the diversity within school EL populations include the following:

- **NEWCOMER:** An EL new to U.S. schooling with emerging English proficiency.

- **RECLASSIFIED FLUENT ENGLISH PROFICIENT (R-FEP):** An EL student who was reclassified to fluent based on local criteria including multiple measures such as an English proficiency exam, writing samples, standardized tests, and/or teacher discretion.

- **LONG-TERM ENGLISH LEARNER (LTEL):** A student who has been in U.S. schools for six or more years and has not been reclassified to R-FEP. Note this definition varies by region. LTELs, and students at risk of becoming LTELs, make up a significant percentage of the EL population in many regions. In California, for example, where LTEL is measured as 7+ years in California schools, 74 percent of secondary ELs are LTELs (Californians Together, 2015).

- **STANDARD ENGLISH LEARNER (SEL):** A student fluent in an English dialect with rules of grammar and syntax that are different from Standard English. African American Vernacular English, Chicano English, and Hawaiian Pidgin are three examples of primary languages that are cultural and linguistic assets for SELs in the United States.

- **STUDENT WITH LIMITED OR INTERRUPTED FORMAL EDUCATION (SLIFE):** This term refers to a small percentage of the EL population who have limited or interrupted formal schooling in their native language and are below grade level in most academic skills. Reasons for limited formal schooling vary widely by students who may be refugees, migrant students, or students who have had limited opportunities for schooling in their home country due to location, poverty, or other variables.

- SEAL OF BILITERACY STUDENTS: Many schools, districts, and states in the United States now award a Seal of Biliteracy to recognize students who have studied and attained proficiency in two or more languages by high school graduation. Both ELs and students who begin school only speaking English can strive for this accomplishment! Dual-language learners are students learning in two languages on a path toward biliteracy.

WHAT IS ENGLISH PROFICIENCY?

English proficiency is what we call the continuum of how well a student understands and communicates in English. Imagine a color spectrum from light blue to medium blue to dark blue with every subtle shade of blue in between. Language proficiency is a similar concept, only instead of color it is a continuum of many subtle shades from no comprehension or use of the language to full academic proficiency to communicate effectively listening, speaking, reading, and writing in any context.

How we measure or label English proficiency varies by school district, region, and country. For ease of communication in this book, I'll refer to stages of English proficiency as three general levels:

- Emerging
- Expanding
- Bridging

If these terms are different from the ones you use, don't worry, as the general concept of chunking proficiency into broad stages is the same. Figure 1.1 is a quick guide to help you connect terms for proficiency levels in this book to ones you might use.

FIGURE 1.1

ENGLISH PROFICIENCY LEVELS

This Book	California ELD Standards	WIDA	ELPA21	Texas ELPS/TELPAS
Bridging	Bridging	Reaching	5	
		Bridging	4	Advanced High
Expanding	Expanding	Expanding	3	Advanced
		Developing		
Emerging	Emerging	Emerging	2	Intermediate
		Entering	1	Beginning

Note: ELD = English Language Development, ELPA21 = English Language Proficiency Assessment for the 21st Century, ELPS = Texas English Language Proficiency Standards, and TELPAS = Texas English Language Proficiency Assessment System. WIDA is the name of the organization formerly known as World-Class Instructional Design and Assessment.

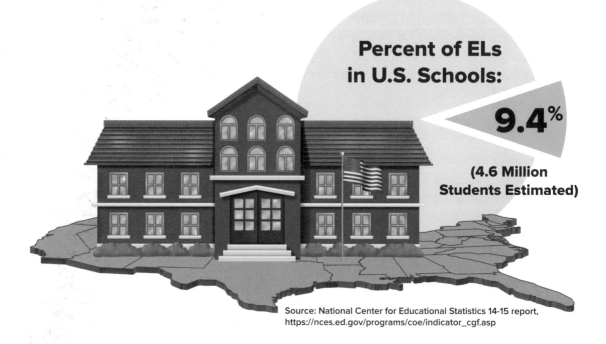

Percent of ELs in U.S. Schools:

9.4%

(4.6 Million Students Estimated)

Source: National Center for Educational Statistics 14-15 report, https://nces.ed.gov/programs/coe/indicator_cgf.asp

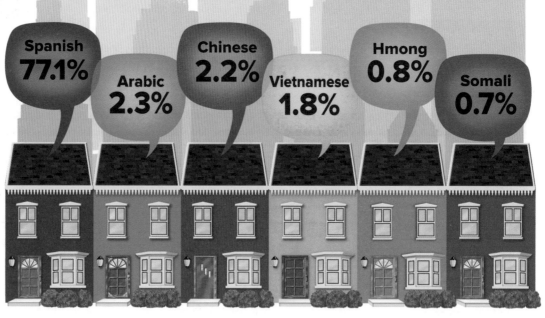

Home Languages of EL Students

Most commonly reported home languages other than English:

Spanish
77.1%

Arabic
2.3%

Chinese
2.2%

Vietnamese
1.8%

Hmong
0.8%

Somali
0.7%

Source: National Center for Educational Statistics 14-15 report, https://nces.ed.gov/programs/coe/indicator_cgf.asp

Birthplace of EL Students in U.S. Schools

KEY: Born in USA   Foreign Born

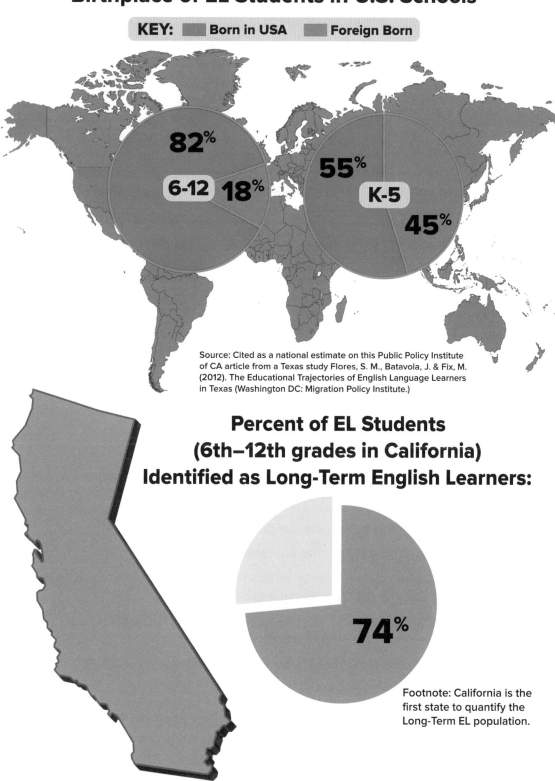

82%
6-12 18%

55%
K-5
45%

Source: Cited as a national estimate on this Public Policy Institute of CA article from a Texas study Flores, S. M., Batavola, J. & Fix, M. (2012). The Educational Trajectories of English Language Learners in Texas (Washington DC: Migration Policy Institute.)

Percent of EL Students (6th–12th grades in California) Identified as Long-Term English Learners:

74%

Footnote: California is the first state to quantify the Long-Term EL population.

LANGUAGE ASSETS: The term *English learner* refers to English proficiency level only. It doesn't tell us anything about how many other languages a student speaks, understands, reads, or writes. Some ELs are bilingual. Other ELs are trilingual! Some ELs are academically proficient at grade level in their primary language. Some ELs are experts at translating on the spot, a complex and creative skill. Some ELs have oral fluency in another language but don't have academic literacy in that language as they have only attended school in English.

In an ideal world, schools help every student be fluent and literate in multiple languages. I certainly wish my local K–8 school provided my own monolingual sons the opportunity to build literacy in multiple languages. I grew up monolingual with a deep desire to be able to communicate in Spanish. U.S. schools didn't help me realize this vision, but thankfully I had the opportunity to immerse myself in Spanish-speaking communities in the United States and to live and work in both Mexico and Guatemala long enough to think, dream, and express in two languages. I am grateful I lived and worked a year in China, long enough to learn basic communication in Mandarin Chinese—and to experience what it is like to be an outsider to the dominant culture, illiterate in the dominant language of my environment. I became multilingual to expand my world, connect to people with different backgrounds, and see beyond the norms of my home community. Imagine if every child had the opportunity to build such global competency in school!

Research shows that effective bilingual programs are among the most powerful ways to ensure ELs thrive with academic English and rigorous core assessment in English (Thomas & Collier, 2002). Bilingual programs that are systematically and strategically structured to reflect the best practices in the field do not slow English literacy or language learning at all. On the contrary, they accelerate it.

Even if you, like most U.S. teachers, teach ELs in an English-only context and only speak English, you can still build on your EL students' language assets. In Chapter 2 and throughout this guide, you'll find strategies to value and build on students' primary language(s) in your everyday teaching.

EVERY STUDENT IS UNIQUE

Every classroom population is unique. Every school population is unique. When we communicate with broad labels like "EL," our classrooms include a wide range of students:

- Students who speak English as their only language (EO)

- Students enrolled in Gifted and Talented Education (GATE)

- Students with individualized education programs (IEPs), enrolled in a resource specialist program (RSP), or receiving special education (SPED)

- Students who qualify for free and reduced-price lunch (students from low-income households)

- Students whose families move across state and national borders for work (Migrant Education Program participants)

When we look beyond labels to get more personal, our classrooms include a wide range of unique personalities, interests, experiences, strengths, and needs. Students often fit the criteria for more than one acronym (e.g., EL and GATE) and defy the definition of each broad category in their own unique ways.

WHAT ABOUT MY STUDENTS WHO AREN'T ELS?

This is a great question most core teachers ask when we talk about EL instruction. It's important because most core classrooms include both ELs and non-ELs.

A common assumption is that to use EL-specific strategies we need to work with ELs in a separate group and get the rest of the students to do something on their own. That's one approach but not the one I emphasize here. In this book, I emphasize teaching the entire class to the high-level expectations of your content and literacy standards and then personalizing instruction based on the unique strengths and needs you identify as students engage in your lessons.

It is not productive to assume that one strategy must be used for all ELs and not for other students. Collaborative conversations, for example, benefit *everyone* every day. Linguistic scaffolds, such as linguistic frames (aka sentence frames), can benefit some ELs and hinder others. It all depends on the task and the students. The key to effective teaching of ELs (and all students) is engaging students in a productive challenge, observing them, and then designing or refining teaching to meet their needs.

You will notice that even though this book emphasizes ELs, many of the specific scaffolds and strategies will be valuable for helping *all* students grow their skills with academic literacy and communication:

- Students not yet at grade-level expectations in literacy
- Students new to making and justifying academic claims
- Students who are silent in class or dominate conversations
- Students who use informal language in academic communication
- Students needing more precise word choice or sentence variety
- Students who benefit from peer conversations to build background, deepen understandings, and build proficiency articulating complex ideas

It is likely that every student in your classroom will benefit from strategies and scaffolds in this book. It is also likely that when you pay close attention to your goals and your students, you notice that ELs and non-ELs may need the same lesson or support. Other times you notice that some ELs need specific attention in one area that other ELs don't need. What support is needed will always change based on the goal, the students, and what they have just learned.

This is why I don't answer the question "What about my students who aren't ELs?" with a specific instructional recipe. Instead, I honor your professionalism as a teacher to reflect continuously on the following questions: What are my goals? What can my students understand and do related to my goals? What instruction and supports will I provide to ensure student success? This flip-to guide helps you engage in this continuous process of reflective teaching to ensure all students, including all ELs, thrive.

TEACHING BEYOND THE "EL" LABEL

Categories such as "English learner" help us group similar needs together and also are often very limiting. When we overgeneralize what students need based on the categories we assign to them, we typically end up teaching in the dark. By "teaching in the dark," I mean we make an assumption and teach to the assumption, not to the students. Assuming, for example, that because a student is EL we must always teach that student using a specific EL strategy is problematic. It's like teaching with a blindfold.

This is why this book, first and foremost, helps you personalize teaching to reach and teach the unique *individuals* in your classroom. Yes, this book will help you integrate the most high-impact strategies for EL achievement into your daily teaching. However, don't expect any one-size-fits-all directives to teach students based on a general label like "EL." We are going to engage all students, watch all students, and in this context get specific about how to help each and every unique EL thrive in your classroom.

CORE PEDAGOGY FOR EL EXCELLENCE

Six essential verbs shape the core pedagogy and organization of this book. The six foundational mindsets and actions are as follows:

1. VALUE: Relationships are at the heart of effective teaching. Effective teachers of ELs foster relationships with ELs based on mutual respect. One way to value ELs is to see students' multilingualism as an asset, not a problem. We value ELs when we recognize that different cultures, languages, and experiences are not inferior to our own and when we are interested in learning the diverse assets each student brings to school.

2. EXPECT: Students rise (or fall) to the level of a teacher's expectations. Low expectations for ELs and students of color are a reality we must be proactive to address. We make high expectations a reality when we value ELs, have clear success criteria, and use supports strategically to help ELs thrive with high-level learning.

3. ENGAGE: No matter how dynamic our lessons, if ELs are in sit-and-get mode, they will not deeply learn content or academic language. Effective teachers use a variety of strategies in every lesson to actively engage ELs and all students including relevance, peer conversations, and actions (e.g., movement, annotation, and writing).

4. OBSERVE: As we engage students, we observe what they do and listen to what they say to learn more about their thinking, strengths and challenges with our content, and language goals. We use every task as an opportunity to gather formative data. When students are silent, unengaged, or struggling, we reflect to change our approach. When students thrive, we notice their strengths and build on them in subsequent lessons.

5. SUPPORT: Effective teachers use supports strategically to engage and challenge ELs. Being strategic is essential and requires paying close attention to students to notice the strengths and challenges they bring to each task. Using real-time data to choose or lose scaffolds is at the heart of effective teaching with ELs.

6. REFLECT: Effective teachers own their impact and continuously reflect to refine how they teach so that all students succeed. Owning impact is the most important mindset for equity and means that when a student struggles, a teacher reflects, "What will I change about *my* instruction to ensure this student succeeds?"

Using these verbs in synthesis is important, as together they shape the continuous process of teaching for impact. Figure 1.2 represents the mindsets and reflective teaching cycle that are essential to ensure everyday excellence for ELs—and all students.

Using this cycle, effective teachers continuously reflect on the following questions:

- **EXPECT:** What are my goals for student learning?
- **ENGAGE:** How will students demonstrate success?
- **OBSERVE:** What can students now understand and do related to my goals?
- **SUPPORT:** What instruction and scaffolds will I provide to ensure student success?
- **REFLECT:** How did my instruction impact student learning? How will I adapt my approach to ensure every learner thrives?

The verb *value* is not a separate step but the ever-present climate we create by valuing all students in our classroom for the assets they bring including their home language(s), cultural backgrounds, and unique experiences. See Chapter 2 for specific actions to create a climate in which every EL feels valued as a scholar capable of excellence. Creating such a climate is as important to learning as oxygen is to breathing. Without it, any instructional approach you use will likely fail.

FIGURE 1.2

ESSENTIALS FOR EL EXCELLENCE EVERY DAY

EXPECT EXCELLENCE

ENGAGE > OBSERVE

REFLECT < SUPPORT

VALUE EL ASSETS

MORE THAN "GOOD TEACHING"

This cycle represents good teaching for *all* students, not just ELs. This emphasis is intentional because effective teaching for all students is the foundation of effective teaching with ELs. In addition to good teaching, ELs need teachers who understand the assets multilingual students bring to their learning and who can build on ELs' linguistic, cultural, and academic strengths. ELs need core teachers who understand the linguistic demands of the texts and tasks they teach and who can use scaffolds and conversation structures to effectively teach content *and* academic language in tandem.

This book emphasizes these EL-specific essentials in the context of the reflective teaching cycle for three important reasons:

1. **It's effective**—High expectations, active student engagement, and data-driven reflective teaching are consistently highlighted in research as essential for instructional improvement (Carrasquillo & Rodríguez, 2002; Darling-Hammond & Schon, 1996; Rosenthal & Jacobsen, 1968). EL strategies used without a data-driven reflective teaching process can actually hinder ELs by watering down expectations or creating dependent learners.

2. **It's connected**—Core literacy teachers, first and foremost, teach all students core literacy. Whether a teacher has one EL or many, the most useful EL strategies are those that directly align with what teachers teach every day. Sections I–III of this book introduces core strategies, and Section IV helps you apply them to specific literacy goals.

3. **It's practical**—The flow of this go-to guide fits naturally with the planning and instructional flow reflective teachers use every day. You can find what you want, when you want it, to both strengthen your reflective teaching for all students *and* meet the needs of ELs.

HOW THIS GUIDE HELPS YOU EVERY DAY

In the context of helping *all* students thrive with your core content, this book helps you excel in reaching English learners. This is a flip-to guide to reference when planning and teaching every day. Here's what you'll find:

Section I: ESSENTIALS FOR EL EXCELLENCE

Chapter 1: INTRODUCTION Learn the core pedagogy for EL excellence and how to use this guide.

Chapter 2: ESSENTIAL MINDSETS Learn three essential mindsets, how we can get stuck, and strategies for immediate action.

Section II: ENGAGE

Chapter 3: ENGAGE EVERY EL Flip to strategies in this chapter to make collaborative conversations and accountable participation central to daily teaching.

Chapter 4: SUPPORT ELs STRATEGICALLY Learn how to support language and concepts strategically without lowering expectations. Gain strategies and a flip-to guide to differentiate with ease.

Chapter 5: BUILD BACKGROUND Use this flip-to chapter to find strategies to connect to students' prior experiences, pre-teach vocabulary, and build conceptual understandings before any lesson.

Chapter 6: SCAFFOLD LANGUAGE DURING A TASK Use this flip-to chapter to find strategies to scaffold students' language use (vocabulary, grammar, or text-level organization) during any speaking or writing task.

Chapter 7: TEACH LANGUAGE BEYOND A TASK Use this flip-to chapter to find mini-lessons to deepen students' understanding of how English works.

Flip-to Tip:
Anytime you are planning for a specific literacy goal (e.g., asking questions, identifying main ideas, or justifying claims with text evidence), flip to the table of contents after the green "IV. Apply" tab. Choose your priority and flip to it to find a wealth of ready-to-use tools that make teaching for EL excellence a breeze.

Section IV: APPLY STRATEGIES TO DIFFERENTIATE ACADEMIC LITERACY

Use this flip-to section to apply the essentials for EL excellence to differentiate close reading, conversations, and writing with text evidence.

Chapter 8: MAKE EL EXCELLENCE ROUTINE Learn a four-step close reading routine to use with any classroom text.

Chapter 9: ANTICIPATE Use Chapters 9–11 to differentiate each step of the routine based on your literacy goals and your students.

Chapter 10: READ TO UNDERSTAND

Chapter 11: READ TO ANALYZE AND INFER

MAKING EL EXCELLENCE ROUTINE

In my work leading professional learning, I see what you see every day: the challenge of applying theory to daily teaching. It's easy to learn new strategies. It's hard to make them central to how we teach every day.

There is also a challenge of initiative overload: too many different demands on teachers coming from too many different directions. It's human nature to get excited about a new silver-bullet solution (e.g., strategy, curriculum, training, or initiative) and much more challenging to synthesize what we know to strategically address the needs of students in our unique teaching contexts.

I address both of these challenges in this flip-to guide by applying my favorite high-level thinking skill: synthesis.

A SYNTHESIS OF BEST PRACTICE

I designed this guide to synthesize research-based practice into user-friendly resources that help you easily enhance what you already teach via a dynamic integration of the following:

- High expectations and critical thinking
- Effective pedagogy for all students
- Effective pedagogy for ELs and SELs
- Designated and integrated language development
- Culturally proficient practice
- Effective use of formative data
- Differentiation to personalize teaching
- Reflective teaching

A SYNTHESIS OF PRIORITIES

In addition to synthesizing best instructional practices, I've intentionally narrowed the focus of instruction in this guide to go deep with two high-priority goals for students:

1. Collaborate in Conversations
2. Make and Justify Claims With Text Evidence

Collaborative conversations are a top-priority strategy to ensure excellence for ELs and build student competencies in collaboration and communication essential for achievement in and beyond school. This guide both teaches collaborative conversation strategies (Section II) and gives you conversation tasks and scaffolds for every literacy goal (Section IV).

Making and justifying claims with text evidence is a high-priority skill for career and college readiness for all students and is embedded with many linguistic challenges for ELs.

Academic argument is at the intersection of the English language arts, math, and science standards (Cheuk, 2013). This makes it an especially high-impact area of emphasis to deepen student and teacher learning across all content areas.

Section IV helps you build student capacity for academic argument through core routines and a flip-to guide to the many subskills of this higher-level literacy goal. Flip to Chapter 11 for an example of how to find specific goals and strategies to help you empower ELs and all learners to make claims (p. 236) and how to help students justify claims with evidence (p. 246). By design, these aren't just strategies in isolation, but a synthesis of strategies organized to help you apply best practices to help your unique students thrive with high-priority academic literacy goals.

WAYS TO USE THIS FLIP-TO GUIDE

You don't have to read this book from cover to cover. I recommend reading Chapters 1 and 2 and then flipping to other chapters as you need them. Here are five great entry points for using this book:

1. **ESSENTIAL MINDSETS.** Do you want to create a classroom and school culture that values diversity and makes high expectations a reality for every EL and every student? Read Chapter 2.

2. **ENGAGEMENT STRATEGIES.** Do you want to learn ways to structure active engagement and academic conversations in your classroom? Read Section II or flip to any strategy in the purple pages to enhance active participation and student conversations in you next lesson.

3. **STRATEGIC SUPPORTS.** Do you want strategies, lessons, and scaffolds to help students learn core concepts, language, and literacy? Read Section III or flip to any strategy in the orange pages when you need new tools to help your students thrive.

4. **LITERACY GOALS.** Are you looking for ways to help ELs (and all students) excel with a specific literacy goal like justifying claims with text evidence? Flip to the chapter in Section IV that aligns with your goal for a wealth of resources organized to make planning and differentiating a breeze.

5. **STUDENT NEEDS.** Listening to student conversations, watching students annotate texts, or reading students' writing, you notice specific areas where they need additional support. To address specific literacy needs, flip to the appropriate chapter in Section IV to find support for both the literacy goals and aligned language goals.

COLLABORATIVE WAYS TO USE THIS GUIDE WITH A TEAM

Any teacher can use this book alone, and the impact amplifies when you use it with a colleague, a team, or a whole school community. Reflect on the entry points listed above and determine your goals together. The following approaches are four great ways to use this book in collaboration with colleagues:

1. **LEARN MINDSETS OR STRATEGIES TOGETHER:** The first four chapters are great for building background together in essential mindsets and strategies. Choose a relevant section or chapter and use the following sequence:

   A. Read.

   B. Discuss. What's most effective? What do you already do? What do you want to try?

   C. Collaborate to plan ways to apply at least one specific strategy to your teaching in the coming week.

   D. As students engage, watch to gather additional formative data.

   E. Meet to compare notes on impact and adapt your approaches together.

2. **PLAN LESSONS TOGETHER:** When planning literacy lessons, choose the chapter in Section IV that best fits your goals and choose strategies within that chapter to integrate into your teaching. When planning *any* lesson, use Chapters 3–7 as flip-to resources for strategies to engage and support ELs.

3. **ANALYZE STUDENT LEARNING TOGETHER:** Prioritize a goal in Section IV. Plan any "ENGAGE" task in Section IV. As students engage, film one pair in conversation or take notes on what they say and do. Choose one or more questions from the "OBSERVE"

questions to focus your observation. Collaborate to compare videos or notes and analyze together with these questions:

- What do we notice students saying and doing relative to our goals? Do we agree on what we see? What trends do we notice in the data?

- When there are successes, what instruction do we infer helped students reach this goal?

- When there are challenges, what instruction will we provide to help students build on what they know to excel at higher levels?

4. **SOLVE A STUDENT LEARNING CHALLENGE:** Together you've identified a challenge or your students' experience with academic literacy or language. You now want to collaborate to plan instruction you anticipate will specifically address their needs. Here's how to use the book in this process:

   A. Identify a challenge you want to solve together and discuss the strategies you anticipate will help students thrive.

   B. Flip to the sections of this book that are most relevant to your challenge and identify at least one specific strategy or lesson you will all try in the coming week.

   C. Collaborate to plan how you will use that strategy and/or to observe as one teacher tries it with a class.

   D. As students engage, watch to gather additional formative data.

   E. Meet after trying the plan with students to reflect on impact and adapt your approaches together.

To deepen your collaborative approach, please read my book *Opening Doors to Equity: A Practical Guide to Observation-Based Professional Learning* (Singer, 2015). It will give you all the tools you need to facilitate peer observation inquiry, a powerful approach to collaborating to plan, teach, observe, reflect, and refine teaching together to solve any learning challenge you prioritize.

REFLECT ON CHAPTER 1

- Who are the ELs in your teaching context? What are the diverse assets different ELs bring to your school? What do you know, or want to learn, about their language proficiency levels, home cultures, and prior educational experiences?

- What are the six verbs in the core pedagogy for EL excellence every day (p. 10)? Which are most central to how you now teach? What is one essential you want to learn more about or make a higher priority?

- How will you use this guide? Will you read it from cover to cover or flip to the sections you need as you need them? Will you read it alone or in collaboration with other colleagues? What do you most look forward to in this guide? Dig in!

CHAPTER 2
ESSENTIAL MINDSETS

"How teachers perceive their students and themselves in relation to them, determine, to a large extent, what the educational experience of students will be."

—Noma LeMoine (2007, p. 6)

MINDSETS MATTER

I start this book with mindsets because they matter more than any strategy.

Seriously.

I can teach at a high level, actively engage students, and use awesome strategies, but none of this will make any difference if I do not value my English learner (EL) students and believe they will succeed.

A CALL FOR HUMBLE REFLECTION

It's really easy to say I value students' backgrounds and have high expectations for ELs. In practice, however, it can be a challenge to consistently live this value in daily teaching. You can be a wonderful, compassionate person dedicated to the teaching profession and, like me, experience a disconnect between your ideal and your reality.

If I am honest and humble, I can reflect honestly that when I started out teaching (in a core classroom in a Title I school with many EL students), I lowered my expectations to meet my students where they were. When I attempted high expectations, my students failed because I didn't have the strategies and tools to bridge the gap.

Lowering expectations was not a conscious decision, but one I realized through day-by-day attempts to engage students with more scaffolds and easier tasks.

Many in our profession call this the "*pobrecito* syndrome." We love our ELs, and we want to protect them from failure. So we lower the bar.

Problem is, a lower bar sets ELs on a different path entirely—a path on which they don't access core curriculum or build fluency in the academic language or higher-level thinking tasks. A low bar leads to ELs going through years of schooling feeling like adults don't believe in them.

I share my story of lowering expectations because I want to invite readers into humble reflection. As humans, we have brains designed to make snap judgments based on whatever information we have. We all have biases. It's part of being human. Most biases are implicit, as in beneath the surface of what we think and unintentional. We don't choose them. Learning our implicit biases is hard. It is also a superpower we can develop with humble inquiry.

One of the toughest challenges with understanding implicit biases is that they don't always align with our beliefs and values (Staats, Capatosto, Wright, & Jackson, 2016). This is where humility matters. Accepting that we carry biases that contradict our own values is part of the journey.

THREE ESSENTIAL MINDSETS

Let's unpack the three mindsets that will help us achieve our vision for all students to succeed. The following mindsets are the focus of this chapter and foundational for excellence with ELs:

1. **Value English Learners' Assets**
2. **Expect Excellence From Every English Learner**
3. **Reflect in Inquiry About Your Impact**

In this chapter, we dive into these mindsets one by one. For each, I offer the vision, the possible sticking points, questions for humble inquiry, and actions you can take to live the mindset. You can read this chapter in sequence or choose one section at a time as a focus for collaborative reading and reflection.

VALUE ENGLISH LEARNERS' ASSETS

VISION: Ensure ELs (and all students) feel affirmed and valued as members of the learning community. Build trusting relationships with ELs that foster safety and belonging, which are foundational to academic risk taking. Value students' home cultures, languages, and life experiences. Help students make intentional connections to their background experiences and home language(s) to deepen their learning.

WHY THIS MINDSET MATTERS

The purpose of this mindset is to ensure every student feels valued and a sense of belonging at school. A sense of belonging is a core psychological need (Maslow, 1943) and impacts student motivation and academic achievement (Goodenow, 1993; Walton & Cohen, 2007).

Without a sense of belonging, human brains go into fight-or-flight mode. Zaretta Hammond (2015) describes the impact of a perceived threat on the brain as an *amygdala hijack*: "When the amygdala sounds its alarm with cortisol, all other cognitive functions such as learning, problem solving or creative thinking stop" (p. 40).

In other words, a student's sense of belonging in a classroom physiologically makes or breaks the learning process. Valuing ELs to foster their sense of belonging in your classroom community is more important than any strategy in this book.

> "We cannot downplay students' need to feel safe and valued in the classroom."
>
> —Zaretta Hammond (2015, p. 47)

The symptoms of a student not feeling valued vary by individual—and are often internal. That a student doesn't feel a part of the classroom community can look to the teacher like lack of motivation or lack of initiative for learning. When a student is silent, opts to follow rather than lead, avoids challenge, or gives up quickly, there can be many reasons for such behaviors that are not about the individual student but about the climate we have created within our classroom for the student to thrive. When ELs exhibit such behaviors in an English-dominant classroom, reflect: Do my EL students feel a sense of safety and belonging in our community of scholars? Do they feel affirmation for who they are as individuals, for their unique life experiences, and for the cultural and linguistic assets they bring? What shifts will I make to ensure every EL feels a strong sense of belonging and value in my classroom learning culture?

WAYS WE MIGHT GET STUCK

Valuing EL assets often means valuing what we don't understand. This can be tough as it requires us to see beyond what we know and our own cultural sense of "normal" to value what is "normal" from others' point of view. This requires both humility to be aware of what we don't know and empathy to find value in how others experience and view the world. We can get stuck easily when we:

- **MISS OUR OWN CULTURAL LENS:** We all have cultural norms and values that are shaped by and shape our reality. These are the lens through which we interpret what is right, normal, just, unjust, important, unimportant, and more. To value students' diverse linguistic and cultural assets, we have to recognize that our lens on the world isn't the only lens or the superior lens. It's hard to do this especially if we have always lived and worked in an environment where our lens is the norm or our lens is given a superior status. When our cultural norms are also the norms of our environment, they are often invisible to us. We need to learn to make the invisible visible. To see beyond our lens and value different lenses our students use to see the world, we need to first become aware that we also have a cultural lens that influences what we see.

- **ASSUME ONE LANGUAGE DIMINISHES ANOTHER:** It feels intuitive to think that expertise in one language comes at the expense of growth in another language. Such assumptions have historically led to problematic policies such as schools forbidding ELs from using their primary language on campus and educators discouraging parents from using their home language with their kids. Research proves these assumptions wrong. In *Promoting Academic Achievement Among English Learners: A Guide to the Research*, authors Goldenberg and Coleman (2010) assert "the best scientific studies we have—those that control for extraneous variables and provide the most confidence in their conclusions—show that in fact using students' primary language (L1) promotes their achievement in English (their L2)" (p. 25). Flip to pages 23–26 for strategies to value and build on students' home language skills as assets for their learning.

- **RELY ON ASSUMPTIONS:** Our brains are wired to make assumptions. We all have implicit, unintentional biases that help us efficiently organize new information. Implicit biases about different cultural groups, ethnic groups, or language groups can lead us to make assumptions about our students that are wrong. Biases, implicit or explicit, can lead us to see other cultures or languages as inferior to our own.

ACTIONS TO LIVE THE MINDSET

1. PRONOUNCE STUDENTS' NAMES CORRECTLY

One easy and essential way to value students' diverse backgrounds is to pronounce students' names the same way their families pronounce their names. This is critically important as our names are our identities. We create a disconnect between home and school when we mispronounce a student's name. For example, a student I worked with as a reading specialist was named Abel (pronounced "ah-BELL" in Spanish, by his family and community). I met him via a family reading club, so I learned his name from his mom. In his classroom, when I called him Abel, he looked mortified. He corrected me to say Abel (ˈābəl) the way his English teachers had called him since the first day of kindergarten. At school, he felt ashamed by the sound of his own name.

This is a disconnect we can prevent easily by making it a norm for every teacher at every level to learn how students pronounce their names. When a name comes from a language you don't speak, pronouncing the name correctly may take several tries. Instead of changing the name to what you can say easily, dare to listen, try, fail, listen, try, and fail as many times as it takes to get it right. In addition to learning names, you model the linguistic risk taking that is essential for learning a new language.

Start the year with a project for all students to research the story of their names. Have students interview family members to learn: Where did the name come from? What does it mean? Have students discuss and/or write to share their name stories along with the pronunciation (and/or nicknames) they want you and peers to use.

2. MAKE CONNECTIONS TO STUDENTS' LIFE EXPERIENCES, CULTURE, AND VALUES

Get to know what your students love and value within and beyond school. Use a getting-to-know-you survey, peer discussions, and/or informal interviews to get to know all students in your class. Open-ended questions such as the following are great for getting insight into students' interests and values:

- What do you like to do for fun outside of school?

- What do you do with your family?

- If you could only save one item from your home, what would it be? Why? (For a rich getting-to-know-you project, have students bring in an item or photo of an item and tell the story of why it matters.)

- Imagine you accomplish something amazing (e.g., win a competition or create something incredible). Would you prefer to accomplish this by yourself or with a team? Why?

Ask questions and watch your students to learn how they experience and understand the world. What motivates them? What makes them proud? What makes them uncomfortable or angry? What makes them comfortable? What brings them joy? These universal questions apply to all students, not just ELs, and open possibilities to learn more deeply how students think about themselves and their experiences in and beyond school.

Seek to understand culture beyond heroes and holidays. To understand and build on cultural differences, look beyond surface aspects of culture (e.g., celebrations, music, and food) that are easy to see, to understand what Hammond (2015) calls shallow culture and deep culture. Shallow culture includes our unspoken rules of what feels "normal" in our communication styles and relationships (e.g., concepts of time, notions of personal space, and ways of handling emotion). Deep culture includes our unconscious beliefs and values such as our notions of fairness or preferences for cooperation or competition (Hammond, 2015). To understand and value the shallow and deep culture of others, it helps to first reflect on what our own culture may be.

The unspoken aspects of our own culture are often invisible to us, especially when we share the same culture as our environment. I've learned the most about my own culture when I've been in cross-cultural situations that challenge my own sense of "normal." For example, I didn't think much about personal space as an aspect of culture until I lived in China for a year and noticed how incredibly uncomfortable I felt in bus lines. Waiting to board a bus, I feel like the strangers around me were incredibly rude to crowd me, press up against me, and even step in front of me to jockey for position to board the bus. Based on my cultural norm, the lack of personal space people gave me felt "rude," but there was no rude or malicious intent. People of all ages were just doing what people did to get on the bus, not just with me but also with everyone. What was comfortable for people used to the culture wasn't comfortable to me based on my own cultural background. I did learn over time to adapt so I could flow onto buses with the crowd— but I never did feel fully comfortable until I boarded and reestablished the amount of personal space that felt right to me.

The following are examples of unspoken aspects of culture with some reflection questions you can use to think about your own cultural values and norms or to reflect on possible differences among you and colleagues or students:

- **PERSONAL SPACE:** How much distance feels comfortable between you and a friend when you are talking? What distance feels comfortable when you walk side by side? What distance is most comfortable between strangers when standing in a line?

- **CONCEPT OF TIME:** When you agree to meet a friend at a certain time, how important is it to arrive by that exact number on the clock? If someone else is ten minutes late, how do you feel? If you are ten minutes late, how do you feel? What's more offensive: someone arriving late or someone getting upset because you are a few minutes late?

- **INDIVIDUALISM–COLLECTIVISM:** Do you feel most comfortable working alone or with a team? Why? How do you feel when you see one person take all the credit for a group project? How do you feel when you see a team get equal credit when some individuals did most of the work?

These questions are not exhaustive but examples of questions to help you and students think about culture beyond holidays and food. Seek to understand the unspoken and invisible aspects of students' cultures so that you can connect across cultural differences in ways that build trust. Know your own culture so you can be intentional to see beyond your own sense of normal to create space for different cultural orientations in your classroom. For example, if you are a teacher in the United States, recognize that the United States is one of the most individualistic cultures in the world and that making learning more collaborative is one powerful way to be a culturally responsive teacher (Hammond, 2015; Hofstede, Hofstede, & Minkov, 2010).

"Our diverse students' knowledge and linguistic abilities are assets that should be integrated into how and what we teach."

—Jeff Zwiers (2008, p. 12)

Beyond beginning-of-year surveys and getting-to-know-you activities, structure collaborative conversations daily in your teaching routines that invite not one right answer but diverse perspectives about the texts students read and concepts you teach. The more you invite students to build their voices in your classroom, the more you learn about their interests and values and the better equipped you become to connect to students' backgrounds in your teaching. Flip to Chapter 3 for peer conversation strategies and Chapter 5 for strategies to connect to students' prior knowledge and experience. Every chapter in Section IV will help you apply these strategies in synthesis to meet literacy goals.

3. BUILD ON STUDENTS' PRIMARY LANGUAGE ASSETS

Learn what students know and can do in their primary language(s). When possible, use primary language assessments or even an informal language survey to learn the unique language assets each EL brings to your classroom. In my home state of California, schools are required to assess primary language within ninety days of when an EL first enrolls in a U.S. school. When I worked as an EL specialist, I administered these assessments to Spanish-speaking ELs and provided this information for teachers. When an EL enrolled with another primary language, since I did not have language resources to assess proficiency in other languages, I used an informal survey to ask parents about student proficiency levels. Download a copy of my informal language survey at www.tonyasinger .com/elexcellence or create your own.

If primary language assessments are given in your district, take full advantage and find those assessment results to know if your EL students are proficient in listening, speaking, reading, and writing. If not, try to interview the student or parents (or have someone fluent in the home language interview parents) with an informal language survey to ask how well the student speaks, understands, reads, and writes the home language.

If you do speak a student's primary language, you can use it to help emerging ELs access your core content:

- Clarify Directions: Even in a lesson in which your goal is full English immersion, you can use primary language strategically to clarify directions for an emerging EL. Don't translate everything, or the EL will tune out what you say in English. Instead be strategic to use the primary language to clarify confusions.

- Check for Understanding: If you have an emerging EL and at least one other student proficient in the same home language, you can have these students talk through an advanced concept in their primary language before speaking in English. Your proficiency in the language helps you check for understanding as they discuss, and helps them build the English they need to express the same complex ideas.

Whether or not you speak a student's primary language, you can tap into ELs' strengths in that language to help them access your core content and learn English:

- Build Background: Have emerging ELs with primary literacy read or watch videos in that language to build background in the high-level concepts and topics you are teaching. When students first build background in concepts and topics in their primary language, they will have an easier time making meaning from your speech and texts on that topic in English. Flip to Chapter 5 for strategies to build background.

- Teach Vocabulary With Cognates: Flip to pages 124–125 for strategies to use primary language cognates to teach new words.

- Encourage Use of Home Language in Families and Communities: Primary language use promotes academic achievement in English (Francis, Lesaux, & August, 2006). The majority of communication and conceptual skills students learn in their primary language transfers to their English learning and literacy. Do not advise parents of ELs to stop using their home language at home. On the contrary, encourage families to read or tell stories together—in the language of the home—and engage in discussions. Encourage students with extended family members in other countries to engage in communication and correspondence with them (via letters, video calls, emails, etc.) to continuously strengthen their bilingual and bicultural skills.

- Learn Language From ELs: With genuine interest in learning the language, without putting students on the spot, create opportunities for ELs to teach words or phrases in their language to you and/or to peers. For example, one teacher with multiple home languages in her first-grade classroom incorporated the words for *good morning* in each language as part of her morning routine. All students chanted all of the different language greetings to start the day. In a high school classroom, a Spanish-speaking EL tutored an English-speaking peer with Spanish homework.

Value nonstandard English dialects. A nonstandard English dialect, like all languages, follows consistent grammatical structures and is powerful for effective communication with others who share the language. The following are examples of the many dialects of English that are part of the rich linguistic tapestry of North America:

- African American English (AAE), also called African American Vernacular English (AAVE)
- Cajun Vernacular English
- Hawaiian Pidgin
- Chicano English

A Standard English learner (SEL) is a student with fluency in an English dialect that is not the same dialect that English students are expected to use in school. Like ELs, SELs have a powerful asset in their fluency with their home language—an asset often undervalued by schools. Honor this asset by first recognizing that what may sound like "incorrect" English to a Standard English speaker is actually a correct application of logical grammar and syntax in the students' home dialect.

"There is nothing inherently superior in the make-up of a 'standard dialect': non-standard dialects have vocabulary, grammar, and pronunciation which are equally detailed in structure, and indeed are often imbued with pedigrees far older than those of the standard variety of the day."

—Oxford Living Dictionaries (2017)

A student proficient in any English dialect that isn't your English dialect may say or write things that sound or look like an error to you but aren't an error at all (LeMoine, 2007; Pullman, 1999). Interpreting such language choices as errors would be like interpreting a French speaker's use of *bonjour* as an error. It's not wrong, just a different language. It has value in one context, and we can build on that value to teach a new way of using language in this new school context.

If you teach students with fluency in nonstandard dialects, seek to learn the history and some of the most common structures of that dialect. Find texts (oral, written, or multimedia) that model effective communication in the dialect and incorporate these into your own reading and your close reading with students. This is a relevant opportunity to engage students in what is already called for in college and career readiness standards—a close analysis of the following questions: What is the audience and purpose for this text? How do the author's linguistic choices impact tone and communication? Students with fluency in more than one dialect have increased background knowledge for this type of analysis and increased linguistic options for communication across diverse contexts for different audiences and purposes. What a gift!

Teaching "standard" English and valuing students' primary language(s) is not an either/or proposition. Having a "yes, and" mindset means we simultaneously value students' home language *and* the academic language we want them to speak in school. We can do this by being curious about the language assets students bring to school and making intentional connections to those assets in our teaching.

4. VALUE "ERRORS" AS FORMATIVE LANGUAGE DATA

When students' English use doesn't sound or look right to you, be curious about the specifics. Be curious about what logical rules students may be applying from their first language. Why did the student make that language choice? Would that use of grammar or vocabulary make sense in the student's primary language or dialect?

I put "error" in quotes for a very important reason: *Error* is a relative term. What sounds like an error in Standard English is often the result of students following the linguistic rules of their primary language. This is true whether a student speaks a language like Spanish, Chinese, or Arabic or a non-standard dialect of English.

When you hear an "error" or what sounds like an awkward use of English, reflect:

- What can I learn from this about the language needed for success with this conversation task?

- What can I learn from this about my students' understanding of how to use language? Would that use of grammar or vocabulary make sense in the student's primary language or home dialect?

- How will I use these data to adjust my teaching? Will I provide one-on-one feedback or a whole-class mini-lesson in the moment? Will I adjust my scaffolds? Will I opt to change nothing in the moment (so critical thinking and risk taking get more emphasis than grammar in this task) and instead use these data to plan a follow-up language lesson to address this need?

If ELs use awkward grammar, is it because they are logistically applying a grammatical structure from their first language? Knowing this is powerful as it helps you validate what students know *and* teach clearly the difference between the two languages.

For example, when I lived in China, people would greet me with a question: "*Ni hao bu hao*." The word-for-word translation is "You good not good."

What?

"You good not good" sounds odd to my English ear for grammar. It is, however, logical and correct grammar in Chinese. If I translated "How are you?" word for word into Chinese, it would sound odd to a Chinese speaker.

Does this mean I have no concept of grammar? Not at all. I have a very strong sense of grammar from my first language and will keep applying those rules to every new language I learn until I see the clear difference and learn different rules.

If a Chinese-speaking EL spends some time with a bilingual dictionary, then says to me, "You good not good," does the student understand grammar?

Yes. And the student also needs to learn the difference in English grammar for this context.

5. USE CONTRASTIVE ANALYSIS TO BUILD ON PRIMARY LANGUAGE ASSETS

Contrastive analysis is a strategy of engaging students in contrasting two ways of communicating the same message for the same purpose, one in the students' home language or dialect and one in the new language (LeMoine & Soto, 2017; Taylor, 1991). In my Chinese example, I guide the student in contrasting the two grammatical structures for "How are you?" by writing the two different versions one above the other, in English, as follows:

> You good not good.

> How are you?

I point to the first example and acknowledge that this grammar is correct in Chinese. I explain that in English we don't use the same structure. Instead, we use a different structure (I point to "How are you?") to ask a question. Then I say, "Let's read it together."

This is one way to have an asset mindset about students' linguistic strengths. We don't just correct what is "wrong" in English; we are curious about what the student already knows and can do in another language that directly relates to this learning. We look to see what grammatical rules the student is applying from the first language, then help the student contrast the two languages side by side to learn the specific difference. Whereas pointing out errors negates students' primary language knowledge, a contrastive analysis approach helps students engage in the high-level process of analyzing how different uses of language are appropriate for different contexts. This is an important concept both for English language arts *and* for effective bilingual communication.

To learn more about contrastive analysis including specific strategies and texts that especially benefit SELs with fluency in African American English, read pages 39–46 of Noma LeMoine and Ivannia Soto's book *Academic Language Mastery: Culture in Context* (2017).

6. CHOOSE "ENABLING TEXTS" FOR YOUR CLASSROOM LIBRARY AND TEACHING

Choosing texts that positively influence and engage ELs and students of color is beyond the scope of this book. That said, the texts we choose are so critical to how we apply the value mindset to everyday teaching, and I recommend readers learn and use Dr. Alfred Tatum's (2009) approach to select "enabling texts." For a brief introduction to this concept, reflect on the following questions I co-created with Zaretta Hammond (personal communication, July 4–7, 2017):

- Do my texts serve as a road map to help students socially and emotionally navigate their everyday lives and the world outside of their immediate community?

- Do my texts focus on self-determination and self-reliance? Do they challenge the victim mentality?

- Do my classroom texts recognize, honor, and nurture students' multiple identities? For example, beyond thinking about one aspect of identity you see (e.g., Spanish speaker), consider how texts honor and nurture the diverse personal, social, academic, and cultural identities students navigate inside and outside of school.

For deeper exploration into choosing texts that engage and affirm students of color, please read Tatum's *Reading for Their Life: (Re)building the Textual Lineages of African American Adolescent Males* (2009).

QUESTIONS FOR HUMBLE REFLECTION

WHAT ARE MY PERCEPTIONS?

- What are my perceptions about ELs in my classroom and school? How do these shape my expectations and my response to ELs as they engage (or are silent) in my classroom tasks?

- What is my primary cultural orientation along the continuum of individualism to collectivism? Is it the same as, or different from, the dominant culture of the school? Is it the same as, or different from, the culture of students in my classroom? How do my cultural norms and values shape my perceptions of students and my teaching?

- What implicit biases affect my assumptions and decisions? Take the Implicit Association Test (IAT) at this link to foster self-reflection: https://implicit.harvard.edu/implicit/takeatest .html.

HOW DO I CONNECT TO STUDENTS' ASSETS?

- What do I know about my students' strengths, home languages, cultures, and life experiences? What more do I want to learn? How will I learn it?

- In what specific ways do I design learning to connect to and build on students' strengths, home languages, cultures, and life experiences? What more do I want to learn about connecting to students' strengths and assets in my teaching?

- How do I engage and value parents as partners in student learning?

ADDITIONAL RESOURCES TO FOSTER THIS MINDSET

Emdin, C. (2016). *For white folks who teach in the hood . . . and the rest of y'all too: Reality pedagogy and urban education.* Boston, MA: Beacon Press.

Hammond, Z. (2015). *Culturally responsive teaching and the brain: Promoting authentic engagement and rigor among culturally and linguistically diverse students.* Thousand Oaks, CA: Corwin.

LeMoine, N., & Soto, I. (2016). *Academic language mastery: Culture in context.* Thousand Oaks, CA: Corwin.

Quezada, R. L., Lindsey, D. B., & Lindsey, R. B. (2012). *Culturally proficient practice: Supporting educators of English learning students.* Thousand Oaks, CA: Corwin.

Rosin, H., & Spiegel, A. (Hosts). (2017, June 9). *The culture inside* [Audio podcast]. Retrieved from http://www.npr.org/programs/invisibilia/532950995/the-culture-inside

EXPECT EXCELLENCE FROM EVERY ENGLISH LEARNER

VISION: Keep rigor of tasks and texts high while providing appropriate scaffolds and supports to engage ELs in building concepts, skills, and language to thrive on a path toward college and career success. When a student struggles, a teacher who expects excellence knows the struggle is temporary, and the student has the capacity for growth.

WHY THIS MINDSET MATTERS

Students rise or fall to the level of teacher expectations. Research clearly indicates a strong correlation between teacher expectations and student achievement (Carrasquillo & Rodríguez, 2002; Darling-Hammond & Schon, 1996; Gershenson, Holt, & Papageorge, 2015; Rosenthal & Jacobsen, 1968). When we have high expectations, we can help students grow toward those expectations. When we have low expectations for students, we limit the impact of our teaching to that low level.

WAYS WE MIGHT GET STUCK

Believing in high expectations for all students and making high expectations a reality are two different things. In theory, it is easy to believe every student can achieve. In practice, it is easy to teach students who currently underperform at low levels. Some of the ways we can easily get stuck include the following:

- **WE MEET STUDENTS WHERE THEY ARE:** It's good teaching to identify where students are currently performing and help them build from their current levels to increasingly higher levels of performance and independent success. The essential word here is *build*. Sometimes, as I reflected at the opening of this chapter, we can get stuck meeting students where they are without also building from that place to help them thrive with rigorous goals. We do this when we adjust the complexity of our tasks and texts so our students don't have to struggle or when we overscaffold so students don't get to apply learning beyond our guidance.

- **WE PROTECT STUDENTS FROM STRUGGLE:** Even if we start with high expectations and challenging tasks, sometimes when students struggle we jump in too soon. We may give an answer instead of letting students figure one out. We may tell students what to do when a prompt may be enough to ignite student problem solving. If students struggle in unproductive ways that lead them to be disengaged, then of course providing immediate guidance, scaffolding, or teaching is important. That said, we must also foster opportunities for students to struggle productively toward ambitious goals. Teaching with high expectations requires both a strategic use of scaffolds and giving students the think time and trial-and-error opportunities needed to solve problems and make meaning through rigorous tasks and texts.

- **WE SORT AND TRACK STUDENTS:** With the intention of addressing specific needs, schools often sort and track students in ways that hinder the learning of underperforming students (Noguera, Darling-Hammond, & Friedlaender, 2015). ELs are often removed from core teaching to engage in low-level, disconnected language instruction. To learn and excel with the academic language essential for content success, ELs need to engage daily in speaking, listening, reading, and writing across the core curriculum. To excel with rigorous academic content, ELs need to access and engage with rigorous academic content. Flip to Chapter 4, pages 86–107, for flexible strategies to differentiate that don't involve tracking.

ACTIONS TO LIVE THE MINDSET

1. BE SPECIFIC ABOUT YOUR GOALS FOR STUDENT LEARNING

Get specific about what you want students to learn and the criteria students need to succeed with the goal. Section IV of this guide helps you get specific about goals for academic literacy and language. For example, for teaching theme, you'll find literacy goals and language objectives as shown in Table 2.1.

To make goals clear, do more than post and say the goals. Engage students in collaborating to explain what they are learning and why. Provide examples of what success looks like, and model how these exemplars demonstrate the learning objectives. Flip to pages 128–129 for a specific routine to model expectations with an exemplar.

Observe students as they engage in conversations and lesson tasks to watch specifically for your teaching goals. This book helps you do this in Section IV by giving you observation questions aligned with each learning goal. Look for the heading "Observe" to focus your

TABLE 2.1

LITERACY AND LANGUAGE OBJECTIVES FOR TEACHING THEME

	LITERACY GOALS	LANGUAGE FOR SUCCESS
Make Claims About Theme	I can make logical **inferences** about the theme and author's message. I can cite the text and author in my claim.	I can communicate my inferences effectively in speaking and writing using precise vocabulary (e.g., general nouns to describe theme). I can express my claim in writing using a complex sentence structure to include the title of the text and author's name with my inference about theme.
Support	I can **support** my thinking with evidence and explanation. I can quote or paraphrase relevant **text evidence**. I can **explain** how the text evidence supports my inference.	I can express ideas in writing using expository organization to support my claims with evidence and explanation. I can use transitions and referents to connect ideas across sentences.

observations, then use your observation data to personalize teaching so students reach success with your high expectations.

2. COLLABORATE TO CALIBRATE EXPECTATIONS

Making our goals clear is important for our communication with our students and their ownership of their own learning. How do we know our goals are appropriate for our grade level and content area? Collaborate with colleagues to answer this question. Powerful processes for teacher teams include all of the following:

- Unpack grade-level content standards to identify the most essential concepts and skills, and design tasks you can use to have students learn and demonstrate success with those concepts and skills.
- Co-create or choose together exemplars of what success looks like for conversations (video exemplar or transcript) and written tasks.
- Co-create a rubric of success criteria to measure success with the task.
- Collaborate to calibrate your scoring of student work (or conversation videos or transcripts) with the rubric. Flip to pages 132–134 for a great protocol to use with colleagues and with students to calibrate your expectations.

Collaborating to make expectations visible and calibrate how you score the same work sample is powerful professional learning that makes your job easier. When we work alone, it is hard to make high expectations a reality. When we work together, we help one another raise the bar in tangible, relevant ways connected to what we teach every day.

3. PRIORITIZE HIGH-LEVEL THINKING TASKS

Make high-level thinking tasks a priority for all students. Remember that perfect English language use is *not* a prerequisite for high-level academic tasks. When an EL uses English imperfectly in the context of a high-level task, don't replace that task with back-to-basics grammar. Instead, encourage the imperfections that are a natural part of students stretching their cognitive and communicative skills, and then listen closely to gather formative data about student assets and challenges. Use this information to plan strategic scaffolds and personalize teaching so ELs thrive with both your high-level tasks and the language they need to effectively communicate their thinking with impact.

"ELs at all proficiency levels are capable of high-level thinking and can engage in complex, cognitively demanding social and academic activities requiring language as long as they are provided appropriate linguistic support."

—California State Board of Education (2012)

Higher-order thinking questions are important not just for the intellectual rigor but for relevance. Most higher-order questions are open-ended, meaning they do not have one right answer. A question such as "What is the author's message in this story?" invites multiple, diverse perspectives. Be open to students having different opinions than you and drawing different inferences from texts based on their own life experiences and cultures.

When you ask high-level thinking questions *and* invite multiple points of view, classroom discussions get interesting! Justifying ideas with evidence becomes a relevant task important for explaining and clarifying thinking. Through higher-level discussions that invite diverse interpretations, you value the unique assets all students bring to their learning. You create a space for every voice in your community of scholars.

Also critical for maintaining high expectations, use scaffolds strategically! When engaging ELs in high-level tasks, use scaffolds to ensure all students can participate, but don't overscaffold. Only use what a student needs. Flip to Section III to learn the core philosophy and strategies for strategic scaffolding, which is central to teaching with high expectations.

QUESTIONS FOR HUMBLE REFLECTION

DO I TEACH WITH HIGH EXPECTATIONS FOR ELS AND ALL STUDENTS?

- Are my goals and success criteria clear to me and to my students?
- Do my goals and success criteria align with grade-level and content-area expectations? How do I know?
- Do I ask questions that require high-level thinking of ELs and all students?
- Do my tasks reflect high expectations appropriate for my grade level(s) and content area(s)? How do I know?

HOW DO I RESPOND WHEN A STUDENT STRUGGLES?

- If an EL struggles, do I blame the struggle on the students' EL status or seek to understand the specific opportunity for growth? Do I lower my expectations or reflect on how I will change my teaching so the student will succeed?
- How is my response to how a student struggles different for different student groups in my classroom (e.g., EL, GATE, low-performing students, white students, black students, boys, girls)? What differences do I notice in what I say, what I do, and the time I wait before stepping in?

Be in inquiry about these questions across a week of teaching. For example, reflect:

- When a high-performing student struggles with a challenge in my classroom, how do I respond?
- When a student who performs well below grade level struggles with a challenge, how do I respond?
- When an EL struggles with a challenge, how do I respond?
- What differences do I notice in the wait time I provide, what I say, or how I say it? What differences do I notice in my nonverbal cues and body language?

ADDITIONAL READING TO FOSTER THIS MINDSET

Gibbons, P. (2009). *English learners, academic literacy, and thinking: Learning in the challenge zone.* Portsmouth, NH: Heinemann.

Saphier, J. (2017). *High-expectations teaching.* Thousand Oaks, CA: Corwin.

REFLECT IN INQUIRY ABOUT YOUR IMPACT

VISION: Reflect in continuous inquiry about your impact. Set clear goals. Look at formative data both to understand how students are learning and to study the impact of your teaching on student learning. When students struggle, ask, "What might I change in my teaching to ensure my students succeed?"

WHY THIS MINDSET MATTERS

Reflective teaching is good teaching for *all* students (Chenoweth & Noguera, 2009; Hattie, 2012; Noguera et al., 2015). Reflective teachers engage in a continuous cycle of inquiry about the impact of teaching on students. Figure 2.1 shows the four essential steps of reflective teaching.

It looks simple enough to apply this cycle to our teaching, and many teachers do so with ease. We plan, we teach, we asses, we look at our assessment data, and then we rethink and refine our plans. However . . .

WAYS WE MIGHT GET STUCK

Every step of this cycle has a possible sticking point when we teach ELs. Our mindset makes the difference. The reflective cycle helps us ensure EL success when we have high expectations for ELs, are curious about the strengths they bring, and have a sense of ownership and responsibility to impact their learning. If, however, we don't believe in

FIGURE 2.1

REFLECTIVE CYCLE OF EFFECTIVE TEACHING

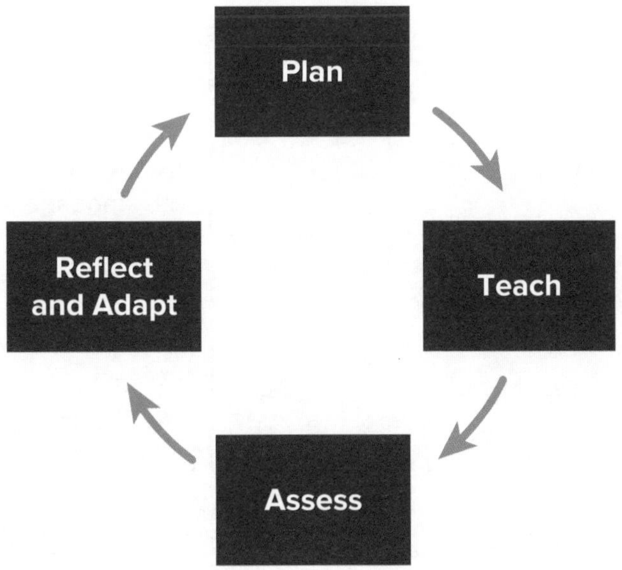

their capacities, assume their learning is another teacher's job, or blame instead of taking ownership for their struggles, the reflective cycle gets stuck. I created Table 2.2 to compare two possible approaches to each step of the reflective cycle. Compare the difference in mindset for each approach.

I have experienced every one of the possible stagnations in the reflective cycle both in my own teaching and in my work helping teachers thrive with ELs. It takes honest, humble reflection to uncover the ways our own unconscious mindsets about ELs might get in our way.

The place in this cycle I'm most likely to get stuck is with the adaptation. When an EL succeeds, I might keep using the same level of supports and challenges. Why? I get

TABLE 2.2

HOW MINDSETS ABOUT ELS HALT OR DRIVE REFLECTIVE PRACTICE

	WAYS TO ENSURE ELS STAGNATE	WAYS TO ENSURE ELS THRIVE
Plan	Lower expectations for ELs. Simplify and water down the curriculum.	Maintain high expectations for ELs. Use supports strategically to ensure success.
Teach	Use *teach* as a verb that only involves teacher action.	Engage students in actively learning via collaborative conversations, action, reading, writing, and relevant inquiry.
Assess	Assess language infrequently or never as it's hard to find an "assessment."	Listen and observe during lessons every day to learn about students' strengths and instructional needs with language and content.
Reflect and Adapt	When an EL struggles, blame the family, the community, or the fact that the student is an EL. When an EL in your class struggles, assume the EL specialist is the only educator responsible for the student's success. When an EL succeeds, keep using the same level of supports and challenges.	When an EL struggles, reflect on what you can change about your teaching to help the student succeed. When an EL succeeds, raise challenges and adjust supports to foster increasing levels of achievement and self-directed learning.

attached to a strategy. It works, so why change it? I get attached to my students succeeding with the tasks I give them. If I take my reflection a little deeper, I notice that I'm also uncomfortable watching ELs struggle. I want to guarantee their success, and as a result, sometimes I overscaffold. Or I don't remove scaffolds as students advance to foster *their* independence and success. It helps to know this about myself so I can actively plan places in the lesson where students may struggle and be intentional about giving them space for that struggle. Instead of jumping in immediately to rescue with scaffolds, I watch closely to learn and see what they can do on their own. I watch to also learn specifically how students struggle (and succeed) so I can personalize my teaching to address their very specific, and evolving, needs.

Reflective teaching is only effective for ELs when used in the context of expecting excellence and valuing ELs' assets. Remember the graphic I introduced in Chapter 1 with the core pedagogy of this guide? Revisit it now in Figure 2.2 below and reflect on the role of mindsets in the core pedagogy of this guide. Which verbs in the graphic relate to mindsets? Which relate to teacher actions? How do you bring these mindsets and actions into synthesis in your everyday teaching?

Compared to the typical graphic we use for talking about reflective teaching in schools (see Figure 2.1), I designed Figure 2.2 with important distinctions to illuminate the essentials for EL excellence. First of all, *expect* and *value* frame the reflective cycle—as these are

FIGURE 2.2

ESSENTIALS FOR EL EXCELLENCE EVERY DAY

EXPECT EXCELLENCE

ENGAGE > OBSERVE

REFLECT < SUPPORT

VALUE EL ASSETS

foundational mindsets that will make or break our impact on ELs. Within the reflective cycle, I also make intentional shifts in word choice and sequence.

- I replaced the words *plan* and *teach* with the student-centered words *engage* and *support* that are more open-ended to incorporate the range of what student learning, and personalized teaching, can be.
- Instead of *assess*, I use *observe* to emphasize the importance of observing students as essential formative data to drive our teaching every day.
- I put the verb *observe* between *engage* and *support* to emphasize the importance of choosing supports based on what we observe that students can already do on their own.

Even though the cycle shows a sequential progression, it's important to remember that teaching for impact is a messy process. Our actions don't always flow in a perfect sequence from *engage* to *observe* to *support* to *reflect*. In the continuous cycle of teaching and reflecting across multiple lessons, these verbs connect in dynamic ways. We support and engage in tandem, we observe and reflect in tandem, and we use all four verbs in different combinations in the humble process of trial and error that is a given when we teach to reach all learners and help them thrive beyond what they already know and can do. No matter the sequence, every verb is essential in every lesson to teach for impact with English learners.

QUESTIONS FOR HUMBLE REFLECTION

Reflect on Figure 2.2.

- Which of these sticking points have I experienced as a teacher?
- Which do I now experience and want to change?
- Which step of the reflective cycle is my greatest strength when teaching ELs? Which is the greatest opportunity for my professional growth?
- When ELs struggle in my classroom, do I blame students and families, refer them to specialists, and/or reflect on what I can change about my own teaching to help them thrive?

ACTIONS TO LIVE THE MINDSET

1. PLAN WITH HIGH EXPECTATIONS AND STRATEGIC USE OF SUPPORTS

Why? Teacher expectations directly affect student achievement (Gershenson et al., 2015; Hattie, 2012). Being strategic about when to use or lose supports is essential for engaging students in the optimal challenge zone for learning (Gibbons, 2009).

How? For ELs and all students, plan lessons to help them realize the high expectations of your grade level and content area(s). Make success criteria visible to students. Use supports strategically to help students realize those expectations while fostering increasing levels of student independence.

- Flip to Section III to learn support strategies to help every EL thrive with rigorous tasks.
- Flip to the "Expect" heading for each literacy goal you want to teach in Section IV, for success criteria aligned to that goal.
- Flip to the "Support" heading for the literacy goal you want to teach in Section IV for supports aligned to that goal.

2. TEACH TO ACTIVELY ENGAGE STUDENTS

Why? The people who do the thinking, talking, writing, and problem solving in a lesson learn the most (Washburn, 2010). Collaborative conversations are essential for language learning (August & Shanahan, 2006; Goldenberg & Coleman, 2010; Zwiers, O'Hara, & Pritchard, 2013).

How? Use peer conversations and active participation strategies in every lesson every day.

- Flip to Chapter 3 to learn collaborative conversation and active participation strategies.
- Flip to the "Engage" heading for the literacy goal you want to teach in Section IV for active engagement tasks aligned to that goal.

3. WATCH STUDENTS AS THEY ENGAGE TO GATHER FORMATIVE DATA

Why? What students say and do during a lesson is the best formative data available in every lesson, every day. Watch and listen to understand what students understand and can do relevant to your goals and to learn what next levels of learning they need. Watch to study the impact of your teaching and scaffolds so you can continuously reflect and refine your approach to reach all learners.

How? Observe students as they engage in learning. Listen to what they say and notice what they do.

- Flip to the "Observe" heading for the literacy goal you want to teach in Section IV for questions to focus your observation specific to that goal.

When students struggle, reflect and adapt your teaching to help them succeed. When students thrive, build on these successes to raise the challenge and/or reduce supports in subsequent lessons.

4. REFLECT AND REFINE TEACHING FOR IMPACT

Why? Teaching isn't about delivery. Teaching is only teaching if students learn. Reflecting and adapting are our superpowers for ensuring our actions lead to student learning.

How? Within every lesson, actively engage students and watch to check for understanding. Notice your thinking and actions when students struggle. When students struggle, take ownership for impact. If students struggle, get specific about what they can do and how they struggle. If students thrive, identify ways to build on strengths to release scaffolds and raise rigor. Use the information you gather watching students every day to adapt teaching within lessons and to plan the future lessons that build on student strengths and address challenges.

- Apply the instructional essentials in Figure 2.2, emphasized throughout this book, to your everyday teaching.
- Flip to the literacy goal you want to teach in Section IV. Use the flow of content to find goal-specific resources aligned to each step of the reflective teaching cycle.

Reflective teaching involves supports strategically based on student data. When students struggle, choose one or more additional scaffolds to help them succeed. When they succeed, remove scaffolds or supports in subsequent lessons to help them build on successes to thrive with increasing levels of challenge and student initiative.

5. COLLABORATE IN CONTINUOUS INQUIRY ABOUT IMPACT

The best way to strengthen your impact for ELs (and all students) is to collaborate with colleagues to co-plan, co-teach, co-reflect, and co-refine teaching for impact. Collaborative inquiry is teacher-driven professional learning that is relevant and connected to what you care most about in your teaching.

My go-to protocol for collaborative inquiry is observation inquiry (OI), a dynamic approach to collaborating with colleagues for equity and innovation. Read my book *Opening Doors to Equity* (Singer, 2015) for a practical, how-to guide to get started. Use OI to collaborate so that ELs—and all students—thrive with the goals that matter most to you and your colleagues.

"The beauty of Observation Inquiry is that it is incredibly applicable and practical. Our ideas go right into action in the classroom. As well, the feedback from team colleagues is meaningful and instructive. We are building a unit of collegiality that encourages teacher growth and teamwork."

—Brigitta Hunter, Teacher, Mark West Union School District

Co-teaching is another powerful approach to collaborative inquiry designed specifically for EL specialists and core teachers working together. Read *Collaboration and Co-Teaching* (Honigsfeld & Dove, 2010), referenced below, to get started.

ADDITIONAL READING TO FOSTER THIS MINDSET

Honigsfeld, A., & Dove, M. (2010). *Collaboration and co-teaching: Strategies for English learners.* Thousand Oaks, CA: Corwin.

Singer, T. W. (2015). *Opening doors to equity: A practical guide to observation-based teacher learning.* Thousand Oaks, CA: Corwin.

REFLECT ON CHAPTER 2

- How do you value EL assets in your everyday teaching? What is one new approach you want to try?

- In what specific ways do ELs in your context access opportunities to realize success with high expectations? What is one action you want to take to make high expectations a reality for all ELs?

- How and when do you reflect on your impact as you teach? How is your approach similar to or different from the cycle in Figure 2.2?

SECTION II
ENGAGE

This section empowers you with strategies to engage every student in active learning every day. Active learning is good for everyone, and also an imperative to ensure ELs thrive in core classrooms.

II. Engage

iStock.com/asiseeit

CHAPTER 3
ENGAGE EVERY EL

"When kids are engaged, when they are active co-constructors of their knowledge, then they are more likely to take ownership, to discover relevance, and to ask why and why not; they are more likely to feel inspired when they realize their voice matters and their questions count more than their answers."

—Kyleen Beers & Robert E. Probst (2013, p. 27)

WHAT IS STUDENT ENGAGEMENT?

We love student engagement. We want more student engagement every day. But what, specifically, do we mean by "student engagement"? Let's build a shared understanding about our goal before digging into the specific strategies of how to make it happen.

Imagine the ideal moment in your classroom when every student is 100 percent engaged. What do you see? What do you notice? What does active engagement look like and sound like? Jot down your ideas, and ideally collaborate with colleagues to compare notes.

When I think of engagement, I think of both students' internal experience as learners and their active participation. Internal experiences include students' thoughts and feelings. Active participation is what students do to engage in tasks. Both are important for engaging English learners (ELs) in core classrooms. Let's dig into each.

ENGAGEMENT FROM THE INSIDE OUT

One way of thinking about student engagement is the engagement that happens inside a learner's heart and mind. As teachers, we can't get inside students' heads to know their thoughts and feelings, but we often get clues in body language, facial expressions, and the things students say or write as they participate in class. Through these clues, we may notice the following types of engagement:

- INTEREST: Wow. This is fascinating. I love this! Cool.
- SENSE OF PURPOSE: I want to learn this because I understand why it is important to help me move toward goals I value.
- RELEVANCE: This is relevant to me. I see myself in this goal.
- CONNECTION: This reminds me of . . . This is similar to . . .
- CHOICE: I choose this book because . . . I want to write about . . . I want to create . . . I want to research this question . . . I want to solve the problem . . .
- CURIOSITY: I wonder . . . ? What will happen if . . . ?
- SELF-EFFICACY: I know I can do this. To move closer to that goal, I'll try . . .

Internal engagement is really the *most* important engagement as it is, in a nutshell, learning. It is the students' brain experiencing safety, relevance, interest, curiosity, and self-efficacy to grow. We foster this type of engagement for ELs in many different ways that I address throughout this book. Figure 3.1 gives you a quick overview of the strategies and where to find them in this guide.

ENGAGEMENT THROUGH ACTIVE PARTICIPATION

Another way of thinking about student engagement is active participation through student actions and expression. The focus in this definition of engagement is on what students *do* in a classroom. You may call this active participation and save the term *engagement* for the thinking/feeling aspects of engagement I described above. No matter the terms we use, the concept that matters is that students don't just sit and listen to the teacher but actively participate in lesson tasks. We teachers structure active participation when we create tasks that require students to engage in the following:

- COLLABORATE IN CONVERSATION: Students collaborate with peers to express ideas, negotiate meaning, and build up ideas together.
- READ: Students preview texts, read for meaning, and reread to analyze and find text evidence to stretch and support their ideas.

FIGURE 3.1

ENGAGEMENT RESOURCES AT A GLANCE

Teacher Actions to Promote Engagement	Resources in This Guide to Help You
Create a sense of safety and belonging for all ELs	Value English Learners' Assets (Chapter 2, p. 20)
Make learning culturally relevant	Value English Learners' Assets (Chapter 2, p. 20) Flip to goals you want to teach in Section IV (p. 171) for lesson-specific examples.
Connect learning to students' background knowledge	Chapter 5 (p. 108) Flip to the goals you want to teach in Section IV. Each goal includes lesson-specific examples of how to connect to students' background knowledge.
Communicate purpose in every lesson	Flip to the goals you want to teach in Section IV. Each goal begins with a clear statement of purpose.

- **ANNOTATE:** Students highlight, underline, and annotate texts.
- **WRITE:** Students write informally and formally alone and with peers.
- **MOVE:** Students take action with hands, feet, or whole body to act out concepts, make choices, and deepen learning.

Structuring active participation for all students is especially important in classrooms with English learners. When we leave participation to chance, ELs and other students often sit silently, passively, in class. Silently listening may help ELs learn some listening skills in English, but it doesn't help them actively use language to process learning and communicate ideas in speaking and writing.

Remember that active participation alone, without internal engagement, is simply compliance. Our goal is to have students collaborate, talk, read, write, annotate, and move in the context of relevant and meaningful learning opportunities. Students listen and read to expand their world. Students speak and write to collaborate, deepen their own thinking, and strengthen the power of their voices in the world. For deep engagement, always structure active participation in tandem with relevant texts, tasks, and topics!

Figure 3.2 shows the many ways this guide helps you structure active participation.

FIGURE 3.2

ACTIVE PARTICIPATION RESOURCES AT A GLANCE

Teacher Actions to Promote Engagement	Resources in This Guide to Help You
Structure collaborative conversations	In this chapter: 3.1 Whole-Class Conversation Structures (p. 52) 3.2 Partner Conversation Structures (p. 54) 3.3 Small-Group Conversation Structures (p. 56) 3.4 Up and Moving Conversation Structures (p. 58) 3.5 Fishbowl Structure (p. 60) 3.6 Listening to Conversations as Formative Data (p. 62) 3.7 Tools to Differentiate Student Conversations (p. 64) 3.8 Linguistic Frames for Conversations (p. 70) 3.12 Collaborate to Write Strategies (p. 80) Flip to the goals you want to teach in Section IV for lesson-specific examples of conversation tasks and scaffolds.
Actively engage emerging ELs	This chapter: 3.9 Strategies to Actively Engage Emerging ELs (p. 72) Flip to the goals you want to teach in Section IV for lesson-specific examples of differentiation by proficiency level.
Structure active participation	This chapter: 3.10 Total Physical Response Strategies (p. 76) 3.11 Read and Annotate Strategies (p. 78) 3.12 Collaborate to Write Strategies (p. 80) Flip to the goals you want to teach in Section IV for lesson-specific examples of active participation tasks.

Let's get started with a focus on peer conversations, the most important strategy for everyday excellence with ELs.

WHY COLLABORATIVE CONVERSATIONS?

If you want to start with the one instructional change that will have the greatest impact on ELs in your classroom while also benefiting *every* student, make it this: structure peer-to-peer conversations in every lesson every day.

WHY PEER CONVERSATIONS ARE THE MOST ESSENTIAL STRATEGY

Anyone? Anyone?

In the classic 1986 movie *Ferris Bueller's Day Off*, a history teacher asks a question to his class full of students who appear bored. "Anyone? Anyone?" he asks after each question. He gets silence. No student raises a hand. No student speaks.

It's funny in the movie, but we who teach know this uncomfortable situation. Even if we are way more effective than the history teacher portrayed in the movie, we know what it's like to ask our students a question and get . . .

silence.

Or, a few students raise their hands to answer. They are the same few students who always raise their hands, not the students who most need this lesson, not the ELs, not the students currently performing below grade level. The students we most need to reach are not engaged.

It's humbling. It's frustrating. What can we do?

STRUCTURE PEER CONVERSATIONS

Peer conversation structures put *all* students in the active role of doing the thinking, talking, and responding to the tasks in our lessons. A peer conversation structure is any partner or small-group discussion structure (e.g., think-pair-share) that has peers discuss a question with peers instead of responding one at a time to the teacher in front of the whole class. See pages 54–61 for a go-to reference to the peer conversation structures to use every day.

With a conversation structure, we make one simple shift: When we ask students a question, instead of calling on individuals in front of the whole class, we have students discuss the question in pairs or groups. For example, if I want to ask students to make a prediction before we read a new text, I might traditionally call on three different students to make predictions one at a time. Now, making the simple shift, I have students discuss their predictions with partners using the think-pair-share structure.

Let's compare the difference in student participation. See Figure 3.3 for a comparison of how students engage when you call on individuals in a whole-group discussion versus when you have partners discuss the same question or task.

WHY PEER CONVERSATIONS ESPECIALLY MATTER FOR ELS

The comparison in Figure 3.3 is relevant to any classroom with any population. Now if we consider the diversity in the classroom and imagine the class includes fluent English speakers, English learners, students who excel with the skills and content concepts

FIGURE 3.3

COMPARE APPROACHES TO CLASSROOM DISCUSSION

	The teacher calls on individual students, one at a time.	The teacher structures think-pair-share.
Who does the thinking for the task?	The few students selected to speak	Every student
Who does the talking for the task?	The few students selected to speak	Every student
Who uses the language required for this task?	The few students selected to speak	Every student
What do students do when not talking?	Hope they don't get called on, or try to get the teacher's attention so they can speak next	Look at their partner and listen to the partner's idea
Who does the teacher get to hear?	One student at a time as they speak to the whole group	One student at a time as they converse with partners and then share as individuals with the whole group

involved in the task, and students who are struggling, what trend might you expect in *who* participates in each scenario?

When a teacher asks a question to the whole class and waits for individuals to respond, who does the thinking for the task? Who does the talking? Who uses, and thus learns, the language for the task?

Who is silent?

When a teacher calls on individual volunteers, ELs are typically silent. Typically, students who struggle with the language, literacy, concepts, and competencies required by the task are the ones who choose to not participate. In other words, the students who most need to engage in this task to build their capacities are the ones who don't actually engage. The ones who already "get it" are the ones who do.

It's a classic case of the "rich" getting richer as the "poor" get poorer, although instead of economics the gap is in learning. Every time we ask questions and wait for volunteers, we widen the opportunity gap for ELs, for students who struggle with what we are teaching, and for any students who are hesitant to take social risks. We widen the gap between the students who already get it and the students who most need the opportunity to learn.

We can change this inequity by drawing names to randomly select students each time we call on individuals (e.g., with Popsicle sticks). This is an important strategy, but it alone doesn't solve the problem that most students are silent and passive every time we ask a question and call on students one at a time. It's a matter of simple math. In a class of twenty, if one student is talking to all, twenty are listening. Even with equitable participation and the teacher only talking as much as students, the average student speaks only 1/21 of the time, or 4.7 percent. In a class of thirty, that average drops to 3.2 percent.

This doesn't even factor in the amount of time a teacher is talking (e.g., giving directions, modeling, explaining) and students are listening, or the amount of time the class spends working silently (e.g., independent reading, writing, or problem solving). Add these factors together, and it is no surprise that many ELs go through entire school days without speaking a word about any academic text, task, or concept in school.

This is a problem you can change with one simple shift in teaching: structure peer conversations instead of calling on individuals with raised hands.

THREE IMPORTANT BENEFITS OF PEER CONVERSATIONS FOR ELS

BUILD ORAL ACADEMIC LANGUAGE: To learn language, we must use language. Listening and reading help us build the receptive language of understanding. Speaking and writing help us build the productive language of expression. ELs who are silent in classrooms may get a high dose of receptive language, but without the opportunities to actively communicate via speaking and writing, they never get to apply the language they are using. Application is essential for deep learning. Daily opportunities to discuss academic ideas are essential for building academic language. ELs need daily opportunities to take risks with language, make mistakes, and learn from the valuable feedback of real-world communication.

BENEFITS OF PEER CONVERSATIONS

Partner and small-group conversation structures have all of the following advantages over calling on individuals:

- Increase the percentage of students who actively engage
- Increase opportunities for students to talk
- Increase opportunities for students to deepen thinking
- Foster academic language development by having all students *use* language to articulate thinking about academic concepts and topics
- Create a low-risk opportunity for ELs to participate
- Create a low-risk opportunity for introverts to participate
- Create a low-risk opportunity for students who may struggle
- Foster collaboration
- Increase your opportunities to listen to students to gather formative data during your lessons

ENSURE ACTIVE PARTICIPATION: One nationwide study found that ELs spent 2 percent of their classroom day engaged in academic talk (Arreaga-Mayer & Perdomo-Rivera, 1996). This 2 percent average means that for every EL who spends twice this average talking, there is another EL who is silent all day, every day, in school. Every teacher can shift this trend by integrating conversations into academic lessons and using peer conversation structures to support and ensure active, equitable participation of all students. This book helps you lead the change.

FOSTER RISK TAKING: Many people fear speaking in front of a group, even in their first language. It is always easier to speak one-on-one or with a small group than in front of a crowd. Foster risk taking by giving students opportunities to build up ideas one-on-one with peers before sharing with the whole class. Listen especially to reluctant participants as they talk with peers, and when you hear a strong response, say, "Excellent idea. I'd like you to share that with the class." Provide specific feedback, if needed, to ensure the student will succeed in sharing with the whole class. Regular peer conversations in tandem with feedback help even the most reluctant participant to take new risks speaking in class.

THE BEST TASKS FOR COLLABORATIVE CONVERSATIONS

The ideal collaborative conversation tasks are open-ended and engage students in authentic collaboration involving all of the following:

- Building up ideas together through multiple exchanges
- Deepening learning specific to the goals of the lesson
- Communicating higher-order thinking
- Sharing diverse perspectives to foster divergent thinking
- Using academic language relevant to the task

The best conversation tasks are interesting and intellectually challenging and merit a real back-and-forth conversation. These include having students collaborate to make meaning from complexity, problem-solve, debate, interpret, evaluate, create, and/or revise.

Sometimes we also structure very short conversations in a lesson for the sole purpose of having students answer a quick question or practice language they have never tried before. For example, when we have students make a prediction and share it with their partner, they usually each just say their prediction, then stop the conversation. There is no back-and-forth communication because the task doesn't call for it. Be clear when structuring these types of tasks. While they have value for active participation and checking for understanding during a lesson, these are not the types of peer conversations that build deep thinking, collaboration skills, or the language of extended academic communication.

Using think-pair-share to have students use a new word is an example of a task that merits only a short conversation. For example, after teaching the word *influence*, we might have students think of one influence smartphones have on our lives. If we provide a sentence frame ("One influence smartphones have on our lives is _____") and structure think-pair-share, it is likely each student will say one idea and then the conversation will end.

Flip-to Tip:
If you want to learn strategies to structure and scaffold conversations and active participation, then keep reading this chapter in sequence. You can also use the table of contents on page 41 to flip to each strategy you want to learn when you want to learn it.

If you want to use conversations to enhance how you teach specific literacy goals, then flip to the goals you want to teach in Section IV.

Compare the previous task to the following: After students brainstorm a list of the many influences of smartphones on our lives, we post our list and have partners collaborate to identify and rank the three influences that are the most beneficial (or harmful). Unlike the first task that just asks students to share one idea, this task requires students to evaluate and prioritize to choose, eliminate, and rank options. By expecting high-level analysis, this task typically engages students in an extended conversation with natural opportunities to agree, disagree, and influence one another's thinking.

When planning conversation tasks, reflect on your primary goal for the task. If you want an extended conversation in which students build up ideas together, agree, and disagree, use a task that merits an extended conversation. Any task that can be answered in one sentence will only lead to peers taking turns answering the question, not an extended discussion. Good tasks for extended conversations include those shown in Figure 3.4.

FIGURE 3.4

EFFECTIVE TASKS FOR EXTENDED CONVERSATIONS

In Effective Tasks, Students Collaborate to . . .	Examples in This Guide
Make meaning from complexity	7.4 Teach Word Relationships (p. 166) 10.1 Identify Main Ideas (p. 206) 10.2 Self-Monitor and Use Context Clues (p. 216)
Argue or debate	11.1 Make Claims About Texts (p. 236) 11.2 Justify Claims With Text Evidence (p. 246)
Co-create	Color-Coded Writing (3.12, p. 80) 7.3 Syntax (or Paragraph) Surgery (p. 164)
Co-evaluate	5.9 Collaborate to Evaluate an Exemplar With a Rubric (p. 132)

NOTES

_____

_____

_____

_____

_____

_____

_____

_____

_____

_____

_____

3.1 WHOLE-CLASS CONVERSATION STRUCTURES

WHAT AND WHY?

In a whole-class discussion, a teacher typically calls on students to speak one at a time to the whole class. Don't rely on this approach alone, but use it as the "share" in think-pair-share or as a follow-up to table group conversations in which students report and discuss ideas with the whole class. Use these structures to enhance whole-class conversations.

STRUCTURES FOR ACCOUNTABLE PARTICIPATION

In most peer conversation structures, first all students talk with a partner or small group, and then a few students share the ideas they discussed with the whole class. No matter the conversation structure you use, it is important to also use accountable participation strategies for whole-group sharing.

To ensure equitable and accountable participation in the final whole-group discussion, use one or more of the following strategies:

- Draw names for random selection (e.g., Popsicle sticks)

- Listen as students discuss with peers, and preselect individuals to share. This is a great approach to use with ELs as you give them time to rehearse their response with you before they are on the spot with the class.

- Invite divergent perspectives. After calling on one to three students, ask for a student who can share a "different idea" or "different perspective" than what has already been shared.

- Have the student who speaks call on the next person to speak. Pay attention to who participates, and call on others as needed to involve all voices.

- As students participate, use a seating chart to tally who speaks. Call on students who have not yet had a voice in the discussion.

TIPS TO BE STRATEGIC

CREATE A SAFE SPACE: When building accountable participation, don't put students on the spot. When you call on a student, give the student the option to pass or call on a different student. When you structure peer conversations, listen especially to students who opt out of whole-group conversations to check for understanding, encourage, and give productive feedback.

DEEPEN DISCOURSE: Often, when sharing ideas in a whole-class discussion, students share ideas one at a time, and there is no extended dialogue. Shift this dynamic by using the Build Ideas Ball Toss strategy.

BUILD IDEAS BALL TOSS

WHY? The Build Ideas Ball Toss strategy is a powerful way to shift the leadership of whole-group discussion from the teacher to students while helping students actively listen to one another to engage in an extended discussion. I use this strategy to help me break my habit of calling on each speaker and responding to each idea. It demands students actively listen to one another, and it's fun!

HOW? Have students stand in a circle or sit at their desks in a circle (ensure nothing fragile is on any desk). Ask an open-ended question, ideally one students have already discussed in pairs. Choose a small ball or another soft item to toss from speaker to speaker.

The rules:

1. Toss a small ball (or another soft item) to the first student you call on to speak.

2. Any student who wants to respond to the idea that student shares (e.g., adding to the idea, providing additional evidence, asking questions, or disagreeing) raises his or her hand.

3. The student with the ball tosses it to any student with a raised hand.

4. As long as students continue to build upon the idea the first student shared, they toss the ball to one another. When a student wants to introduce a completely new idea, the ball must first go back to the teacher.

5. The teacher cannot speak unless holding the ball, except to clarify the rules. Do your best to honor this rule as it helps you democratize the discussion so students can truly take the lead.

EXAMPLE IN A LANGUAGE ARTS LESSON: This is a great structure to use when discussing a high-level open-ended question about a text (printed, digital, video, or other) that is relevant to students. For example, we used this in eighth grade to discuss the author's message in Rhina P. Espaillat's poem "Bilingual/Bilingüe." First, students watched an online video of a student reciting the poem. Next, they read a printed copy and annotated their own thoughts. Then, students discussed with partners. As a fourth step, we gathered in a circle and used the Build Ideas Together Ball Toss strategy to discuss ideas from the poem including main ideas and message. The discussion was rich with students' unique thinking, justification with text evidence and life experiences, questions, and divergent perspectives.

3.2 PARTNER CONVERSATION STRUCTURES

WHAT AND WHY?

Partner structures are the go-to strategy for engaging all students in a conversation during any lesson. Partner structures are the easiest to use and are the most time-efficient way to give all students opportunities to talk and actively listen. Use partner conversation structures every day instead of calling on individual students with raised hands.

STRUCTURES FOR PARTNER CONVERSATIONS

Think-Pair-Share: Partners first think silently and then discuss ideas together. Finally, some students share idea(s) from their partner discussions with the whole class.

Think-Write-Pair-Share: First, students think and write independently. Then, they discuss with a partner. Finally, some report to the whole group. Writing first gives students additional think time before the conversation. This structure supports reluctant speakers. You can also use "think-annotate," "think-sketch," or "think-jot" phrases in a graphic organizer as variations to "think-write."

Think-Pair-Write-Share: Partners first think silently and then discuss ideas together. Next, students write a response independently. Finally, some students share what they wrote with the whole class. In this variation, the partner conversation helps students build up ideas together before the writing part of the task. This structure supports reluctant writers.

Partner Conversations in Context: There are unlimited tasks and contexts possible for partner conversations. Here are a few examples: Before reading a picture book aloud, a primary teacher shows students the cover illustration and title and uses think-pair-share to have students predict what the story will be about. During the reading, she has students revisit and/or revise their predictions with a partner. In a high school math class, the teacher uses think-write-pair-share to have students first sketch or solve a solution to a problem and then discuss their approach with a partner. During a middle school science lab, a teacher structures think-pair-write-share to have students collaborate to describe

the chemical reaction they observe orally, write observations in their lab notes, and then share observations together with the class. Replace traditional hand raising with partner conversations in every lesson, every day.

FLIP-TO TIP:
Flip to page 80 for "Color-Coded Writing," a powerful strategy for peer conversations.

Barrier Game: Put a visual barrier between partners, such as two file folders taped together to make a self-standing screen. Give each partner the same items to manipulate, such as pattern blocks (e.g., two parallelograms, three squares, and one triangle), or cut up sections of a text. Partner A lays out the items in a specific way and then describes the layout to a partner. Partner B listens and asks clarifying questions in order to lay out the items in the same way. When both partners believe they have the same layout, they lift the screen to check. This is a great game to promote active listening. Note: Unlike the other partner structures, the barrier game doesn't work for all conversation tasks.

NOTES

_____

_____

3.3 SMALL-GROUP CONVERSATION STRUCTURES

WHAT AND WHY?

Small-group conversation structures are great for engaging a table group or any small group of students in a collaborative conversation. Unlike in a partner conversation, where the student listening will always be the next to talk, in a small-group conversation there are many possible dynamics for turn taking and building up ideas together. Use small-group conversations when you want to add variety or complexity to how students collaborate to discuss ideas.

STRUCTURES FOR SMALL-GROUP CONVERSATIONS

Numbered Heads: Have students at each table count up from one so that each student has a number (1, 2, 3, etc.). Ask a question to elicit discussion. When time is up, select a number and have the student with that number from each table report to the class. This is a go-to structure to give every student an accountable role while leaving conversation dynamics open-ended. A student can opt to be silent during the small-group conversation and still have an important role to listen and be prepared to report for the group.

Numbered Heads in Context: After reading and annotating a text about ocean pollution, a teacher uses the numbered heads strategy to have students to discuss the effects of human pollution on the ocean environment. First, students discuss the effects in their small groups. Next, the teacher spins a projected spinner to randomly choose which number will report to the whole group. She calls on number 3, and has each student with that number show a silent thumbs-up or thumbs-down if ready to share. If any thumbs are down, she gives the table groups an extra minute to prepare the reporting student to share. Student number 3 from each table then reports an effect of ocean pollution to the group.

Talking Chips: Ask a question to elicit discussion. Each member receives the same number of chips (plastic markers, pennies, etc.). Each time a member contributes to the conversation, he or she tosses a chip into the center of the table. Once individuals have used up their chips, they no longer speak. Continue discussion until all members have exhausted their chips. This structure helps students build awareness about how often they speak in a group and gives them a tool to ensure everyone has a voice in the conversation. Try it occasionally for this purpose, then drop the structure to create room for the natural flow of authentic conversations fueled by engaging topics and texts.

Pass the Stick: At each table group, students pass a "talking stick" or other class-adopted object to designate the speaker. When holding the stick, each student takes a turn contributing to the conversation. This is the most structured approach for ensuring every student has a turn, and it's valuable for accountable participation. The flip side of this structure is it does not encourage students to respond to one another in a natural conversation.

Pass the Stick in Context: To build community, use the pass the stick strategy with getting-to-know-you questions like "What is one thing people may not know about you?" or "What is your favorite song?" Pass the talking stick and give all students an opportunity to share or pass when the stick comes to them. Start the year asking surface-level questions about favorites, and build toward deeper questions to check in with students' emotions, reactions to a current event, or priorities in the world. To review key concepts at the end of any lesson, use the pass the stick strategy to have students reflect in small groups, "What is one thing you want to remember from this lesson?" If you are reading this chapter with colleagues, try the pass the stick strategy to each reflect, "What is one strategy you want to try in your classroom?"

NOTES

_____

_____

WHAT AND WHY?

Use up and moving structures as an energizing movement break and to engage students in talking with peers who aren't seated at the same table. The question you ask, and the time you provide for the discussion, will determine how shallow or deep these conversations become.

STRATEGIES FOR UP AND MOVING CONVERSATIONS

Clock Partners: This is a variation on think-pair-share to add movement and vary partners. To prepare for this strategy, have each student draw a simple clock with the times 12, 3, 6, and 9 written on the circle. Have students move around the room to find four different partners who are available for an "appointment" at a specific time on the clock.

Clock Partners in Context: Once you have established the clock partners structure, you can use this at any time as a variation from "turn to your neighbor" think-pair-share. For example, after annotating a paragraph of science text about photosynthesis for main ideas, a ninth-grade biology teacher has students explain the key concept to their "3 p.m." clock partner. Students find their 3 p.m. partners, discuss standing up, and then return to their seats for the next part of the lesson.

Collaborative Brainstorm: Ask any question that elicits a range of possible short answers. On the collaborative brainstorm reproducible (flip to p. 285 in the Appendix), students write one or more of their own responses. Then, the teacher sets a time limit (three to seven minutes) and has students mingle to share responses with different individuals in the room. Students write each new idea they hear in a different box.

Collaborative Brainstorm in Context: A social studies teacher uses the collaborative brainstorm after a unit on the impacts of colonization on North

America to have students create a list of important impacts together. In a language arts class, after students read "Sally" by Sandra Cisneros, they use the collaborative brainstorm to generate many possible adjectives they can use to describe Sally. After the brainstorm, they star one adjective they will justify with text evidence in a literary response, and have a deeper discussion with a partner to build up ideas in preparation for writing.

Inside Circle/Outside Circle:
Students stand in two concentric circles. Half the students are on the outside facing in, and half are on the inside facing their partners. Teachers ask any question that elicits a range of possible short answers. Partners discuss. When the teacher gives a signal, students in the inside circle take a step to the right (clockwise) to change partners. Have students discuss the same question with multiple partners or ask a different question before each rotation.

Traveling 4-by-4: First, have students stand in groups of four around the periphery of the room. Number students in each group from 1 to 4. Next, ask a question for all the small groups to discuss at the same time. Signal for students to pause their discussion, then call a number between 1 and 4. Students with the number called rotate one group to the right (clockwise) and summarize their last group's ideas with their new group. The teacher then asks a new question and repeats the process.

3.5 FISHBOWL STRUCTURE

WHAT AND WHY?

The fishbowl structure is a useful strategy for modeling and reflecting on peer discussion dynamics as a whole class. With fishbowl, you position one peer discussion (pair, small group, or half the class) in the center of the room, and have all other students observe the discussion with a specific focus.

DIFFERENT WAYS TO USE FISHBOWL

Use Fishbowl to Model Expectations: One way to use fishbowl is to put a group or pair in the center that you are confident will model a conversation skill you want others to use. You might rehearse the skill with the students before the fishbowl or simply observe their success before choosing the students to be in the fishbowl.

Use Fishbowl to Reflect on Conversation Dynamics: When you use fishbowl to model, you preselect the inner conversation group and have observers watch to learn a specific skill. By contrast, make fishbowl more open-ended by inviting any students to participate

in the inner conversation and having observers watch to reflect on what they see. Use the following active observation tasks to enhance this approach.

Enhance Fishbowl With Active Observation: Make fishbowl more dynamic by giving observers an active observation task. Choose an observation task relevant to conversation skills you are teaching, such as one of the following:

- Note when speakers give text evidence. Write the phrases they use to reference evidence, or highlight the part(s) of the text they reference.

- Note participation. Tally who speaks or note what people say to bring one another into the conversation.

- Note active listening. Write phrases you hear that show you a speaker is responding to what someone else has said, or note nonverbal listening observed.

- Notice the building of ideas together. When people speak, tally whether they introduce a new idea or build upon what someone has just said.

- Notice questioning and prompts. Write questions peers ask of one another or prompts (e.g., "Tell me more") they use in conversation.

Use Fishbowl for Teachable Moments: Do a spontaneous fishbowl when you notice a pair or table group excelling with a conversation skill or dynamic. First ask the students if they are willing to rewind and replay that part of their conversation (to the best of their memory) in a fishbowl. Then ask the class to freeze and turn to watch the team. Make this brief. Encourage other pairs/teams to integrate the skill they just observed into their conversations.

NOTES

_____

_____

_____

_____

_____

_____

_____

_____

3.6 LISTENING TO CONVERSATIONS AS FORMATIVE DATA

WHAT AND WHY?

What students say and how they say it in conversations with peers is rich data about how they learn, what they understand, what they misunderstand, and how they collaborate. It is also a go-to formative assessment for language use.

STRATEGIES TO LISTEN TO CONVERSATIONS AS FORMATIVE DATA

Focus on a Few Students: In each peer conversation, listen to a few students. You won't have time to hear every conversation, so be strategic about listening to different partners or groups each time students discuss. Prioritize listening to students who do the least talking in whole-group discussions, especially ELs, so you have real-time formative data on their strengths and instructional priorities to excel with the goals of your lesson.

Focus on Priority Learning Goals: Listen for one or two aspects of the conversation that are most important for you right now to shape your instruction. For example, as students make inferential claims about a character, you may choose to listen for a literacy goal, a language objective, or a conversation skill such as one of the following:

Literacy goal:

* Do students make claims that involve an inference or analysis beyond what is literally stated in the text, or do they read from the literal text?

Language objective:

* Do students use effective word choice to communicate their thinking about characters? Do they use general adjectives or precise words to talk about character emotions or traits?

Conversation skill:

* Do students each say one idea and then stop talking, or do they build up ideas together in an extended conversation?

To make gathering formative data easy, I've included questions like these for every literacy goal in Section IV of this guide. Look for the heading "Observe" for questions to help you focus your observation of peer conversations to gather formative data.

Listen for literacy goals when you want to check for understanding with the primary content goals for your lesson. Listen for language use to learn about the linguistic assets students bring to the task and the aspects of language you may need to teach or scaffold to ensure their success. Watch and listen for conversation dynamics to learn more about students' ever-evolving skills to collaborate in extended academic conversations.

Use a Rubric to Quantify Conversation Data: In addition to taking qualitative notes on conversations, you can quantify observations with a rubric. Figure 3.5 is one example of a rubric quantifying the question "Do students each say one idea and stop talking, or do they build up ideas together in an extended conversation?" Be sure to use a high-level task that motivates an extended conversation when you use this rubric.

FIGURE 3.5

SAMPLE CONVERSATION RUBRIC FOCUSED ON EXCHANGES

BRIDGING 4	Student collaborates to converse with more than five exchanges on the topic. For example: • Support with evidence • Paraphrase • Synthesize
EXPANDING 3	Student collaborates to converse with three or four exchanges on the topic. For example: • Elaborate • Ask/answer questions • Agree/disagree • Build on an idea
EARLY EXPANDING 2	Student shares one idea with a peer in a sentence or two. There is occasionally an extended conversation.
EMERGING 1	Student shares one short answer with a peer in a highly structured task. There is no extended conversation.
0	Student is silent in peer conversations.

Download a more comprehensive rubric for collaborative conversations at www.tonyasinger.com/elexcellence.

3.7 TOOLS TO DIFFERENTIATE STUDENT CONVERSATIONS

Effective differentiation always begins with high expectations and close observation of how students engage. For any conversation task relevant to your teaching, choose at least one conversation goal (see "Expect") and a question to focus your observation (see "Observe"), then use the data you observe to *differentiate supports*. Here is a flow of resources you can use.

EXPECT

Use your local standards and goals to set high expectations and clearly communicate your learning intentions. Goals for conversations include, for example, the following:

CONVERSATION GOALS	
Conversations	• I can take turns in conversations with peers.
	• I can ask questions related to what peers discuss, and respond to others' questions and comments.
	• I can discuss disagreements respectfully to both explain my point of view and learn from others' points of view.
Text-Dependent Conversations	• I can read closely and annotate to prepare for conversations.
	• I can refer to the text to support and justify my thinking.

ENGAGE

Ask a high-level, open-ended question or provide a conversation prompt that is relevant to your lesson objectives. Use a partner or small-group structure from pages 54–57 to invite all students into the peer discussion.

OBSERVE

Choose at least one question from the following examples to focus your observation:

- Who participates? Do all students take turns contributing to the conversation and listening to others?

- Do students engage in an extended back-and-forth dialogue or each just say one idea, then stop talking?

- What conversation skills do you observe? Do students express opinions, ask questions, clarify, support their ideas, and/or discuss disagreements? Do they paraphrase or synthesize ideas?

- In text-dependent conversations, do students reference their annotations or the text to support their ideas?

SUPPORT

Use what you learned from observing students to prioritize what you will teach and support to help them thrive in collaborative conversations with peers.

PERSONALIZATION CHART

IF STUDENTS . . .	THEN TRY ONE OR MORE OF THESE STRATEGIES:
Are silent	• If students who are silent are emerging ELs, use the Strategies to Actively Engage Emerging ELs on p. 72. • To engage any student who is silent, try every strategy in this section. • Use highly engaging, relevant conversation topics and tasks. • Build a safe classroom culture that fosters risk taking and values diverse points of view.
Don't look at peers or seem to listen to them when talking	• Model nonverbal listening: look and learn. • Model ways to respond to a partner's idea, including asking a clarifying question, agreeing or disagreeing, or prompting for evidence. Flip to p. 70 for linguistic frames. • After partners discuss, expect students to report their partner's idea to the class. • Use the Numbered Heads strategy on p. 56 to structure accountable listening in small-group discussions. • Use the Build Ideas Ball Toss strategy on p. 53 to structure accountable listening in a whole-class discussion. • To build listening skills, play the barrier game on p. 55, which gives students an authentic opportunity for listening closely to one another.
Dominate the discussion while others are silent	• Structure partner turn taking as detailed on p. 67. • Structure small-group turn taking with the talking chips strategy on p. 57. • Try also the strategies listed above to engage silent students.

CONTINUED

CONTINUED ⮕

IF STUDENTS . . .	THEN TRY ONE OR MORE OF THESE STRATEGIES:
Don't engage in extended conversations, but say one idea and then stop talking	• Make sure the conversation task is high-level and open-ended and requires more than just sharing "one answer." • Model expectations for an extended conversation using the fishbowl strategy on p. 60 or the exemplar strategy on p. 128. • Teach students to prompt and ask questions of one another in peer conversations. Flip to pp. 70–71 for prompts. • Provide students enough talk time for an extended conversation. Make sure they aren't feeling rushed to finish and move on to a second task.
Only speak if given a linguistic frame	• Plan conversation tasks on topics that are highly relevant and engaging to your students. • Build on success with familiar topics to expand students' risk taking in conversations. • If students are emerging ELs, use the Strategies to Actively Engage Emerging ELs on p. 72. • Emphasize meaningful communication over grammatical perfection.

STRATEGIES TO SUPPORT AND DIFFERENTIATE CONVERSATIONS

Model Expectations: Model the specific conversation skills you expect by acting out a conversation with another student, using the fishbowl strategy (pp. 60–61) or analyzing a video exemplar of a conversation with your class. Examples of skills you might model include active listening, asking clarifying questions, building up ideas together, and disagreeing respectfully.

Structure Who Discusses Together: A powerful management structure for any classroom is to preassign partners and small groups for peer discussions. For example, when students are in a table of four, set up three easy structures for discussions:

a. Elbow partner (partner discussion with person next to you)

b. Face partner (partner discussion with person across from you)

c. Table group (small-group discussion with table group)

Seat Students Strategically: Enhance peer conversations with the following seating recommendations:

Flip-to Tip: Flip to pages 52–57 to learn specific strategies to structure partner, small-group, and whole-class conversations.

- Pair reluctant speakers with patient, encouraging students who don't dominate a conversation.

- Plan pairs and groups to be heterogeneous, with a range of academic levels and proficiency levels. A moderate range (e.g., lowest with middle level, middle with high) is typically more productive than an extreme range (e.g., lowest with highest).

- Ideally, have emerging ELs participate in a trio during routine partner discussions. When using English is the goal, the emerging EL can listen first to the other two students, then either share a new idea or repeat an idea already shared. When content expertise is the goal, ideally have the emerging EL discuss content concepts with another student fluent in that language before engaging in the English conversation task. (This is not an option if your EL is the only one in the class proficient in the home language.)

Structure Turn Taking: If some students dominate and others are silent, use one or both of the following scaffolds to structure turn taking:

1. Assign students roles (e.g., A/B partners) and specify who speaks first.
2. Time how long each partner has to speak.

Either structure helps ensure reluctant students participate and confident speakers don't dominate. The flip side of both structures is they hinder the natural back-and-forth exchange of ideas that is our ultimate goal for peer conversations. Use this scaffold to increase participation, then lose it as soon as possible to empower students to initiate turn taking and engage in natural exchange of ideas.

Start With "Think-Write": When you begin any peer conversation with a "think-write" step, this slows the process in a way that benefits ELs, introverts, reluctant speakers, and any student who engages best with more think time. Starting with "think-write" also gives the teacher an opportunity to scan written responses for a quick formative assessment. On the flip side, adding a writing step to a peer conversation requires one to two minutes of additional time. It can also lead to stilted conversation in which students only read what they wrote, without any back-and-forth exchange of ideas. Vary when you add "think-write" to a peer conversation based on your timing and priorities and to learn more about what works best for different students in your classroom.

Provide Linguistic Scaffolds: Provide linguistic frames or word banks to help students with language specific to the topic, task, and conversation moves you expect. Flip to page 70 for examples of linguistic frames for basic conversation moves relevant to any conversation. Flip to Section IV for many more specific frames and word banks relevant to each literacy goal.

For examples of how to differentiate conversation supports see Figure 3.6.

FIGURE 3.6

QUICK GUIDE TO DIFFERENTIATE PEER CONVERSATIONS

	STRUCTURE PEER TALK	SCAFFOLD LANGUAGE USE
BRIDGING Light or No Support	Structure multistep tasks that require collaboration, but don't structure each conversation and step. For example, have students collaborate to research and create a podcast about the effects of pollution.	Use scaffolds occasionally to validate students' strong language choices (e.g., start a word bank with words students use) or expand how they use language (e.g., add new words to that word bank that include nuanced shades of meaning).
EXPANDING Moderate Support	Structure specific conversation tasks using partner or small-group strategies that let students initiate turn taking. For example, after reading a text about pollution, structure numbered heads to have students discuss effects.	Provide a range of linguistic frames representing a variety of sentence structures and/or a bank of words that are optional for students to use during the task. Encourage students to go beyond the scaffolds.
EMERGING Substantial Support	Structure turn taking in peer conversations. For example, after reading a paragraph about pollution together, give each partner one minute to share one effect. Give partners roles (A/B) and tell partner B to begin.	Model and guide students in doing the task using one linguistic frame and a word bank that can be used to complete the frame. Structure peer practice so all students use the scaffolds you modeled.

QUESTIONS TO REFLECT AND ADAPT TEACHING

Watch students as they engage in conversations and reflect on their strengths and priorities for learning.

Reflect:

- Do students engage in back-and-forth conversations building up ideas together?

- What impact does the task I structure have on how students engage in conversations? Which types of tasks and topics lead to the best collaborative conversations?

- How do the scaffolds I use impact student engagement and learning? Do they advance or hinder student participation? Advance or hinder learning? Advance or hinder critical thinking? Advance or hinder language use?

- What shifts will I make in my teaching and scaffolds to build on the strengths I see in my students and to help them thrive with collaborative conversations across the curriculum?

GUIDE TO ADJUST CONVERSATION SUPPORTS ACCORDING TO NEED

If . . .	Then . . .
Some students don't participate	⬆ Increase supports
Some students dominate the conversation	⬆ Increase supports
Students struggle unproductively with the task	⬆ Increase supports
Students actively engage in learning through challenge	*Keep this sweet spot!*
Students take risks to build up ideas together	*Keep this sweet spot!*
Students (above emerging EL) only copy your model	⬇ Decrease supports
Student responses are predictable or canned	⬇ Decrease supports
Students don't get to struggle, think, or problem-solve	⬇ Decrease supports
You want to assess student conversation skills	⬇ Remove supports

3.8 LINGUISTIC FRAMES FOR CONVERSATIONS

WHAT AND WHY?

Use the conversation prompts and linguistic frames provided in Figure 3.7 strategically to help students learn and apply conversation skills to both prompt peers and respond in the natural flow of student-driven conversations.

FIGURE 3.7

PROMPTS AND FRAMES FOR EXTENDED CONVERSATIONS

Focus	Conversation Prompts	Possible Linguistic Frames
Express Ideas Make Claims	What do you think? What's your point of view? (See also every prompt in Section IV such as "What do you infer about this character?")	I think _____. I believe _____. In my opinion, _____. It's evident that _____. According to _____, _____.
Clarify	What do you mean by _____? Are you saying that _____? I'm confused. Please explain.	What I'm trying to say is _____. I mean _____.
Support	What's your evidence? How do you know? What evidence supports your idea? What clues gave you that idea?	I know _____ because _____. One text detail that **shows** this is _____. The quote "[quote text]" shows me that _____. The author **demonstrates this point** when [paraphrase text evidence].

Focus	Conversation Prompts	Possible Linguistic Frames
Agree and Disagree	What's your perspective? Do you agree or disagree? Why?	I agree. I also think that _____. I disagree. I think that _____. You have a point. However, I think that _____. I disagree with your idea that [paraphrase]. Instead, _____. I agree that [paraphrase]. However, I disagree with your idea that [paraphrase]. Instead, _____.

TIPS TO BE STRATEGIC

Prioritize Meaningful Communication: Response frames can tragically reduce peer conversations to scripted exchanges devoid of thinking or authentic engagement. Avoid this by making your tasks, topics, and texts engaging and inviting conversations *without* frames before offering frames as an optional resource to expand how students already naturally communicate.

Focus on One New Skill at a Time: When introducing prompts and frames for conversations, focus on one skill (e.g., clarify) at a time. Choose a relevant context to apply the skill that is connected to your curriculum. Model the skill, post the frames, and engage students in practicing the skill to deepen their content discussions.

Build Student Capacity to Prompt Deeper Discussions: Traditionally, the teacher prompts a conversation, and students respond. Change this dynamic by empowering students with prompts and questions they can ask of one another within peer conversations.

NOTES

_____

_____

_____

_____

3.9 STRATEGIES TO ACTIVELY ENGAGE EMERGING ELS

WHAT AND WHY?

When emerging ELs are learning academic content in English, it is important to use intentional strategies both to make your instruction comprehensible *and* to foster active participation. When possible, also use emerging ELs' primary language (flip to p. 24 for specific strategies) to help them access content and build on their linguistic assets to thrive with both your content and language learning goals. These pages emphasize strategies you can use when teaching content in English or teaching the English language to students who are new to English.

STRATEGIES TO MAKE YOUR TEACHING COMPREHENSIBLE

Model and Demonstrate: As you speak, make sure students see as well as hear your message. For example, if you want students to look at the heading of a nonfiction text, project the text and point to the heading as you give your verbal directions. If you want students to take turns in a peer conversation, act out turn taking in a conversation or show a short video of a conversation and point to the specific actions you want to emphasize. When you give oral directions, also write them on the board. When you explain your expectations for a written task, also share an exemplar of what success looks like. Ideally, give students a copy as well and engage all in pointing, underlining, or highlighting the specific parts of the exemplar you want them to notice. Modeling benefits all students, not just emerging ELs. Flip to page 126 for more specific strategies to model.

Give Directions Orally and in Writing: For some students, listening is more challenging than reading. For others, reading is more challenging than listening. Provide directions orally and in writing to give emerging ELs (and all learners) two access points to directions for any classroom task. With access to the internet, an emerging EL can also type directions into a translation site as needed to use primary language assets to comprehend.

Rephrase: In other words, say things in more than one way (like I just did). Rephrasing is especially important when you use vocabulary students may not understand or an idiomatic expression (e.g., "That's a piece of cake") that could be especially confusing for English learners.

Avoid Idiomatic Expressions: When possible, avoid idiomatic expressions as emerging ELs will try to make meaning from the literal translation and miss the meaning you intend. If you let one slip, use rephrasing to clarify your meaning. When idiomatic expressions are part of classroom texts or communication, teach the meanings of these expressions directly using images, explanation, examples in context, and images.

Chunk Your Speech: When giving directions to an emerging EL, chunk your speech so you say one sentence at a time clearly. Pause between sentences to allow think time.

Use Visuals: Use pictures, real objects (aka realia), or your own quick sketches to help you communicate concrete vocabulary (e.g., pencil, bridge) with ease. Use graphic organizers to represent concepts visually and demonstrate how texts are organized and how to organize ideas into written texts. A picture is worth a thousand words!

Preteach Important Vocabulary: Teach important vocabulary before your lesson (flip to pp. 114–125 for strategies) and also quick teach words that can be taught in the moment with a sketch, demonstration, or cognate (p. 124).

Check for Understanding: It's not enough to make what you say comprehensible. In addition to these many important strategies to make your talk comprehensible, use strategies to foster active participation to facilitate two-way communication so you can check for understanding.

STRATEGIES TO
FOSTER ACTIVE PARTICIPATION

Use one or more of the following strategies to adjust a lesson task so that emerging ELs can actively participate with a verbal or nonverbal response even before they feel comfortable speaking a full English sentence on their own. If you get silence with an open-ended conversation task, use one or more of the following approaches to adjust the task so the student can actively participate and you can get valuable formative data about student comprehension and learning.

Total Physical Response: Use physical gestures and movement to make your communication comprehensible to emerging ELs. Also structure opportunities for emerging ELs to respond with a motion, a low-stress entry point to participate without words.

Examples:

Act this out with me [model and guide an action as you teach a word].

Point to the _____.

Touch the _____.

Put the _____ on the _____.

Open to page _____.

Clap if _____.

Turn around, stand up [etc.].

Choose Between Two Options: To encourage emerging ELs to move from silence to taking risks to speak in English, create tasks that ask for a choice between two options.

Yes/No Examples:

Is this a/an _____?

Is _____ a kind character?

Do you like _____?

Either/Or Examples:

Is this hot or cold?

Is the character mean or nice?

Respond With a Simple Frame and Word Bank: Post a list of words with colors and the frame "I like _____." Ask, "Which color do you like?"

Post a list of emotion words. Teach each word with a picture and total physical response. Post the frame "I feel _____." Ask, "How do you feel?"

Post a word bank of prepositions of location (e.g., under, on, in) and the frame "The pencil is
_____ the table." Move the pencil under the table and ask, "Where is the pencil?"

STRATEGIES TO ENGAGE
EMERGING ELS IN PEER DISCUSSIONS

Group Emerging ELs Strategically: When structuring partner or small-group conversations,
ideally pair an emerging EL with at least one student with strong English skills who is
fluent in the EL's home language. If this is not possible, at least ensure that students paired
with emerging ELs are good role models for classroom expectations and are patient at
encouraging peers to take risks to participate.

Invite Primary Language Use: When conceptual understanding and higher-level thinking is
the goal, ideally have emerging ELs engage in the conversation task with other student(s)
fluent in the ELs' home language. If this is not an option in your classroom population and
the emerging EL has primary language literacy, give the emerging EL an opportunity to
research the concept in the primary language online before engaging in a lesson on the
topic in English. These are powerful strategies to ensure emerging ELs access core content
and also to value the linguistic strengths of multilingual students.

Create Low-Risk Opportunities to Speak: When English language use is the goal, have the
emerging EL listen first to the other students in the group, then repeat back words, phrases,
or a full-sentence response another student has shared. For an additional scaffold, provide
a response frame and/or word bank for the emerging EL and guide practice.

Use Flexible Grouping: If you have multiple emerging ELs, vary your small-group
configurations so that for some tasks emerging ELs are in heterogeneous groups with
fluent speakers to hear and use English peers and for other tasks they are together with
you for personalized instruction at their language level.

NOTES

_____

_____

_____

_____

_____

3.10 TOTAL PHYSICAL RESPONSE STRATEGIES

WHAT AND WHY?

Total physical response (TPR) is a strategy to have all students move together for a task. You can use TPR to guide all students in the same movement (e.g., when teaching the word *reject*, have students push a hand away while saying "reject"). You can also invite different TPR responses (e.g., "Show me a facial expression that reveals how you infer the character feels") or have students create their own movements to demonstrate a concept they learned.

STRATEGIES FOR TOTAL PHYSICAL RESPONSE

Point To: This is the most basic TPR move and especially valuable to engage emerging ELs in demonstrating comprehension without words. It also benefits all students. Here are some ways to use "Point To" every day:

- When you *give directions*, have students point to what you describe. For example, when you are talking about using headings, have students point to a heading in the text in front of them. This benefits all students with an active listening task and gives you a quick read on comprehension of your directions.

- When you *teach vocabulary* related to classroom objects or anything represented in pictures, use this strategy to reinforce learning and check for understanding. For example, when teaching basic classroom objects to an emerging EL, saying "point to the marker" or "point to the pencil sharpener" is a great way to reinforce vocabulary and check for understanding even before the student feels comfortable saying the word in English. Use the same strategy with fluent speakers after teaching new concrete vocabulary such as "point to the bibliography" or "point to the footnote."

- When you want students to *use text evidence to support a claim* and you aren't having them mark or highlight the text, structure think-point-pair-share and use the "point" step to visually check for understanding before students begin their discussions.

Act Out a Word Meaning: There are many approaches to act out a word meaning from teacher-directed to student-directed. Acting out a word meaning helps students understand the word. Having students copy your action as they say the word helps students remember the word. Having students create their own action to demonstrate a word's meaning helps them deepen learning and gives you an opportunity to check for understanding.

Thumb Vote: Use this quick, silent TPR strategy to have students show you one of three answers to a question: (1) thumbs-up, (2) thumbs-down, or (3) thumbs to the side to answer any yes/no/maybe question. One daily way to use this strategy is to do a thumb vote after giving directions to get a quick read on students' readiness to begin. With a thumb at the chest, students can quickly show you their answer:

Thumb up = Ready.

Thumb to the side = I have questions but will ask my peers.

Thumb down – Help! I need more clarity from the teacher, please.

Do a quick scan of the room to determine next steps. If there are many thumbs down, clarify and reteach with everyone. If there are only a few, go support students at their tables or bring them into a small group with you for a brief mini-lesson to address their questions and confusions.

Also use the thumb vote to get a quick read on students' opinions on a topic before, during, or after a class discussion. Have students show you with their thumbs if they agree, disagree, or are undecided.

Finger Rubric Vote: A finger rubric vote is like a thumb vote with more options. Use a finger rubric when you want students to choose among four or five options. For example, you might ask students how well they know a word and have them vote with fingers to show their response on the following rubric scale:

1. I haven't seen or heard it.

2. I've seen or heard it before.

3. I know it somewhat.

4. I know it well and use it.

Also use the finger rubric vote when you analyze exemplars of student work (writing, conversations, multimedia, etc.) with a rubric. Start with a rubric of the success criteria that ideally you've developed with your class. Have students analyze an anonymous example of student work in silence or with a partner to determine the best rubric score. Next, use the finger rubric vote to have all students simultaneously show the score they think the work exemplifies. Notice the range of responses. Follow the silent vote with a peer discussion structure in which students make a claim about the ideal rubric score and justify and debate their claims with evidence from the work and the rubric. To calibrate your expectations for scoring, keep discussing until all agree on the score within one point.

Vote With Your Feet: Use this great movement strategy during any whole-class discussion on a debatable topic. State an opinion and have students stand along the wall on the right side of the room if they agree, along the left side if they disagree, or along the back wall. Call on students from each side to speak in support of their opinion and persuade others to agree. After students hear diverse viewpoints, give all an opportunity to move again if they have changed their minds. Use this beyond traditional debate topics (e.g., "We should have cell phones in class") for any classroom discussion involving disagreement (e.g., "This story is suspenseful," "This text is politically biased," or "This essay exemplifies a 3 on our rubric").

3.11 READ AND ANNOTATE STRATEGIES

WHAT AND WHY?

Reading, of course, is another form of active participation in our classrooms. Use these structures, in addition to peer conversations, to foster active, accountable interaction with texts.

STRATEGIES TO READ AND ANNOTATE TOGETHER

Read Together: Independent reading is important. In classrooms, we also read texts together for many reasons: enjoyment, to learn new content, to learn comprehension strategies, to analyze authors' craft, and more. When reading a shared text together, choose one or more of the strategies shown in Figure 3.8 according to your goals.

FIGURE 3.8

STRATEGIES TO READ TOGETHER

Strategy	What and Why?
READ-ALOUD	Read aloud to enjoy a text together, model fluent reading, and make complex texts accessible to students not yet reading at the level of the text.
RECORDED READ-ALOUD	Some digital texts include a "read-aloud" option for students to listen to the text as they read. This may be a simple audio or audio combined with highlighting each word being read in the text.
CHORAL READING	Have all students read a word, phrase, or sentence with you chorally. Use choral reading to emphasize part of a text and/or to create an easy participation opportunity for emerging readers or emerging ELs.
ORAL CLOZE	Read aloud, stop at about one word per paragraph, and have students chorally read that one word aloud before you continue. This takes some practice to get started and reinforcement to engage every student. Use this strategy to build fluency after reading aloud for meaning and/or before silent reading for deeper comprehension.
PARTNER CLOZE	When your class knows the oral cloze strategy, you can have students take turns leading the strategy with a partner. Use this activity to build fluency and encourage multiple readings of a text.

Strategy	What and Why?
READ-ANNOTATE-DISCUSS	Sharing a text doesn't have to mean reading aloud, as the strategies above all imply. Especially in upper grades, when rereading a text closely with a shared comprehension focus, use the read-annotate-discuss strategy to have students reread a section of text in preparation for a peer discussion.
CHUNKING TEXT	When having students read to annotate or reread to look for text evidence, you can easily adjust the challenge of the task by focusing on a small or large chunk of the text. Focus on one paragraph at a time for maximum support or a full article for minimum support.

Read Together in Context: A fifth-grade teacher uses a sequence of read together strategies to engage students in closely reading a narrative in her anthology. First, she reads the text aloud as students listen to enjoy it and think about the main ideas or confusions. Next, she chunks the text to focus on one meaningful section and uses oral cloze to reread that section with a specific comprehension focus (e.g., on character or author's craft). She then has students reread the section independently to find specific text evidence to back up their claims.

Flip-to tip:
Flip to Chapters 9–11 for annotation tasks specific to each literacy goal.

Annotate: Annotation is a go-to strategy to note thinking while reading and prepare for peer discussion about text. There are many different approaches to annotating, and there is also value in sharing a common language of annotation in your classroom. My go-to approach is to have students

- Highlight main ideas
- Circle unknown words or confusing phrases
- Write reactions, reflections, or inferences in the margins
- Underline text evidence relevant to the task and your claim(s)

When reading texts that can't be marked, choose an alternative approach such as one of the following:

- Use a "wiki-stick" to temporarily underline text evidence relevant to the task.
- Draw a line down the center of a page (or make a two-column table in a digital document) to create a double-entry journal. Write text evidence on the left side and a corresponding inference, interpretation, or question on the right side. Repeat.
- Have students write their inference on a self-stick note and place it on the page next to the text evidence that supports it.
- Have students write their inference in a graphic organizer (p. 290) and write each piece of text evidence on a self-stick note that will fit in the organizer.

COLLABORATE TO WRITE STRATEGIES

WHAT AND WHY?

In addition to teaching writing, integrate short written responses into everyday tasks to foster active participation, support language development, and check for understanding. Have students write before, during, or after conversations. Depending on your goals and timing, have students write independently or in collaboration using one of the following strategies:

STRATEGIES TO COLLABORATE TO WRITE

Color-Coded Writing: Give each pair or small group a large piece of paper and a different-colored marker for each student. Have students collaborate to write a short response (sentence to paragraph) to any task. Invite students to collaborate to write in any way they choose with these parameters: each person must write with his or her own unique color, and all colors must be part of what students write together.

Differentiate how you structure Color-Coded Writing with these tips:

- First try this strategy with partners. When students are successful, try it with trios or small groups.

- When more structure is needed, have students take turns writing every other word in a single-sentence response.

Gallery Walk: As a follow-up to Color-Coded Writing, post each collaborative piece of writing around the room. Have groups rotate together to read what other groups posted. Give them a specific task for reading and reflecting such as one of the following:

- Identify and underline strong word choice, or recommend a strong word choice on a self-stick note and put it over a word.

- Write a check next to each example of text evidence, or write "What's the evidence?" on a self-stick note and put it next to an unsupported claim.

- Collaborate to analyze the response based on the success criteria. Write one strength and one goal for revision on a self-stick note.

Writing Online Together: I use this strategy professionally to co-author articles. Have students collaborate to create an online document (e.g., Google Doc) using separate log-ins and devices to contribute. This is the most efficient way to write and revise longer writing or multimedia together. Unlike Color-Coded Writing, which fosters conversations, this is not a good strategy for fostering oral communication. Using Google Docs, there is no need to color-code to track how each person contributes to the work. Accountability is built in. When students log in and write from different computers onto the same Google Doc, a teacher can use the "see revision history" feature to see how each student contributed to the work.

Peer Editing With Track Changes: I use this strategy professionally to collaborate with editors. Unlike the other collaborative strategies, this strategy begins with one student creating a digital document using Microsoft Word. The collaboration is the second step, when the student has a peer edit or make revisions within the document. Within Microsoft Word, choose "Tools/Track Changes/Highlight Changes." Every change the editing student makes in the document will be visible. The author can then "accept" or "reject" changes to revise the document. Tip: Turn Track Changes off when creating the final copy.

TIPS TO BE STRATEGIC

Choose Digital or Paper Based on Your Goals: Be clear about your goals when choosing your approach. What's your top priority? Efficiency? Conversations? Digital skills? Digital collaboration is most efficient in part because students usually write without talking at all. If conversations are your goal and the written task is a paragraph or less in length, use color-coded writing. If efficient collaboration is your priority to create a document or multimedia product, use online collaboration. If you want peers to edit documents created or pasted into Microsoft Word, use Track Changes.

NOTES

_____

_____

_____

_____

REFLECT ON CHAPTER 3:

- How and when do I structure peer conversations in my classroom?

- What is working most effectively in my current approach to structuring peer conversations?

- What is my next level of learning, and/or my students' next level of learning, to improve peer conversations in my classroom?

- Which strategies in this section will help me build from what I'm already doing to help my students thrive with conversations in new ways?

APPLY LEARNING TO TEACHING

- Plan a peer conversation task for an upcoming lesson. Plan your own task, or choose one from Section IV of this book. Choose one conversation structure from pages 54–61 to use for this task. Choose supports from pages 64–71 and/or participation strategies from pages 72–81 you anticipate will help your students thrive. Structure the task and watch students as they engage. What do you notice in terms of students' content understandings, conversation skills, and/or academic language use? How will you use this formative data to adjust how you structure and teach peer conversations?

COLLABORATE WITH COLLEAGUES

- Co-plan the previous task. Each try the task in your own classrooms and film one pair of students (including at least one EL) as they engage. Meet again to watch the videos together to reflect on student successes and challenges with the conversation task including content understandings, conversation skills, and academic language use. What trends do you notice among all students? What trends do you notice specific to ELs? How will you adjust teaching to build on successes and address challenges?

RELATED READING TO EXTEND YOUR LEARNING

Crawford, M., & Zwiers, J. (2011). *Academic conversations: Classroom talk that fosters critical thinking and content understandings.* Portland, ME: Stenhouse.

Singer, T., & Zwiers, J. (2016). What conversations capture. *Educational Leadership, 73*(7). Retrieved from http://www.ascd.org/publications/educational-leadership/apr16/vol73/num07/What-Conversations-Can-Capture.aspx

Zwiers, J., & Soto, I. (2017). *Academic language mastery: Conversational discourse in context.* Thousand Oaks, CA: Corwin.

SECTION III

SUPPORT

III. Support

iStock.com/monkeybusinessimages

CHAPTER 4

SUPPORT ELS STRATEGICALLY

"We must meet children where they are, we must understand them well to teach them well, and we must offer the right amount of supports and challenges to grow."

—Jennifer Serravallo (2015, p. 19)

When we talk about supports for English learners (ELs), we often lose the forest for the trees. Strategies, supports, and scaffolds are shiny and inviting. They are nouns of teaching ELs—a concrete solution to a complex challenge. They are easy to collect in trainings, books, and new curriculum. They are easy for administrators to look for in classrooms.

Supports are important to learn and use, and for this reason, I give them significant emphasis in this guide. Chapters 5–7 are your flip-to friendly resource for support strategies you can use to support ELs before, during, and after any lesson. Chapters 8–11 are provided to help you apply these supports to your academic literacy routines to teach specific literacy goals.

Before we get specific about *what* supports to use, let's focus on *why* and *how* to use supports so that they help our ELs thrive, rather than getting in their way.

Too many supports, or the wrong supports, can be problematic for ELs. If we overmodel, overguide, and overscaffold, we hinder student thinking and self-directed learning. When a support such as the linguistic frame is the norm in every student conversation year after year, students begin to rely on what was meant to be a temporary scaffold. Supports we use with good intentions get in the way of our goals. On the flip side, if we don't ever provide supports, we let our most vulnerable students flounder and fail.

So how do we use supports strategically? How do we use supports to help ELs build upon their assets to thrive in, and beyond, our classrooms? This is the essential question, the forest to always keep in mind as we focus on individual trees. The purpose of supports is embedded in that essential question: "to help ELs build upon their assets to thrive in, and beyond, our classrooms."

To realize this purpose, we get must specific about our goals and where students are in relation to our goals and then choose, lose, or adapt supports according to each student's assets and needs. In this chapter, I give you mindsets and tools to help you strategically support ELs every day. I organize the content with the following three questions:

What Supports Do ELs Need?

How Do I Personalize Supports?

How Do I Differentiate With Ease?

Let's start with the first question.

WHAT SUPPORTS DO ELS NEED?

There is no one answer to this question that is true for every English learner because ELs are a diverse group with a wide range of strengths and needs, and every lesson has different challenges and opportunities. There is, however, one process to answer this question that will help you find the right supports every time. Find the right supports for your unique students to thrive with four essential steps:

1. **EXPECT:** Get specific about your goals for students in this lesson.
2. **ENGAGE AND OBSERVE:** Engage ELs in a task related to your goals to identify their assets and needs for support with those goals.
3. **SUPPORT:** Choose and use instructional supports that will help ELs build from their assets to thrive with your goals.
4. **REFLECT:** Reflect on the impact of your supports on EL learning, and refine your approach to foster increasing levels of student-directed success.

Look familiar? Yes, these are the same essentials of reflective teaching that I keep emphasizing throughout this guide. To support ELs strategically, in ways that accelerate rather than remediate their learning, it is critical that we choose and lose supports within the context of reflective teaching.

This is true for supporting *all* students. Now let's get even more specific about the unique needs of ELs in core classrooms by focusing on two simultaneous goals we have for ELs: (1) excel with content learning and (2) learn language for success within, and beyond, school.

FIGURE 4.1

ESSENTIAL QUESTIONS TO CHOOSE AND ADJUST SUPPORTS FOR ELS

	Content Learning	Language Learning
EXPECT	What are my goals for student learning?	What aspects of language must students understand and use to excel with these goals?
ENGAGE AND OBSERVE	What do students say and do as they engage? What do their words and actions reveal about what they can understand and do related to my goals?	What language choices do students make? What do these reveal about their strengths and needs with language essential for success with this task?
SUPPORT	What instruction and supports will I provide to help students build from current understandings to succeed with the goal?	What instruction and scaffolds will I provide to build and support language connected to these goals?
REFLECT	How did my instruction and supports impact students' content understandings and success with my goals?	How did my instruction and supports influence students' understanding and/or use of language?

Thriving with **content learning** means excelling with the high expectations we have for all learners to excel with our content learning expectations. Your local standards and curriculum including texts, tests, and tasks drive your content learning expectations. The literacy demands of your content tasks are also an essential part of your content expectations. One reason to design supports for ELs is to help ELs excel with core content expectations, including high-level listening, speaking, reading, and writing tasks about academic content. Content learning supports for ELs include building background in concepts, connecting to students' prior knowledge and home language, modeling, using graphic organizers, and structuring collaborative conversations to deepen thinking.

Learning language for success within school means developing and using the academic language essential for listening, speaking, reading, and writing across the curriculum. We support language before, during, and beyond lesson tasks to help ELs understand and use language effectively. Examples of language supports (aka linguistic supports) include teaching vocabulary, teaching how language is used in a text, scaffolding language use with linguistic frames or word banks, and structuring conversations to develop oral academic language in meaningful ways.

Figure 4.1 expands the reflective teaching cycle to address these two simultaneous goals we have for ELs: content learning and language learning. These are your go-to questions to design and refine strategic supports for ELs. Read Figure 4.1 and reflect:

- For each essential verb (e.g., *expect*), how are the reflection questions the same for teaching content and teaching language? How are they different?
- Which questions do I regularly ask myself when planning or teaching?
- Which do I want to incorporate into my everyday approach?

To engage in reflective teaching with a focus on language, we first need clarity on the abstract question, what is language?

WHAT IS LANGUAGE?

To get specific about how to support language, we need to be clear about our goal. We often have more clarity about our content learning goals (e.g., reading standards or science standards) than our language learning goals. Why? Language is complicated, and for many of us who live and communicate in our primary language, it is invisible. It is the air we breathe as we communicate, not what we actually are thinking about or talking or writing about. It is like water to a fish.

What is language? is a big question that is still debated among linguists. For practical purposes, I'm going to be as precise as possible to share current thinking relevant to your everyday teaching with ELs.

"Academic language is the set of words, grammar, and organizational strategies used to describe complex ideas, higher-order thinking processes, and abstract concepts."

—Jeff Zwiers (2008, p. 20)

Language is more than vocabulary and grammar. Language shapes how we think and how we communicate and connect in the world. We can't isolate language from thinking and interaction—it is more complex than that. Language is action (van Lier & Walqui, 2012). Language is connection. To tease out a small aspect of language (e.g., vocabulary words) into a simple worksheet is like choosing one plant sample from a rain forest. Watering the isolated sample won't re-create the rain forest. Teaching language in isolation from rigorous academic content literacy won't empower ELs with the language they need to thrive with rigorous academic content literacy.

To learn academic language, ELs need opportunities to actively participate in meaningful, high-level learning and communication in core classrooms. They need opportunities to use language imperfectly in speaking and writing as they make meaning from complex texts, problem-solve, and express their own thinking with high-level tasks. ELs benefit from language teaching and scaffolds that help them make meaning from complexity and communicate effectively in academic conversations and tasks across the curriculum.

ESSENTIAL SHIFTS FROM TRADITIONAL LANGUAGE TEACHING

It's important to recognize that what we traditionally think of as language teaching is not effective to help ELs thrive in rigorous academic contexts. Read Figure 4.2 to understand the important shifts we need to make to be effective. This guide helps you apply current research and theories of language learning to your teaching every day.

FIGURE 4.2

CORE SHIFTS IN HOW WE UNDERSTAND AND TEACH LANGUAGE

Traditional Theories	Current Theories Central to This Guide
• Simplify activities and texts to teach language as a precursor for rigorous content learning.	• Teach language through active interaction with complex texts and cognitively challenging content tasks.
• Focus on what is correct as the primary goal.	• Focus on interaction and communication first, with scaffolds to guide appropriate linguistic choices.
• Teach language as discrete skills in a linear scope and sequence.	• Facilitate language learning as a complex, nonlinear dynamic process that centers on meaningful communication.
• Teach grammar as rules isolated from meaningful communication.	• Teach grammar in the context of the academic conversations, reading tasks, and writing tasks you structure every day. Understand grammar includes discourse, text structure, vocabulary, and syntax.

Source: California State Board of Education. (2012). *California English Language Development Standards Grades K–12*. Retrieved from http://www.cde.ca.gov/sp/el/er/documents/eldstndspublication14.pdf

SUPPORT PRODUCTIVE AND RECEPTIVE LANGUAGE

When thinking about supporting ELs with language in your classroom, it is helpful to think of the two main ways we use language—to receive information from others via listening or reading, and to produce clear communication via speaking and writing. We refer to these as receptive language and productive language.

RECEPTIVE LANGUAGE: Do students understand me? Do students understand one another? Do students understand classroom texts, multimedia, and other classroom materials?

PRODUCTIVE LANGUAGE: Do students communicate their ideas effectively in speaking and writing? Do they use effective word choice, grammar, and text organization appropriate for the purpose and audience?

Students use receptive and productive language in every classroom, every day. Reflect on the content in Figure 4.3. Which of these are expectations you have for all students in your classroom?

FIGURE 4.3

LANGUAGE DEMANDS OF EVERYDAY LEARNING IN CORE CLASSROOMS

	Receptive Language		Productive Language	
	Listening	**Reading**	**Speaking**	**Writing**
Ways ELs Must Use Language to Thrive	Listen to understand the teacher talk about academic topics, concepts, and texts. Listen to understand peers in collaborative tasks.	Read to understand the literal meaning of texts and task directions. Read to research and learn new concepts and content. Read critically to go beyond the literal meaning of texts.	Speak to express thinking about academic topics, concepts, and texts. Collaborate with peers to problem-solve, research, and create.	Write to communicate thinking about content topics, concepts, and texts. Collaborate to create and revise writing with peers.

Reflect on Figure 4.3 as it relates to your classroom expectations and your students:

- Which of these uses of language must all students master to thrive with your everyday teaching?

- In which of these uses of language do English learners in your class demonstrate the greatest ease and success? In which do they demonstrate the greatest challenge?

- Which of these aspects of language use are the highest priority for you to effectively teach, scaffold, and support so that ELs thrive in your classroom every day?

It helps to consider all the domains of classroom communication when thinking about the language demands of our curriculum. Language is more than an academic word list or a grammatical rule. The ultimate goal of supporting ELs with language is to help ELs thrive across all the domains of speaking, listening, reading, and writing in diverse academic contexts.

LISTENING, SPEAKING, READING, AND WRITING

The best lessons and the best language-learning opportunities engage students in using productive and receptive language in synthesis to communicate. We listen and speak in collaborative conversations. We read texts closely, discuss them with peers, and write our interpretations to communicate our ideas with others. We take notes to prepare for our conversations, or use conversations to generate ideas for writing. All four domains of listening, speaking, reading, and writing work together—and I demonstrate this synthesis in the lesson routines and strategies in Section IV of this guide.

TEACH HOW ENGLISH WORKS IN THE CONTEXT OF MEANINGFUL COMMUNICATION

What about grammar? What about vocabulary? How do we help English learners build vocabulary and improve their understanding and use of English grammar? I give so much emphasis to meaningful communication within academic learning contexts, you are likely asking these important questions. ELs do need to learn how English works at the level of words, sentences, and texts, so how do we teach these elements of language to ELs?

The short answer is that the best way to teach ELs how English works is within the context of meaningful communication. The best way to build academic language is within the context of academic learning and academic communication. The long answer—with clear examples relevant to your everyday teaching goals—is how I organize supports for ELs in Section III and help you apply them to the context of everyday academic literacy in Section IV of this guide.

You'll notice I don't organize the scaffolds in the next chapters based on domains of language (listening, speaking, reading, and writing) or based on levels of language to teach—word level (vocabulary), sentence level (grammar), and discourse level (text structure and cohesion in different genres of communication). I organize supports for ELs into three categories based on *when* you use them:

BEFORE: Strategies to Build Background

DURING: Strategies to Scaffold Language During a Task

BEYOND: Strategies to Teach Language Beyond a Task

Chapters 5–7 go deep in each of these three areas. Flip to those chapters to learn individual strategies to use before, during, and beyond any lesson to support ELs.

In Section IV, I help you apply these strategies to meet specific literacy goals. Within the "Support" section for each literacy goal, you'll find a menu of supports to choose or lose based on the needs of your students. These are organized in the same three categories of the chapters: Before, During, and Beyond.

The support strategies in this section are the same strategies introduced in Chapters 5–7, with a twist: Every strategy is a ready-to-use example designed to support the specific literacy goal. In the section on theme, for example, instead of learning about the word bank strategy, for example, you'll find actual word banks specific to theme that you can use with your students right away.

What you teach is primary—the relevant, meaningful tasks you structure to help all learners thrive with your specific content goals. The supports I provide throughout this guide are at your service to amplify how ELs learn your content *and* language to thrive within (and beyond) your lesson tasks.

So, in your planning as you ask yourself the essential question of this section, "What supports do my ELs need?," consider both your content learning goals and the aspects of language students need to thrive and to excel with the listening, speaking, reading, and writing tasks you structure about your content. Start with a big-picture look at the meaningful communication you expect—and the language needed for success—and then choose (or lose) supports based on how they help ELs reach that destination.

As you plan, ask:

1. *What are my content and language goals for student learning?* Envision what a strong response to your task(s) looks like. (EXPECT)

2. *What can students understand and do relevant to my goals?* Anticipate the strengths ELs bring to the task(s) and possible challenges they may have. Or, engage students in a task that gives you current formative data to answer this question. (ENGAGE AND OBSERVE)

3. *What instruction and supports will I provide to help students build from current understandings to succeed with the goal?* Choose from the strategies in the next three chapters to plan supports that build on their assets to address their challenges so that they thrive with your specific content and language goals. (SUPPORT)

HOW DO I PERSONALIZE SUPPORTS?

You know your goals, you choose supports you anticipate will help students reach the goals, and you try them in the classroom. During the lesson, however, you notice some students are just copying your examples or using the response frames and word banks you provided to give a predictable response. Other students are silent. The supports that seemed ideal, in theory, aren't working.

Sound familiar? There is no go-to support that works for every student, every time. A strategy that empowers a student in one moment interferes with the student's original thinking and self-directed learning the next. How do we adjust the supports we choose, continuously, so they are at the just-right level for each learner?

A VISION FOR STRATEGIC SUPPORTS

The gold standard for using supports strategically is engaging students at the optimal level of challenge. We don't support to help ELs do a task. We support to help ELs grow beyond what they already understand, know, and can do on their own.

When a task is challenging with the optimal level of supports, students are in the learning zone. You likely know this as the zone of proximal development, or ZPD (Vygotsky, 1978). It is the sweet spot you experience when "ahas" happen, students grow, and your teaching makes a difference.

We love that zone. We get there by maintaining high expectations and using the right supports at the right time to help all students excel.

In the complex art of teaching, the challenge level of our tasks and the supports we use are always in flux. Learning how to adjust these two levels intentionally is key to being an effective teacher for ELs and all students.

Challenge refers to the complexity of the tasks we have students do and the texts we have students read and write. The following are examples of the factors we adjust to raise or lower the challenge of a task:

Low-level question–High-level question

Teacher directed–Student directed

Simple text–Complex text

Familiar topic–Unfamiliar topic

Short text–Long text

Supports are scaffolds and strategies we use to help students excel with any challenge. Supports help us differentiate without lowering the expectations of tasks and texts. We adjust the level of supports from substantial to moderate to light, as best fits the needs of each learner in our classroom.

These essentials in tandem help us bring all learners into the ideal learning growth zone, the upper right quadrant of Figure 4.4.

THE RIGHT SUPPORTS AT THE RIGHT TIME

Use scaffolds and supports to help stretch students to learn beyond what they already know and can do. Remove them any time students will be able to realize their own success via problem solving, productive struggle, and self-directed learning.

FIGURE 4.4

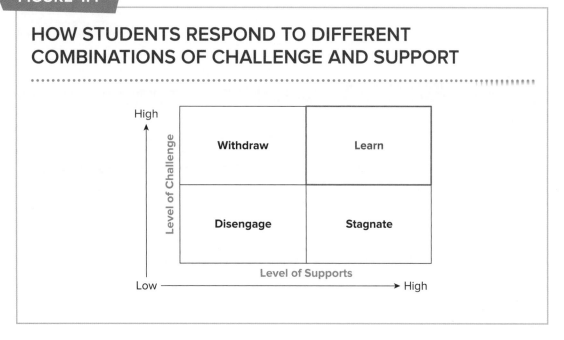

HOW STUDENTS RESPOND TO DIFFERENT COMBINATIONS OF CHALLENGE AND SUPPORT

- Too many supports all of the time lead to passive learners dependent on teacher direction.

- Too few supports can lead to students failing and disengaging from school.

So how do we find the optimal level of supports every time?

EXPECT, ENGAGE, OBSERVE

The answer lies in the same cycle of reflective teaching I emphasize throughout this guide. We start with high expectations, actively engage students, observe students as they engage to gather formative data, and then adapt our teaching based on what we see.

Start with high expectations. Use your high expectations to plan a task students will do to demonstrate their prior knowledge, successes, and/or challenges with those expectations. Make sure the task requires collaborative conversation and/or writing so you get formative data about student thinking and language use.

To plan that first engagement task, anticipate the right level of supports based on what you know about your students. This is a best-guess situation as you can't know for sure if your supports are at the optimal level until you watch students in action. When in doubt about how much, or how little, to support, I like to first err on the side of undersupporting to give students an opportunity to show me what they can do without me.

In other words, I take a risk. I plan a task that I think will stretch my students and thus open the opportunity for some student problem solving and productive struggle. I hope it will be a productive struggle—a struggle that engages students in active thinking to make meaning and figure something out to learn. I can't be certain, however, that their struggle will be productive. It is possible they will try the task and give up or be silent. It is possible they will do it with ease. I don't know. I am going to structure the task and find out.

When I'm pushing the edge of what I believe is the right edge of learning for my students, I always have this mindset. It is a combination of optimism, uncertainty, and curiosity.

ENGAGING FOR FORMATIVE DATA VERSUS DIRECT INSTRUCTION

My approach to planning this first engagement task is very different from my approach to planning explicit direct instruction, also a valuable approach for addressing identified needs. With explicit direction instruction, by contrast, I begin with substantial supports and help students succeed with me before I have them attempt the task without me. I teach with the following steps in sequence:

> **I DO:** I model what I expect students to do. For example, I project the text I want students to reread closely to make inferences about a character. I use the think-aloud strategy to model my thinking as I read. I model annotating the text—I underline details that help me make inferences about the character and write my inference in the margin.

> **WE DO TOGETHER:** Together we read the next section of text that I have selected because it is strong for practicing this skill. I have students think silently and put their finger on one piece of evidence that helps them make an inference about the character. I check visually that students are each pointing at evidence and ready to discuss with a partner. If they are not, I provide more modeling to ensure they are ready. If they are, I structure a partner interaction to have students discuss the evidence they found and their inferences. As students report out from their partner conversations, I use their examples to model additional annotations (by projecting their annotations or adding them to my own model text), and I write or project strong student responses as additional models (in this context, the responses are one to two sentences that express an inference about a character and include justification with text evidence).

> **WE DO:** I have students read the next section on their own and annotate in preparation for a peer discussion. I use the think-annotate-pair-share strategy (p. 54) to have students collaborate to discuss their ideas, and then I use the Color-Coded Writing strategy (p. 80) to have students work with partners to write a response together. I check for understanding as students annotate, discuss, and collaborate to write.

> **YOU DO:** I have students read a new text or section about a new character, then annotate and write a short response that communicates an inference about a character and justification with text evidence. I use the think-write-pair-share strategy so students are first accountable to do the complete task on their own (think-write) and I can gather formative data about what individual students have learned relative to my goals. In the pair-share discussions, students share ideas and collaborate to refine their responses based on my goals as I listen in and/or provide strategic support to one or more pairs that demonstrate a need.

The I DO—WE DO—YOU DO sequence of direct instruction is an essential approach to effective teaching. It is also not the *only* approach. It is important we use direct instruction strategically when this pedagogy matches our goals and the specific needs we observe in our classrooms. Use direct instruction when

- You are introducing a process or skill that is new to students—and you don't know how to structure an experience that will help them learn it via problem solving or student-directed learning
- You attempted to engage students in a task requiring this skill, and you observed them give up, check out, or flounder unproductively

Direct instruction is efficient. It leverages your expertise as a teacher to help show your students what you expect and how to be successful. Use it to make your expectations visible and to teach students strategies they can use to be successful with your expectations. Use it to address gaps you observe between what your students already understand and can do without you and what they need to thrive with your goals.

If direct instruction is our *only* approach with ELs, however, it is easy to overscaffold every lesson, every time. We also miss an opportunity to learn what our ELs can do on their own. When substantial scaffolding and guidance is the norm, our students often internalize the expectation that the teacher must first model and guide before they are to try. In many districts, I hear teachers lamenting that ELs are waiting to be spoon-fed before they participate. If that's the reality in your local context, reflect beyond the individual students as the cause of this phenomenon and ask, "How might our pedagogy influence how ELs engage?"

EXPLORE THE CONTINUUM OF LEARNING

With any task I structure (e.g., read, annotate, and discuss), I have a choice:

- Do I assign the task and see what students already know and can do on their own? (YOU DO, first)
- Do I explicitly model, guide, and structure practice to guarantee all students are prepared to succeed before I have them do this task? (I DO, WE DO, YOU DO)

I recommend alternating between these choices continuously so that you get the best of both. Start with student engagement (and minimal modeling) to gather formative data about what students can do without your guidance. Notice strengths and challenges and use these to determine the best next steps within and beyond the lesson. If students are silent or struggle unproductively, stop the task. You have relevant, timely data in a matter of minutes. Use these data to immediately shift your approach to model and guide students toward success with explicit direct instruction (I DO–WE DO–YOU DO).

If students engage productively and yet demonstrate some challenges with aspects of the task, give in-the-moment feedback to address those challenges in the lesson and/or plan an explicit lesson specific to those challenges the next day.

We have two primary approaches for *when* to personalize supports:

1. The moment we observe a need

2. In a future lesson

Both are important. Every need we observe within a lesson helps us anticipate the best level of supports in future lessons. Also, within lessons, we need to be nimble to change course immediately when we see that students are not productively learning and engaged.

PERSONALIZE SUPPORTS WITHIN A LESSON

When you structure a task that gives students an opportunity to engage with open-ended conversation or writing tasks relevant to your goals, you have an opportunity to gather timely formative data. How do you respond, in the moment, to adjust your approach?

EXPECT AND ENGAGE FIRST: To personalize supports within a lesson, first ensure you structure an opportunity for students to engage in a possible productive struggle and show what they understand and can do. (If their only task is to listen to a lecture or raise their hand if they want to share, for example, you will have no specific data to use to personalize.) Flip to the "Engage" heading for every literacy skill in Section IV for examples of tasks you can use to gather formative data specific to your instructional goals.

OBSERVE: As students engage with a lesson task (e.g., collaborative conversation about a text-dependent question), take a quick count of how many students are engaged in learning through the challenge and how many need additional supports to fully engage and learn. Also listen to what students say and watch what they do as evidence of their strengths and challenges with your goals to identify priorities for support.

REFLECT AND ADAPT: Use what you observe to adjust your teaching both in the moment and beyond the lesson. In the moment, we make a quick assessment about needs and whether to continued as planned or make a quick in-the-moment shift in our approach. Use Figure 4.5 as a quick reference to adjust teaching in the moment to address observed needs.

Notice Figure 4.5 is not EL specific, as no matter your student population, the general approach to figuring out the most logical way to leverage your time to address diverse needs is the same. You may notice that both ELs and non-ELs struggle with the same aspect of a task. In that case, group those students together to provide the same support. As you provide that support, you may notice that ELs have a strength they can build upon that a non-EL doesn't have, or you may notice that an EL needs a specific language support the non-EL doesn't need. Always be curious, for all students, about the strengths and challenges they experience with a task—and use what you notice to continuously refine the supports you provide.

Our EL-specific insights and supports come through this process as we pay specific attention to how ELs engage in our tasks and get specific about both their assets and their challenges specific to our instructional goals. The better we understand our goals for content and language and where our ELs are in relation to our goals, the more skilled we become at choosing the right support every time.

PERSONALIZE SUPPORTS BEYOND A LESSON

Many of my "aha" moments about the best supports for my ELs come after the lesson. I noticed some ELs struggled. I did my best in the moment to adjust my teaching to address the needs I observed. And I'm looking at ELs' writing or reflecting on what I observed with continued curiosity about the gap between where they are and where I want them to be.

FIGURE 4.5

QUICK GUIDE TO ADJUST SUPPORTS IN THE MOMENT

If	Then
Most students are engaged and experiencing a combination of success and productive struggle	Keep the task the same and use this opportunity to gather more information about the students' strengths and challenges with this task
One to three students struggle yet the rest of the class is productively engaged in the task	Provide one-on-one feedback to the individuals who need support as others productively engage
Three to seven students struggle yet the rest of the class is productively engaged in the task	Pull the students who need additional support to meet with you as the rest of the class continues to engage with the task and, with this small group, provide additional modeling and/or increase scaffolds and supports
Most students are not engaged or are struggling in ways that are counterproductive	Change course immediately for the whole class by adjusting the task, providing additional modeling, and/or increasing scaffolds and supports

Student writing is a great snapshot into language use. When I read ELs' written responses to a task, especially in comparison to highly proficient responses in my classroom, I get "aha" insights about the aspects of language use this task requires—and which of those aspects of language my ELs have yet to learn.

For example, I see generalized word choice in one EL response and compare that to strong word choices in a response that exemplifies my expectations. In a paragraph response to a text-dependent question, for example, the proficient response includes many specific words to reference the text (e.g., *poem*, *stanza*, *line*). The EL response uses *poem* every time. This comparison gives me an "aha" about the type of vocabulary that is needed to excel with this type of communication in this context—vocabulary I can teach explicitly (see the strategy on page 120) and/or encourage students to use by providing a word bank (see the strategy on page 144) relevant to this task.

When I initially planned the lesson, even though I tried to anticipate the language demands, I didn't even think about this aspect of word choice needed for success for this task: a whole category of words—nouns to reference the text. Now that I see this language learning priority, I can address it in a follow-up lesson on revising for precise word choice. For example, I might project an exemplar response with strong word choice, highlight the words, and use these words to start a bank of words that can be used to reference different types of texts or parts of texts. Next I have students collaborate to identify additional words to add to the word bank, and then I have all students revisit their first-draft responses to change at least one word for a stronger word choice.

In future lessons, each time students engage in a new task to justify their thinking with text evidence, I post the word bank students co-created together. I encourage students to use it or add to it as we discuss and write about different types of texts across the year. The ideal linguistic scaffolds are ones we co-create with our students to build on their strong language choices to help them use language in new, more nuanced ways.

When we plan a lesson, we always ask, "Which scaffolds are best for this moment in time?" The answer ideally is part of a continuous, multilesson journey we experience with our students. Remember this each time you see a need within a lesson you don't feel possible to address in the moment, or whenever you have an "aha" moment after a lesson in which you reflect, "I should have . . ." Use those insights to personalize supports and adapt your approach moving forward, as you and your students continue to learn.

"Planning for your lesson is valuable, but being willing to let go of that plan is even more so. It is only on the path away from where you started that you can get to where you want to go."

—Christopher Emdin (2016, p. 207)

If you are asking questions about your goal, your students, and the best level of support—and humbly reflecting and adapting when things don't go as planned—you are on the right path. Humility and inquiry are all part of the process of using scaffolds strategically so ELs thrive.

HOW THIS GUIDE HELPS YOU PERSONALIZE SUPPORTS

When you flip to each literacy skill you want to teach in Section IV, you'll find all the tools you need to personalize supports for your students. The content flows with your natural reflective cycle across five headings—"Expect," "Engage," "Observe," "Support," and "Reflect"—to help you use supports within the context of continuous inquiry connected to your instructional goals. All of the supports are organized by when you use them before, during, and beyond a lesson.

The high-utility skills I emphasize (e.g., read for main ideas) are the types we build across multiple lessons and opportunities for students to engage with texts. This means you get to choose the supports that feel right today and observe, reflect, and use the data you gather to adjust your approach today and tomorrow. There are many tools for you to choose and lose over time, as your students continue to reach higher levels of achievement and self-direction with your goals.

HOW DO I DIFFERENTIATE WITH EASE?

One of the biggest challenges in personalizing supports isn't so much knowing what students need as it is figuring out logistically how to address the wide range of needs in our heterogeneous classrooms. The essential question is, how do we help every student experience the optimal level of support and challenge when students have such a wide range of needs in the classroom?

To answer this, we need more than data about our students and great strategies to use. We need some logistical strategies to best use our instructional time, often as the sole teacher, to address many different needs.

LOGISTICS FOR EVERYDAY DIFFERENTIATION

Logistical structures for differentiating within your classroom fall into two categories:

1. FLEXIBLE: These are strategies a solo teacher can use to differentiate teaching flexibly in every lesson, every day. We use these to provide just-in-time feedback and lesson adjustments.

2. SCHEDULED: Scheduled small-group rotations make differentiating lessons easy, when we have first established routines for the rest of the class to engage in productive, self-directed learning. This approach works for part of a day (e.g., literacy centers), not for every content lesson, every day.

In this guide, I am giving the most emphasis to flexible strategies to differentiate, as we can use these in any lesson with any group of students all day long.

STRATEGIES FOR FLEXIBLE EVERYDAY DIFFERENTIATION

The most important strategy for everyday differentiation is the core pedagogy of this book, specifically the sequence I detailed in the previous section under the heading "Personalize Supports Within a Lesson." In a nutshell, we first engage students with a task through which they can demonstrate success or challenges with our goals, next observe to gather formative data, and then make adjustments within and beyond the lesson to address students' needs.

This process does more than help us gather formative data; it also creates a context for us to differentiate the levels of support we provide. By starting with minimum levels of supports, we get a quick read on which students are ready to productively engage with light supports. *And*, we get them started with a productive task.

That last point is important, and not something I emphasized in the previous section. When we start a task with minimum supports, we give all of the students who can do the task with minimum supports something to do. This creates an opportunity for us to address other needs we observe right away—as students who don't need follow-up support continue the task. If I structure a task and notice, for example, that six students are struggling, I can pull those six to a table and provide additional modeling, guidance, and/or scaffolds to address their needs.

What about the other students in the class? This is the big question we always have to answer when providing one-on-one or small-group instruction. We answer this question easily when we begin with a task that challenges our students.

By engaging first, we create an opportunity to identify and address needs we see via one-on-one or small-group teaching as the other students engage. Many supports, such as providing an additional model or linguistic frames, don't actually take much instructional time. We can provide them quickly to students who need them, as others continue to productively engage.

Refer back to Figure 4.5 for a quick guide to adjusting our approach mid-lesson based on how many students demonstrate a need for additional support.

There are many other strategies for flexible mid-lesson differentiation, including the following four I'll detail in this section:

1. Provide Tiered Supports

2. Personalize Feedback During a Whole-Group Task

3. Personalize Supports as Peers Discuss

4. Strategic Partnering

PROVIDE TIERED SUPPORTS

A quick differentiation strategy in any whole-group lesson is to post a range of possible supports. For example, if you are providing response frames for students to use when making predictions, provide a range of options from simple to complex such as the following:

- I predict that _____.

- I predict _____ because _____.

- Based on the illustration, I predict _____ because _____.

Post all the frames and read them aloud before having students think-pair-share to discuss their ideas. Encourage them to use a response frame or their own unique sentence to make a prediction. Listen for the language choices students use, and celebrate any variations from your scaffolds by acknowledging students' original choice and adding their example to your range of frames. For example, if you hear a student say, "I used the title to predict that this story is going to be a mystery," you might add "I used _____ to predict that _____" to your list of response frames. This validates student language choices, invites students to take risks beyond the frames, and democratizes the creation of linguistic scaffolds in your classroom.

PERSONALIZE FEEDBACK DURING A WHOLE-GROUP TASK

Every time students engage (e.g., talking, writing, problem solving), you have an opportunity to provide personalized just-in-time feedback. As students write, you read over a student's shoulder and provide one-on-one feedback to prompt one student to indent or another student to include text evidence in a literary analysis. As students discuss with partners, you compliment a pair on building up ideas together, then help a pair of students who misunderstood the task reengage. These small moments of just-in-time feedback are part of your differentiation tool kit. Effective one-on-one just-in-time feedback includes any of the following:

- Validate a specific way the student is demonstrating success criteria
- Prompt to remind a learner to apply something you have taught
- Support with additional scaffolds you didn't provide for the whole class
- Question to encourage self-reflection and goal setting
- Challenge a student to extend beyond the first task

PERSONALIZE SUPPORTS AS PEERS DISCUSS

Every time you structure a peer conversation, you have a moment to listen to a few partners discuss or support a pair of students. You don't have time to focus on *every* partner, of course, but this is a golden opportunity to provide additional supports to a pair in need or challenge a pair to extend their conversation in new ways. When you structure peer conversations in every lesson, as I recommend, these brief opportunities to personalize support add up.

Support Emerging ELs or Students Who Are Silent: As students begin to talk with partners, lean in to support a pair involving a student who is silent or an emerging EL. For an emerging EL, guide choral repetition of the simple response frame and use of the frame, or give the student two responses to choose from and guide the student in pointing or repeating to make a choice. For a student with higher proficiency who is silent, ask questions to engage the student in conversation.

Prompt Students to Go Beyond Supports: When we provide supports to the whole class (e.g., response frames and modeling), some students who don't need these supports get stuck using them. They repeat our model rather than thinking for themselves or just use our response frame in a way that limits their expression. When you see this, challenge students to try expressing their ideas without the frame (or expressing an idea different from what you modeled). Or ask them a critical thinking question to expand their conversation in new ways.

If the majority of the class is silent or needs to go beyond the supports, don't just lean into one pair. Instead, stop the discussion, adjust the supports for the whole class, and start again. (This is the "trial and error" part of differentiation. It's not even error. It's *the* process of good teaching.)

STRATEGIC PARTNERING

Setting up how students partner for peer conversations (or group for peer group conversations) is also part of your differentiation tool kit. For everyday peer conversations, have students turn to discuss with someone who is at a different level of academic and English proficiency. Ideally, don't pair extremes (highest with absolute most struggling), and do pair reluctant participants with peers who are encouraging. This structure helps students learn from each other so *you* are not the only one they rely on for differentiation support.

Strategic Partnering With an Emerging EL: When you have one or more emerging ELs in a mainstream classroom learning rigorous content in English, it is ideal to structure a trio of students for each emerging EL. The trio matches the EL with two peers who are encouraging and have enough English proficiency to fully engage in classroom tasks. Ideally, if possible, one of the students is also fluent in the same primary language as the EL.

Every time you structure a pair-share conversation, the pair should speak first, and then the emerging EL has a choice of adding a new idea or repeating an idea that one in the pair shared. Repetition is a great first step to participating actively, and while not a way to build critical thinking or content success, it helps the emerging EL get comfortable risking pronouncing new words in a new language with peers.

If one person in the trio also is fluent in the home language of the emerging EL, you can also encourage that student to use the primary language to help build background and/ or engage the EL in trying the task first in that language. With advanced concepts, using primary language (via peer conversations, reading, or access to multimedia online) is how you engage an emerging EL in thinking and learning the core content of your lesson, rather than just parroting what someone else has said. Use this approach when content concepts are your primary goal. When a specific English language objective (e.g., ask a question in English syntax) is your goal, then make sure partners also practice that skill in English in their conversations.

STRATEGIES FOR SCHEDULED DIFFERENTIATION

We've explored four tools reflective teachers use to flexibly differentiate within whole-group lessons. Now let's look at ways to schedule opportunities for a teacher to work with a homogeneous group of students grouped according to similar instructional needs.

SCHEDULED SMALL-GROUP ROTATIONS

Scheduled small-group instruction is another go-to strategy for differentiation that teachers most commonly use for guided reading or leveled reading groups. With scheduled small-group instruction, students learn a routine for rotating between independent activities and small-group instruction with the teacher. The teacher works with one small group at a time as students engage in literacy centers, personalized learning with technology, or other independent work.

When students are in homogeneous groups, such as for guided reading, it makes it easy to differentiate because students in each group have similar instructional needs. For each group, a teacher chooses texts, tasks, and supports that are at the optimal learning zone for students in that group.

Scheduled small-group instruction is powerful, especially as a go-to routine in literacy to ensure all students get to engage with texts at their optimal reading levels.

It is valuable for *any* learning goal, including teaching language mini-lessons to ELs, but there is always one big challenge working with a small group: What does the rest of the class do?

To even begin working with scheduled small groups, we either need a team of assistant teachers or must first establish routines for students to engage in high-quality independent tasks. Quality independent tasks in a literacy classroom may include independent reading, writing, word work, and one-to-one technology. Many teachers use a framework such as The Daily Five™ to engage students productively throughout rotations.

Even if we *love* leading a regular routine for small-group teaching (e.g., guided reading and The Daily Five™) in literacy, we are daunted by the idea of trying to set up additional small-group structures to differentiate content and language learning across the curriculum.

Scheduled small-group instruction is a tool in your differentiation tool kit, not the *only* way to differentiate. We have to break the myth that this is the gold standard of differentiation for ELs because, honestly, it's not practical to always have 75 percent or more of the class work independently all day long. It's not realistic. It would also be problematic for both language learning and 21st century learning goals if students were doing silent, independent work 75 percent of the day.

Use scheduled, small-group rotations when

- You have instructional assistants, specialists, or parents in your room at a regularly scheduled time
- You have established routines for students to engage productively with self-directed learning tasks
- You teach guided reading (or other leveled reading) and have established literacy center routines or The Daily Five™

In every other lesson, be fluid and flexible in pulling a small group to support as needed. Whenever the majority of students are engaging in a task and three to eight students need additional support to engage, pull those students into an in-the-moment small group to provide the supports they needs to productively engage.

SUBSTANTIAL TO MODERATE TO LIGHT: A RANGE OF OPTIONS

Beyond learning flexible and scheduled approaches to meeting different needs, it's helpful to also recognize that most supports exist on a continuum. Often students don't need entirely different supports, but they need different levels of the same types of supports. This understanding makes differentiation so much easier to navigate in a classroom with diverse needs. Often we don't actually need to provide different instruction to every different level, but need instead to make nuanced shifts in the supports we provide.

In many EL frameworks, and this book, we look at supports on a continuum from substantial to moderate to light. We align this continuum to English proficiency levels as illustrated in Figure 4.6.

Good news for teachers who also teach non-ELs: When we get specific about what each level of support means for individual supports, we start to see that this continuum of supports also is relevant to our non-ELs. I'm not saying that ELs and non-ELs always have the same needs. What I am saying is that the actual strategies we choose or lose, the actual strategies we use at a substantial or light level, are often also valuable for meeting needs of non-ELs. Let's get more specific as it is through the details that this big idea will become clear.

FIGURE 4.6

ALIGNING PROFICIENCY WITH SUPPORTS

English Proficiency Level	Optimal level of support
BRIDGING	Light or no support
EXPANDING	Moderate support
EMERGING	Substantial support

SUPPORTS ALONG A CONTINUUM

Let's explore this continuum of substantial to moderate to light supports with one type of support that benefits all students: modeling. In Figure 4.7, I detail three levels of modeling in a continuum of supports. Think of each continuum as a volume lever on a sound mixing board. In any lesson, you can move the lever toward substantial supports or toward light supports. You try to anticipate the right level of supports as you plan, and then during teaching you make adjustments up and down the continuum to help students build from where they are toward increased self-directed learning, problem solving, and success with your rigorous goals.

FIGURE 4.7

QUICK GUIDE TO DIFFERENTIATE MODELING

	Model
BRIDGING Light Support	1. Engage students first. Invite productive struggle, and observe to check for understanding. 2. Only prompt or model to address specific needs you observe. Don't model what students will be figuring out via productive struggle and collaboration.
EXPANDING Moderate Support	1. Model the minimum needed to ensure students understand task expectations. 2. Engage students. Observe to check for understanding. 3. Use what you observed to personalize support. Provide light or substantial support to small groups or the whole class as needed.
EMERGING Substantial Support	I DO–WE DO–YOU DO 1. I DO: Model expectations and how to do the task. 2. WE DO: Guide students in doing the task with you. 3. YOU DO: When students demonstrate they are ready, have them do the task without you.

Modeling is only one of many supports in our tool kit for EL excellence. Other essential supports are structuring conversations (Chapter 3), building background (Chapter 5), scaffolding language (Chapter 6), and teaching language (Chapter 7). In Chapters 9–11, I show you how to use all of these supports in synthesis in the context of helping students excel with rigorous academic literacy goals. In those chapters, you'll find continuums of supports that align with your teaching goals and many specific supports you can choose or lose as your ELs—and all students—continue to build on their assets to thrive.

To help you apply the continuum of supports concept to your everyday planning and teaching, I've also created for you a one-page "Quick Guide to Differentiate Supports" that you can keep at your fingertips as you plan and teach. Use it to easily adjust four supports (Build Background, Model, Structure Talk, Scaffold Language) along the continuum from light to moderate to substantial as you differentiate your teaching every day. Download this go-to tool at www.tonyasinger.com/elexcellence. The just-right levels for each support will always change, as your goals and tasks change and as your students continue to learn and grow. Sometimes, when introducing a new, abstract concept, we move all the supports we use toward substantial support for all students. Other times, we move them all toward light support to invite student-directed learning and gather formative data. Often, we adjust our supports in different ways for different students using the flexible differentiation strategies in this chapter.

The continuum concept of differentiating supports helps us think globally about how to adjust supports strategically. No matter the specific supports we use, the big concept is the same.

REFLECT ON CHAPTER 4

- How do you approach determining the best supports for ELs in your classroom? How is your approach similar to or different from the recommendations in this chapter?

- Which aspects of language are your greatest priority to support to ensure ELs thrive with your content lessons and listening, speaking, reading, and writing tasks?

- How do you differentiate to meet diverse needs in your classroom? Which differentiation strategies do you now use? Which do you want to try?

CHAPTER 5
BUILD BACKGROUND

"Knowing what is known is the starting place for new learning."

—Diane Lapp, Doug Fisher,
and Nancy Frey (2012, p. 8)

WHAT AND WHY?

We build background and help students connect to prior knowledge to help them learn new concepts, make meaning from texts, and succeed with classroom tasks. We build background in concepts, in language, and often in both at the same time. Strategies to build background include all of the following:

- Build upon students' prior knowledge and experiences
- Build new background knowledge important to what you teach
- Model what you expect students to do and how to do it

- Pre-teach vocabulary for a text or a task
- Pre-teach language for a text or a task

Notice that the strategies for building background are about both supporting language and teaching new concepts, skills, and task expectations. These are strategies to choose from when students need teaching *before* they engage in a task to engage productively and build from what they already know to excel in new ways.

WHEN DO I BUILD BACKGROUND?

Plan to build background when you introduce a new concept or topic and before having students engage in a new task to apply a new skill. Plan every lesson with at least one way to build background or connect to students' prior knowledge—even with something as simple as asking students to share with a partner, "What do you know about this topic?"

Use build background strategies mid-lesson when you observe a need. You cannot always anticipate the ideal amount of background to build, and you often notice the need for building background when you see students struggle with a task in your lesson. When you observe that some students seem lost or are struggling unproductively, stop the task and use building background strategies to model, teach, and help students build from what they already know to succeed.

WHO BENEFITS FROM BUILDING BACKGROUND?

Most of these strategies are good teaching for every student. All benefit struggling readers. All benefit English learners (ELs). The most important distinction with ELs is that to connect to their prior knowledge and experiences, we must value their linguistic strengths and cultural assets. We must value strengths ELs bring—instead of only seeing through our own cultural lens reflecting the background knowledge we value that ELs don't have. Flip to pages 20–28 in Chapter 2 for more specifics on valuing EL assets.

STRATEGIES TO BUILD BACKGROUND

TIPS TO BE STRATEGIC

Don't rob students of productive struggle. Building background prepares students for success. Too much of a good thing can also have a negative effect. If you pre-teach vocabulary from a text, for example, you make it easier for students to read the text for meaning. You also rob them of the opportunity to use strategies such as context clues to figure out words as they read. Aim to build enough background for students to productively engage while also keeping enough challenge for students to hone their skills in meaning making and problem solving.

Be strategic. Flex how you use this strategy based on your goals and your students' ever-evolving abilities. The "just right" balance of how much background to build is an ever-changing equation that will vary by student, by concept you teach, and by what students have just learned.

Engage in reflective teaching to continuously use observation data to reflect and refine your approach.

NOTES

_____

_____

_____

_____

_____

_____

_____

_____

_____

_____

_____

_____

5.1 CONNECT TO STUDENTS' BACKGROUND KNOWLEDGE AND EXPERIENCES

WHAT AND WHY?

Connecting your teaching to students' prior knowledge and experiences is powerful on many levels. Connecting to students' prior knowledge (1) makes your teaching relevant to your students, (2) values students' backgrounds, and (3) helps students build on what they know to learn new information (Emdin, 2016; Marzano, 2004; Washburn, 2010).

STRUCTURE A QUICK PEER DISCUSSION BEFORE READING OR TEACHING

Having students talk about a text before reading it, or about a concept before learning it, gives you valuable data about the background knowledge they bring. It also activates their thinking about what you are about to read or teach, a great way to prime the brain for learning and making meaning from texts. Good questions for a quick discussion include any of the following:

- What do you know about _____?
- What do you want to know?
- What do you notice? (when you show students any visual related to what they will read or what you will teach)
- What do you predict this will be about?

BUILD BACKGROUND FROM A FAMILIAR TO ACADEMIC CONTEXT

1. **START WITH A FAMILIAR CONTEXT:** If you want to teach a new concept such as how to justify a claim with evidence, begin with a context that is familiar and relevant to all of your students. To teach argument skills, for example, create a real opportunity for the class to collaborate to make a decision together. For example, I tell students that on Friday I'll bring any snack they choose (within my budget and school snack policies). The one catch: the entire class must first agree on the snack I should bring.

2. **ENGAGE:** Structure a conversation task that actively engages students in discussing the concept in a familiar context. To help students argue to reach a shared agreement, for example, I structure peer conversations to engage students in making claims about the best snack and justifying their claims with evidence.

3. **OBSERVE AND BUILD ON STRENGTHS:** As students negotiate ideas with peers, I listen for strong examples of justification and write these down (or use the fishbowl structure described in Chapter 3, p. 60) to model for students. When we narrow down the top choices, I use the Vote With Your Feet strategy (p. 77) to help students stand by their claim and try to convince others to join them. I then pair students with similar perspectives to write a short persuasive paragraph using the Color-Coded Writing strategy (p. 80).

   Through this process, we choose a snack for Friday, but more importantly, I teach students how to collaborate in making and justifying claims. I engage students in creating written examples of arguments on familiar topics.

4. **EXTEND TO AN ACADEMIC CONTEXT:** I build from this shared experience the next week to engage students in applying the same concept of argument to make and justify claims about character (flip to p. 256) or theme (flip to p. 266).

OTHER WAYS TO BUILD FROM STUDENTS' PRIOR KNOWLEDGE TO NEW LEARNING

- **BUILD FROM PRIMARY LANGUAGE TO ENGLISH:** Even if you don't speak a student's primary language, you can encourage an emerging EL with primary language literacy to read or watch videos in that language to build background in the high-level concepts and topics you are teaching. This is a great way to use students' linguistic strengths to build background knowledge in essential concepts before you teach these concepts and related academic language in English.

- **BUILD FROM MULTIMEDIA TO TEXT:** When teaching students to make inferences about characters or themes, begin with a familiar movie or TV show students love. This only works if all students know the multimedia, you show it in your class, or you work with a small group of students who share the same background experience. Have students collaborate to make inferences about characters in the show and justify their claims with evidence from the show. Then extend this same concept to reading comprehension by having students make and justify inferences about characters in a text. Use the same visuals and linguistic supports in both lessons to explicitly connect the two tasks.

- **BUILD FROM PICTURES TO TEXT:** For example, build on students' natural ability to make predictions by having them first make a prediction about a short video, a sequence of pictures, an engaging picture book such as *The Mysteries of Harris Burdick* by Chris Van Allsburg, or any enticing cover of a picture book. When needed, label the nouns in the picture to create a word bank students can use to explain their thinking about the picture. Then have them apply that knowledge to do a similar task to make a prediction based on a text on a familiar topic. Use the same visuals and linguistic supports across both lessons to help students connect the concept of predictions from one context to the next.

TIPS TO BE STRATEGIC

Don't make assumptions about students' background experiences. There is so much diversity within cultural groups that even our own expertise with a culture may be a mismatch for students' experiences. Don't rely on an abstract generalization about what "EL students" or "Mexican American students" or "Hmong students" do. Instead, use surveys, peer conversations, and observation to get to know your unique students. What do they love to do beyond school? What do they value? What makes them uncomfortable? When are they most motivated to take a risk to grow? Every time you have students discuss, listen to learn. Listen for their questions and confusions as well as their personal stories and connections they make.

5.2 TEACH CONCEPT VOCABULARY WITH THE FRAYER MODEL

WHAT AND WHY?

Directly teach students the essential vocabulary they need to understand the central concept(s) of your lessons. Concept words are often general nouns for an abstract concept (e.g., *theme*, *main idea*, *claim*) or process verbs (e.g., *justify*, *compare*). Pre-teaching these words explicitly prepares ELs, and all students, to understand the most essential concepts of your lesson.

FIGURE 5.1

COMPLETED FRAYER MODEL

Student-Friendly Definition: The message or central idea of a story	Characteristics: • A big idea • Something you infer after reading or watching the whole story • What the author wants you to learn, feel, or value
THEME noun	
Examples: The theme of the story is • Justice • Honesty • Courage • Determination The theme/message of this story is • Be yourself • Be kind to others • If you fail, try again	Nonexamples: The story is about • A bull • A bull who doesn't want to fight A theme is *not* a specific detail from the story. A theme is *not* stated in the text.

HOW?

PREPARE: Choose one or more words from your content standards, lesson objectives, and/or task directions that are core concepts students must understand for your lesson. Complete a Frayer Model graphic organizer (see p. 286) for the word, such as the example in Figure 5.1.

There are a variety of ways to use the Frayer Model from teacher-directed to student-directed methods. For direct instruction with active student participation, create a note-taking scaffold such as the example in Figure 5.2. A note-taking scaffold is a completed organizer with one to two blank spaces per box for the teacher and students to take notes during direct instruction.

FIGURE 5.2

FRAYER MODEL WITH A NOTE-TAKING SCAFFOLD

Student-Friendly Definition:	Characteristics:
The _____ or central idea of a story	• A big idea • Something you _____ after reading or watching the whole story • What the author wants you to _____ _____
THEME noun	
Examples: The theme of the story is • Justice • Honesty • Courage • Determination The theme/message of this story is • Be yourself • Be kind to others • _____	Nonexamples: The story is about • A bull • A bull who doesn't want to fight • _____ A theme is *not* a specific detail from the story. A theme is *not* stated in the text.

HOW TO DIRECTLY TEACH A
WORD WITH THE FRAYER MODEL

1. **PREPARE:** Use the Frayer Model graphic organizer on page 286 to prepare a note-taking scaffold such as Figure 5.2. Project it and give each student a copy.

2. **TEACH THE WORD:**

   a. Say the word. Have students repeat it chorally. Call on three individuals to repeat the word.

   b. Say the part of speech.

   c. Explain the word using a student-friendly definition. Have students write the missing word in the note-taking scaffold to demonstrate listening comprehension, or for substantial support have them write it as you write it in your projected model.

   d. Explain the characteristics and have students complete the note-taking scaffold.

   e. Give examples in the context of familiar stories or movies students know.

   f. Give nonexamples. Have students collaborate with a partner to discuss other nonexamples and add one nonexample to the note-taking scaffold.

3. **ENGAGE STUDENTS IN USING THE WORD:** Provide a response frame and structure think-pair-share to have all students use the word in a familiar context.

EL Excellence Every Day

TIPS TO BE STRATEGIC

OMIT CONTENT STRATEGICALLY IN YOUR NOTE-TAKING SCAFFOLD. There are two types of blanks to create in a note-taking scaffold: (1) a one-right-answer blank that students copy as you teach the word, and (2) an open-ended blank that students complete with a peer conversation or writing task to apply word learning. Use the first type when omitting words from a definition. For example, I omit the word *message* in Figure 5.2 as this is essential to the concept of the word *theme*. In teaching the word, I say the full definition including *message*, and students write it to reinforce what they hear. For an extra scaffold, I write the word as I say it and copy what students see or hear. Use the second type for at least one blank in characteristics, examples, or nonexamples that you anticipate partners will be able to collaborate to generate together. The first type is best for efficient, direct teaching with new concepts and examples. The second type is best for engaging students in using the word to deepen understanding and give you an opportunity to check for student understanding. A combination of both is typically ideal for the right balance of clarity, efficiency, and active student learning.

MODEL CONCEPTS IN ADDITION TO TEACHING THE CONCEPT VOCABULARY: In tandem with vocabulary teaching, it is important that you also model the concept words in the context of academic tasks. For example, to learn *theme*, students need more than a vocabulary lesson. Also model reading closely for theme, annotating for theme, discussing theme, and writing about theme. Flip to pages 126–127 for modeling strategies to use in tandem with vocabulary teaching when building background in new concepts and skills.

NOTES

_____

_____

_____

_____

_____

_____

_____

_____

_____

_____

5.3 A COLLABORATIVE APPROACH TO THE FRAYER MODEL

WHAT AND WHY?

This collaborative approach is a great way to facilitate student-driven learning and deepen word knowledge. Use this when students have at least a basic understanding of the meaning of a word, not to teach a new word. Have partners collaborate to complete a blank Frayer Model Organizer for a word you choose (e.g., *justify*). Use the Color-Coded Writing strategy (p. 80) to foster accountable participation to create one shared organizer between every two students.

HOW TO FACILITATE THE COLLABORATIVE APPROACH

1. **PREPARE:** Pair students and give each pair one blank Frayer Model Organizer (see the Appendix, p. 286) and two different-colored pens.

2. **INTRODUCE THE WORD:**

    a. Say the word. Have students repeat it.

    b. Say the part of speech.

    c. Explain the word using a student-friendly definition. Have partners collaborate to write a definition in the organizer.

3. **ENGAGE STUDENTS IN THE COLLABORATIVE TASK:** Have students collaborate using the Color-Coded Writing strategy to complete the rest of the Frayer Model together. Ask for a minimum of two characteristics, two examples, and two nonexamples.

4. **OBSERVE:** As students collaborate, listen and watch to check for understanding of the word, the task, and collaborative conversation skills.

5. **FACILITATE PEER REFLECTION:** After pairs create their own Frayer Models, have each pair collaborate with another pair to compare what they have written. Use the following questions and a small-group conversation structure (p. 56) to facilitate the four-person discussion:

    a. How are our notes similar? How are they different?

    b. What can we learn from our different approaches? What will we now revise in our own Frayer Model?

    c. What questions do we still have about this word?

6. **ENGAGE STUDENTS IN COLLABORATIVE REVISION:** Have partners use insights from the previous discussion to make at least one revision to their Frayer Model or write one new sentence using the word.

TIPS TO BE STRATEGIC

CHOOSE YOUR APPROACH BASED ON GOALS, STUDENTS, AND TIME AVAILABLE: The collaborative approach is more time-intensive than explicit teaching and not the best way to build background with a new concept. Use it strategically for high-utility words students know at least superficially. If students don't have any experience with the word or struggle unproductively with the task, switch to an explicit approach to build background with clarity.

BE INTENTIONAL WITH OUTSIDE SOURCES: To encourage face-to-face collaboration and assess prior knowledge, have students first collaborate without any outside sources. Without digital screens between them, students will have a more collaborative conversation to access prior knowledge. To deepen vocabulary knowledge and encourage savvy research skills, invite students to use print or online dictionaries, thesauruses, or other relevant research tools. Choose one approach or use both in sequence to have students first discuss prior knowledge, then research together, as needed, to answer questions or deepen understandings.

NOTES

_____

_____

_____

_____

_____

_____

_____

5.4 DIRECT INSTRUCTION VOCABULARY ROUTINE

WHAT AND WHY?

A direct instruction routine is the most efficient and clear way to teach new academic vocabulary to students. This explicit vocabulary routine is similar to the Frayer Model except it doesn't include characteristics or nonexamples. These differences make the routine slightly more efficient, an asset when you are teaching more than one word at a time. Use Figure 5.3 (also available in the Appendix, p. 287) for this routine.

WHEN TO USE?

Use this routine to pre-teach four to seven high-utility academic words, also known as Tier II words (Beck, McKeown, & Kucan, 2002), that students need to understand to access your lesson concepts, directions, or texts. Don't use this routine for words you can teach quickly with a picture or for obscure words students won't need beyond one context. Use it to teach essential words for lesson concepts and tasks (e.g., *justify, evidence, quote*) or to pre-teach words from a text that are essential for comprehension and can't be figured out with context clues.

FIGURE 5.3

DIRECT VOCABULARY INSTRUCTION ORGANIZER

WORD	PART OF SPEECH	EXPLAIN	EXAMPLE(S)

Use the Word

WORD	PART OF SPEECH	EXPLAIN	EXAMPLE(S)

Use the Word

STEPS FOR DIRECT VOCABULARY INSTRUCTION

As with the Frayer Model, you can teach new vocabulary with a blank organizer, a completed organizer, or a note-taking scaffold (see Figure 5.4). These steps are for using a note-taking scaffold, my favorite approach.

1. PREPARE: Prepare a note-taking scaffold including essential content and leaving strategic blank spaces for students to write key words or additional examples. Distribute a copy of a note-taking scaffold for the words you are teaching. Project your copy for all to see.

2. TEACH THE WORD:

   a. Say the word. Have students repeat it chorally. Call on three individuals to repeat the word.

   b. Say the part of speech and explain it in student-friendly language (*noun*—a person, place, thing, or concept; *verb*—an action word; *adjective*—a describing word; etc.).

   c. Explain the word using a student-friendly definition. Guide students in taking notes and add words to the blanks in your projected note-taking scaffold.

   d. Provide two examples of the word in contexts the students will understand. The first example should be a very familiar context, ideally connected to students' everyday experiences. The second should use the word in an entirely different context. Guide students in taking notes.

3. ENGAGE STUDENTS IN USING THE WORD: Provide a response frame and structure think-pair-share for students to use the word orally in a sentence and then write the sentence using the word. Select many students with strong examples to share their sentences.

4. REPEAT FOR EACH NEW WORD (adapted from Kinsella & Singer, 2010).

FIGURE 5.4

DIRECT INSTRUCTION NOTE-TAKING SCAFFOLD EXAMPLE

Vocabulary	Part of Speech	Explain	Example(s)
evidence	noun	_____ or information that shows an idea is true	1. Crumbs on the counter are _____ that someone ate a cookie. 2. Sally biting someone's ear is text evidence that _____.

Use the Word:

_____ is evidence that _____.

TIPS TO BE STRATEGIC

CHOOSE HIGH-UTILITY ACADEMIC WORDS: This routine takes time, so be selective. Don't use this routine for words students only need for one context (e.g., *photosynthesis*) or words that can be taught quickly with a picture (e.g., *canoe*). Do use it for general academic words that are useful across many contexts (e.g., *impact, infer, courage, reference*). Read *Bringing Words to Life* (Beck et al., 2002) to deepen your expertise in choosing and teaching Tier II academic vocabulary.

DON'T ROB STUDENTS OF USING CONTEXT CLUES: When pre-teaching words from a text students will read, prioritize words that are essential for comprehension and cannot be figured out using clues within the text. For strategies to guide students in using context to figure out word meaning, flip to pages 216–221.

DEEPEN WORD KNOWLEDGE. This strategy is only effective for introducing words. To deeply understand and use words, students need multiple opportunities to engage with the words in different contexts. Flip to pages 166–167 for follow-up strategies to deepen knowledge of words you teach.

USE TECHNOLOGY: Have partners each choose one sentence to type into a Google Form, then collaborate to read all submitted sentences and identify which most clearly demonstrate the word meaning.

NOTES

_____

_____

_____

_____

_____

_____

_____

_____

_____

_____

_____

_____

_____

_____

_____

_____

_____

_____

_____

_____

_____

_____

_____

5.5 TEACH VOCABULARY WITH COGNATES

WHAT AND WHY?

When students have fluency in a romance language (e.g., Spanish, French, Italian), they can use cognates in their language to quickly learn academic words in English.

A cognate is a word that has similar spelling and meaning across two languages. For example, the following are examples of English–Spanish cognates:

English	Spanish
education	educación
idea	idea
theme	tema
inference	inferencia

It is estimated that one-third to half of the vocabulary of an educated person has cognates in another romance language (Holmes & Guerra Ramos, 1995). Some estimate that 80 percent of English words, and even more in the context of science teaching, have cognates (Bravo, Hiebert, & Pearson, 2007). When ELs have primary language expertise in a romance language, using cognates is a powerful way to tap into their linguistic assets to learn new words (August, Carlo, Dressler, & Snow, 2005).

HOW TO USE THIS STRATEGY

Identify at least one student in your classroom who can be a cognate helper and read the cognate you write with the accurate pronunciation.

STEPS TO TEACH VOCABULARY WITH A COGNATE

1. Explain that a cognate is a word that has a similar spelling and meaning in two languages.

2. Write the cognate under the word you are teaching.

3. Ask your cognate helper to read the word aloud. Repeat it and have the class repeat it. (If you don't speak the language, repeating the word is a great way to model risk taking with new vocabulary—and show you value the language. Repeat it until all feel confident with the pronunciation.)

4. Ask students to compare the words and notice the similarities and differences. Even non-ELs will benefit from this collaborative analysis task.

5. Underline similarities in both words and help students use the language they know to learn the meaning of the cognate.

For more explicit teaching, model comparing the words by thinking aloud:

> "This word, *tourist*, is similar to the word *tourista* in Spanish. *Tourista* means a person who travels and visits places, so I think *tourist* means the same thing."

To provide substantial scaffolding, write out a response frame students can use to compare the cognates, such as the following:

This word is similar to the word _____ in my language. That word means _____, so I think this word means _____.

TIPS TO BE STRATEGIC

ONLY USE IF STUDENTS KNOW THE COGNATES IN A PRIMARY LANGUAGE: Use this strategy only when you have students with fluency in a romance language. Note that some ELs who speak Spanish as a primary language but have attended school in English since kindergarten don't have sufficient academic fluency in Spanish to know the Spanish cognates. Flip to page 23 for tips to learn students' home language proficiency.

Flip-to Tip: Flip to examples of the cognate strategy for specific literacy goals on pages 187, 210, 219, 226, 249, 270, and 277.

NOTES

_____

_____

_____

_____

_____

_____

_____

_____

_____

_____

_____

WHAT AND WHY?

Modeling is at the core of good teaching for all students, and also essential for ensuring ELs understand both your content and language expectations for your tasks. We model to help students envision what success looks like so they can drive their learning. We model through think-aloud and demonstration to teach a process or skill. Adjusting how much or how little we model is a go-to strategy to differentiate teaching in any lesson.

STRATEGIES FOR MODELING

MODEL BY DOING: Use demonstration, think-aloud, acting out, and other strategies to model what you want students to do and how you want them to do it. Model what is challenging for students to help them realize higher levels of learning. The following are examples of modeling language or literacy goals through action:

- **Model a conversation skill** such as negotiating a disagreement by acting out the conversation with a student or using the fishbowl strategy (p. 60).
- **Model figuring out a word** by projecting a sentence that has context clues and using think-aloud to make your thinking visible. (Flip to pp. 216–221 for more on content clues.)
- **Model interacting with text** to make meaning, analyze, or infer by projecting the text, modeling rereading, and using think-aloud to make your thinking visible. (Flip to pages 210, 260, 270, and 278 for examples aligned to specific reading goals.)
- **Model annotating a text** by projecting the text, modeling rereading for a specific purpose, and annotating (e.g., highlighting, underlining, taking notes) for that specific purpose.
- **Model note taking** by taking notes or demonstrating writing key words or phrases in a graphic organizer.
- **Model writing** a sentence, a paragraph, a paragraph from a graphic organizer, or longer multiparagraph text by writing in front of students.
- **Model revising** by projecting a text, using think-aloud to reflect, and demonstrating a specific revision in front of students.

HOW TO MODEL WITH THINK-ALOUD

Think-aloud is an effective strategy to model any thinking skill that is otherwise invisible. Use the think-aloud strategy to model cognitive goals like problem solving to make meaning from a complex text or analyzing text to make inferences. Use think-aloud with the following steps and tips.

PREPARE: Choose a short passage of text (one to four paragraphs). Preread the text and take notes about your thinking and strategies you notice yourself using as you read it. Prioritize what you will emphasize in your think-aloud.

1. Project the text so all students see what you are reading.

2. State the skill you are modeling and why it is important

3. Read aloud and stop at one or more places in the text to model your thinking with informal "I" statements. What you say will vary depending on what you are modeling. Two different examples follow:

   - **EXAMPLE FOR USING CONTEXT CLUES:** A third-grade teacher reads, then stops at an unfamiliar word, and says, "I don't know this word. I'm going to reread the sentence to look for clues to figure this out." The teacher then rereads aloud and stops to underline a clue that helps him figure out the word. He uses think-aloud to model using the clue to figure it out: "This clue makes me think the word might have something to do with _____."

   - **EXAMPLE FOR CHARACTER INFERENCES:** A middle school teacher uses an excerpt from "Sally" in Sandra Cisneros's *House on Mango Street* (1991) to model making an inference about a character. She stops at a showing detail and shares her thinking: "Wow! When I read she bit her ear, I thought, 'Wow, Sally is mean!'" then write your inference (*mean*) in the margin of the text.

4. Annotate the text if appropriate during your think-aloud to model how you use annotation in tandem with the thinking skill.

5. Always follow up your think-aloud with an opportunity for students to try the skill and discuss their thinking with peers as you listen to check for understanding.

TIPS TO BE STRATEGIC

TAILOR MODELING TO THE NEEDS OF YOUR STUDENTS: Model what is challenging for your students and will help them reach new levels of engagement, achievement, and language use. Don't model what students can do on their own or figure out through productive struggle and risk taking in a high-level collaborative task.

DON'T MODEL WHEN YOU WANT FORMATIVE DATA: Do you want to know what students already understand and can do with the skill or concept you are about to teach? When gathering data is your priority, start with the minimum amount of modeling necessary for students to engage in the task. Watch for understandings, confusions, and how students approach the task to learn what assets to build from and what needs to address. Listen for students' natural language choices before scaffolding or modeling how they communicate. Build from this formative data to prioritize what and how you will model.

ALTERNATE GRADUAL RELEASE WITH FLIPPED GRADUAL RELEASE: Gradual release is a direct instruction process that begins with modeling and follows this sequence: (1) Model, (2) Guide Practice, (3) Structure Peer Practice, and (4) Structure Independent Practice. This is a powerful process, but if it is the *only* process you use with ELs, they will be dependent learners. Use it when you are clear you need to model a specific skill, then engage students in a new problem-solving task to apply that skill in a new context. Flip the sequence so students first engage in problem solving via independent or peer practice as you watch to gather formative data. Guide and then model, as needed, to address priorities.

5.7 MODEL EXPECTATIONS WITH AN EXEMPLAR

WHAT AND WHY?

An exemplar is an example of the work product you expect. For example, a written sentence, paragraph, or essay is a written exemplar. A video of a conversation could be an exemplar of conversation moves you want students to use. An exemplar may be student created, teacher created, or a published work (aka mentor text or model text). Use exemplars to make your goals and success criteria visible for students.

HOW TO MODEL WITH AN EXEMPLAR

PREPARE: Choose an exemplar that demonstrates your success criteria for your literacy goals. For example, a seventh-grade teacher chose the following exemplar by her student Aeriel Woodson to model her success criteria for a single-paragraph response to the question, "What is the theme of the poem?"

SUCCESS CRITERIA

- Make a logical inference about theme.
- Write a thesis statement that communicates the inference and names the text.
- Cite relevant text evidence to support the claim.
- Explain how text evidence supports the claim.

EXEMPLAR

Rhina P. Espaillat's message in "Bilingual/Bilingüe" is that being bilingual strengthens her instead of weakening her. The narrator shows her father's fear in the second stanza "that words might cut in two his daughter's heart (el corazón) and lock the alien part." This means her father believes Spanish and English are two different cultures and your heart should only belong to one. The narrator then teaches herself Spanish at night without her father's consent. When she writes, "And still the heart was one," she is telling her father that being bilingual didn't break her, but made her stronger

STEPS FOR INSTRUCTION

1. Distribute a copy of the success criteria and exemplar for each student and project your copy on a screen.

2. Use highlighting and text-marking strategies to guide students in actively finding the success criteria in the exemplar. For example, have students

- HIGHLIGHT logical inference and the thesis statement in green
- UNDERLINE relevant text evidence that supports the claim
- WRITE A CHECK ✓ next to each sentence that explains how text evidence supports the claim

EXEMPLAR WITH MARKED SUCCESS CRITERIA

Rhina P. Espaillat's message in "Bilingual/Bilingüe" is that being bilingual strengthens her instead of weakening her. The narrator shows her father's fear in the second stanza "that words might cut in two his daughter's heart (el corazón) and lock the alien part." ✓ This means her father believes Spanish and English are two different cultures and your heart should only belong to one. The narrator then teaches herself Spanish at night without her father's consent. When she writes, "And still the heart was one," ✓she is telling her father that being bilingual didn't break her, but made her stronger.

TIPS TO BE STRATEGIC

USE EXEMPLARS FROM A DIFFERENT, SIMILAR TASK: When modeling expectations before students write, don't use an example of the exact task they will do—as that will kill the motivation to write it. Instead model a similar task with a different topic.

BUILD FROM TEACHER-DIRECTED TO STUDENT-DIRECTED: The first time you use this strategy, use direct instruction to guide the process by explaining each connection and modeling how to mark the text. Once students know this routine, have them collaborate to find and mark success criteria with each new exemplar.

FOCUS YOUR ANALYSIS: Every exemplar is rich with opportunities for teaching literacy and language learning goals. Be selective. When introducing a new genre, emphasize the essential features. To address a need you see in students' writing (e.g., explaining text evidence), emphasize only that aspect of the exemplar in your analysis. To teach language choices, prioritize word choice, a grammatical structure, or the organization of the text as the sole focus of your analysis lesson.

COLLECT EXEMPLARS EVERY YEAR: Every task is an opportunity to collect student exemplars that demonstrate your expectations and/or common challenges you want to help students address. Save exemplars from prior years to use anonymously with new students. Crease a common permission form all parents and students can sign to give permission to use their writing beyond the classroom, and give them the option to include or exclude the author's name with the exemplar (some young authors want credit!). When you are securing permission, collaborate with other teachers in your district to collect and share exemplars.

5.8 COLLABORATE TO CONTRAST EXEMPLARS

WHAT AND WHY?

Engage students in collaborating to compare two exemplars that are similar but distinct in at least one way you want to emphasize for their learning. Unlike the previous strategy to directly model expectations with one exemplar, this approach is more student-directed and engages students in the higher-level thinking process of comparing and contrasting. This is a great strategy to engage students in reflecting on how changes in language impact changes in meaning and tone.

HOW?

1. Provide students with two or more short exemplars that differ in at least one specific area you want to emphasize.

2. Post discussion questions such as "How are they similar? How are they different?"

3. Give students time to read, think, and annotate the exemplars to prepare for the partner discussion.

4. Use a peer conversation structure to have students collaborate to compare the exemplars with questions such as the following:

   - How are they similar? How are they different?
   - Which is more effective for this audience and purpose?
   - Which would be more effective for [a different specific audience and purpose]?

EXAMPLE

If you are teaching students to build from simple topic sentences about theme to more complex sentences that name the author and title of the work, you may give students the following two exemplars to compare:

A. Rhina P. Espaillat's message in "Bilingual/Bilingüe" is that being bilingual strengthens her instead of weakening her.

B. The message is you should be bilingual.

Give students time to read and highlight differences in the examples, then structure a peer discussion with questions such as the following:

- How are they similar? How are they different?
- Which is more effective for a peer conversation? Why?
- Which is more effective to start a paragraph or essay about theme? Why?

See Figure 5.5 for examples of goals and tasks for contrasting exemplars.

FIGURE 5.5

EXAMPLES OF GOALS AND TASKS TO CONTRAST EXEMPLARS

If you want students to	Have students
Understand how explaining evidence impacts an argument	Compare • One paragraph that includes a claim, text evidence, and an explanation • The same paragraph without the explanation Reflect on and discuss • Which paragraph is more convincing and why
Understand the impact of punctuation on a reader	Compare • One paragraph that uses effective punctuation • One paragraph with no punctuation Reflect on and discuss • Which paragraph is easier to read and why
Reflect on how word choice impacts meaning and tone	Compare • One sentence with precise word choice • The same sentence with general, vague words
Reflect on differences between oral language use in their home dialect and the academic language used for a specific academic task	Compare • One "text" you've transcribed from a student communicating an academic concept effectively using a home dialect • A text you create that communicates the same message using the academic language of school Reflect on and discuss • When, and for which audience, each approach is most effective (If you were explaining this concept to a friend after school, which approach would be most effective? If you were explaining this concept in writing in an academic journal, which would be most effective?) • What specifically is similar or different about grammatical structures or word choice (What can we learn from these differences to build our fluency with the dialect or language or school?)

5.9 COLLABORATE TO EVALUATE AN EXEMPLAR WITH A RUBRIC

WHAT AND WHY?

Engage students in analyzing writing (or a conversation transcript or video) with a rubric to get specific about success criteria and build self-reflection and peer revision skills. This strategy helps students (and teachers) calibrate expectations and identify specific priorities to revise writing to meet those expectations. This strategy builds background for students (and teachers) to give excellent feedback to self and others specific to the success criteria.

HOW?

PREPARE: Provide students with a rubric, ideally one you have created together, to clarify the success criteria of your writing (or conversation) task. Have students use the whole rubric, or make this an easier, skill-focused task by having students use only one aspect of the rubric (e.g., word choice). Choose one shared exemplar to use the first time you teach this strategy.

1. *READ THE SAME WRITING SAMPLE SILENTLY.* Give every student a copy of the same writing sample. When students know the routine well, partners can use this routine to co-evaluate samples of their own writing together.

2. *USE THE RUBRIC TO SCORE THE WRITING.* The first time you do the routine, have students only score one row of a rubric for one aspect of the writing (e.g., word choice). Each student identifies a score between 1 and 4 for word choice and writes it in a secret place the partner cannot see.

3. *COMPARE SCORES AND DISCUSS.* Have students compare scores and discuss why they chose the score they did. Encourage them to justify their score with evidence from the writing and in the rubric.

4. *CALIBRATE BEYOND PARTNERS.* When all students are scoring a copy of the same essay (such as an exemplar a teacher provides), use a finger rubric vote (p. 77) to have all students show the scores they choose for the writing. Facilitate a whole-group discussion to have students justify their scores with evidence and convince one another of their perspectives. Keep the conversation going until all students agree on the same score within a range of 1 point.

See Figure 5.6 for conversation prompts and scaffolds to compare exemplars. Figure 5.7 provides suggestions for personalizing this strategy.

FIGURE 5.6

CONVERSATION PROMPTS AND SCAFFOLDS TO COMPARE EXEMPLARS

Focus	Conversation Prompts	Possible Linguistic Frames
EVALUATE	What score would you give this for word choice? How did you score this on our rubric?	This essay is a _____ for word choice.
JUSTIFY	How do you know? What evidence do you have to support your score? What do you see in the writing to support your score? Which specific rubric criteria does this writing demonstrate?	I choose a score of _____ because I saw in the essay _____ and this is an example of _____ in the rubric. I choose a score of _____ for word choice because the author used the words_____ and these are examples of what the rubric calls specific academic words.

FIGURE 5.7

PERSONALIZE THE EVALUATE AN EXEMPLAR STRATEGY

If students	Then
Score based on factors that are not in the rubric (e.g., spelling when you want them to focus on organization)	Model highlighting the specific aspects of the rubric in a written model Model scoring with a rubric and justifying your score by quoting and highlighting success criteria in the rubric and the aspects of the rubric you find in the writing
Have a wide range of scores	Foster extended discussion and debate until all agree to a score range within 1 point and model, using the tips above, as needed to ensure all are using the rubric to score

TIPS TO BE STRATEGIC

TRY THESE TASKS WITH YOUR COLLEAGUES: Analyzing exemplars with colleagues is a powerful way to build shared understandings about expectations and success criteria and shared approaches to scoring. Use a shared rubric and collaborate to calibrate how you score exemplars. Justify your thinking with evidence from the exemplar and rubric for a rich, professional discussion.

REFLECT ON CHAPTER 5

- How do you approach learning about your students' prior experiences, home language assets, and prior knowledge? Which strategies do you find most effective for helping students connect new learning to what they already know?

- How do you determine what background knowledge is essential for a lesson you teach? Which strategies do you use to build students' background knowledge of a concept or topic before a lesson or reading of an academic text?

- How do you determine which vocabulary is essential to teach when you introduce a new concept or text? Which strategies do you find most effective to build vocabulary knowledge?

- What is one familiar strategy you want to improve upon or one new strategy you want to try next week?

iStock.com/FatCamera

CHAPTER 6

SCAFFOLD LANGUAGE DURING A TASK

"Critically examining how language is currently being used in one's own classroom will assist not only second language learners but also many of their monolingual-English peers."

—Pauline Gibbons (2002, p. 11)

WHAT AND WHY?

We provide linguistic scaffolds during a task to increase student engagement, guide effective language use, and help students communicate in new ways. Linguistic scaffolds, such as linguistic frames and word banks, offer a low-risk way for emerging English learners (ELs) and reluctant participants to communicate in speaking and writing. When used strategically, they can also help students at all levels expand their use of academic language.

When we scaffold language effectively,

- Students use language appropriate to the task, audience, and purpose—including having opportunities to use language imperfectly as they problem-solve or collaborate to build up complex ideas together
- Students communicate their unique thinking effectively
- Students feel a sense of agency to build on their own linguistic assets to take risks and use language in new ways
- Scaffolds are temporary
- Scaffolds help students build on the language they already can use on their own, and do not limit student thinking or language use

STRATEGIES TO SCAFFOLD LANGUAGE DURING A TASK

HOW TO DESIGN EFFECTIVE LINGUISTIC SCAFFOLDS

The right amount to scaffold a task is always changing based on our tasks, our students, and their ever-changing needs. Finding the just-right amount of scaffolding always involves some trial and error, or what we professionally call reflective practice. This is great news as it means we don't need a new process to design linguistic scaffolds; we just need the instructional essentials provided in Figure 6.1 with a focus on language. Does this figure look familiar? Notice the four verbs in the cycle are the same as the four steps to designing linguistic scaffolds.

FOUR STEPS TO DESIGN JUST-RIGHT LINGUISTIC SCAFFOLDS

1. **ENGAGE** students in a task through which they can demonstrate successes or challenges with your goal. Provide the minimal level of linguistic supports necessary for ELs to participate.

2. **OBSERVE** student actions and conversations (or writing) as a quick formative assessment. To inform language scaffolds, listen specifically for students' language use with the following tips:

   - **Get Specific About Language Needed for Success:** Listen to strong responses to get specific about effective language use in this context. Notice: What

FIGURE 6.1

ESSENTIALS FOR EL EXCELLENCE EVERY DAY

does a strong response sound like? Is it informal or formal? What word choices are needed for success? What types of grammatical structures do students need to communicate effectively in this task for this audience and purpose?

- **Understand ELS' Language Assets and Set Goals for Language Learning:** Listen to ELs in a conversation task to notice: Does each EL communicate in a way peers understand? What effective sentence structures and word choices does each EL use? If there are errors, do they interfere with communication? What patterns in language use do you notice? What do these tell you about students' linguistic strengths and the aspects of language you need to teach or scaffold to ensure ELs thrive with this task?

- **Consider Different Aspects of Language:** Vary which aspects of language you listen for as you identify priorities to support. As you listen to students, consider the following:

  - **Discourse:** Do students each say one idea, then stop, or do they have an extended conversation? Do students negotiate ideas? Ask questions? Build up ideas together?

  - **Sentence:** Do students use sentence structures and grammar appropriate to the task, audience, and purpose?

  - **Word:** What word choices do students make? Do they use academic vocabulary or precise word choices appropriate for the task?

3. **PERSONALIZE SUPPORT:** Plan linguistic scaffolds based on students' needs and your instructional goals.

   - If students have strong responses, have them continue via student-directed engagement. Build on this success in future lessons to raise rigor and/or release responsibility.

   - If you want to help students respond with more linguistic complexity or variety, write response frames that will help students elevate their responses to higher levels of thinking, success, and/or language use.

   - If you want to build on students' word choice, create word banks that help students communicate with more specificity.

4. **REFLECT:** Engage students in a task using your revised scaffolds and watch again to see how they engage and the language choices they make. Use these new data both to help you understand your students and to reflect on the impact of your new scaffolds.

   - How do the scaffolds impact student thinking and engagement? How do they impact student language use?

   - Do they help students use higher levels of language than they already use on their own?

   - Are the scaffolds I provide open-ended, or do they narrow responses to only a few possible answers?

   - Have I made it clear that using these scaffolds is optional and that students can respond in their own unique way?

ANTICIPATING THE JUST-RIGHT LEVEL OF SCAFFOLDS

Rather than starting a task without scaffolds to gather data, it is often more efficient and effective to plan scaffolds based on what we observed our students say and do yesterday and last week. The more we know our students, the easier it becomes to anticipate the just-right level of scaffolds as we plan. Here are three questions to help you use your prior knowledge about students to plan scaffolds for a task:

1. **EXPECT:** What are my goals for student learning? What does an ideal response sound like or look like?

2. **ANTICIPATE:** How do I anticipate my EL students (and range of all students) will respond?

3. **SUPPORT:** What is the gap I anticipate between how students might respond and the goal? What scaffolds and instruction will help me close that gap?

When you plan scaffolds through anticipation, always be humbly prepared to have your assumptions challenged. It happens every day: students exceed our expectations or have needs we never anticipated. Use the reflective teaching cycle to observe, reflect, and refine based on student needs.

REMEMBER THAT "ERRORS" ARE VALUABLE

When listening for language use, it is very important to keep in mind that perfect grammar is not a prerequisite for high-level thinking in rigorous academic tasks. It is essential that ELs have daily opportunities to engage in academic communication tasks that stretch their current levels of thinking, literacy, and language use. Grammatical errors and awkward language choices in the context of high-level tasks are evidence that you are stretching your students. Don't take the data of hearing language "errors" as evidence to stop stretching ELs academically or to replace high-level tasks with low-level back-to-basics grammar.

Do take these data to help you learn the answers to three golden questions for choosing the right language scaffolds for ELs:

* What aspects of English language do students need to excel with this task?

* What aspects of this language can my students effectively use on their own?

* What aspects of language must I teach or scaffold to ensure their success?

Answering these questions as we plan a lesson can be really tough, as we have to see through the topics, texts, and tasks in front of us to understand the language within them. This is like going to Times Square, standing in the middle of all the catchy neon signs, and trying to notice the air. We breathe it. It fills the spaces between everything we see. And yet it is so essential to our reality that we don't see it. This is especially true if we, like most teachers in our English-speaking schools, only speak one language: English. It's tough to see the aspects of language that might be tricky for ELs—tough, at least, until we see or hear our ELs stumble with that language.

USE "ERRORS" TO LEARN THE LINGUISTIC DEMANDS OF YOUR TASKS

The best way to scaffold *our learning* about the aspects of language ELs need to thrive in our classrooms is to listen to students (and read what they write) to see how they use language.

When something doesn't sound right, it's really easy to notice it. A student's awkward use of English is a gift to us if we use it to deepen our understanding. It is a gift to us if we see a language "error" not as a failing on behalf of a student but as an opportunity to identify the aspects of language we can scaffold or teach to help the student thrive.

There are many out-of-classroom approaches to training teachers to write and teach language objectives. I lead such trainings as they build awareness about language and empower teachers with a skill. That said, let me be clear: the very best way to become an expert in *understanding* the specific aspects of language ELs need in order to thrive in your class comes down to three essentials you already do every day as you teach: EXPECT EXCELLENCE, ENGAGE, and OBSERVE.

This is great news for teachers who have ELs and non-ELs in the same classroom. Why? Expecting excellence and engaging students is already central to your everyday teaching for all students. You also already listen to students and read their responses to check for understanding. You naturally notice when students use English in awkward ways as well.

The only new step here for designing language scaffolds is to also notice students' effective language choices. We make a subtle, but important, shift from noticing only the language "errors" that need fixing to using them as clues to help us understand the aspects of English language use that are essential for success with this task. Clarity about the language demands of our tasks and the language choices students make helps us design and refine linguistic scaffolds strategically to build on what students already know to help them use language in increasingly effective ways.

TIPS TO BE STRATEGIC

BUILD ON STUDENTS' LANGUAGE CHOICES: When you listen to students in conversation, notice their effective language choices, not just the errors and needs for growth. When you want to provide linguistic frames, first create linguistic frames from students' strong uses of sentence-level grammar with the task. Show students the effective language choices they are already using on their own. When you want to support student word choice with a word bank, begin the word bank with words you hear students using. This validates students' linguistic choices and helps students see the relevance of your scaffolds to their communication.

WHEN IN DOUBT, UNDERSCAFFOLD: It's hard to get the level of scaffolding right every time. When trying to decide how much or how little to scaffold, err on the side of providing fewer scaffolds. Watch students as they engage and then make mid-lesson adjustments based on what you see. This approach helps you create more opportunities for student risk taking and continuously test your own assumptions about what your students can do. Dare to invite imperfection. It's how we push the edge of what we know and can do.

DROP SCAFFOLDS WHEN THEY GET IN THE WAY: If your linguistic supports lead students to mimic without thinking or to disengage, your supports are too limiting. Drop the scaffold and work to generate original thought and authentic participation—no matter how incorrect the grammar. Then use more complex, varied, and open-ended supports to help students stretch their thinking and language use in new ways.

6.1 LINGUISTIC FRAMES

WHAT AND WHY?

A linguistic frame, also known as a sentence frame or response frame, is a partially completed sentence or paragraph that students "fill in" in their oral or written responses to a task. A linguistic frame guides students to use a specific sentence structure and vocabulary when they converse with peers or write in response to a task.

EXAMPLES OF LINGUISTIC FRAMES

I disagree with the idea that _____ because _____.

That's an interesting point. However, you might consider _____.

I agree with your idea that _____. However, I propose _____.

In the article "_____," the author argues that _____.

The most important message in _____ by _____ is _____.

WHEN TO USE LINGUISTIC FRAMES

Use linguistic frames when they help students deepen their thinking and precision with language. Don't use frames when they limit student thinking or language use. Flip to Chapters 9–12 for specific examples of linguistic frames you can use to scaffold students' conversations before, during, and after reading academic texts.

EXAMPLES OF HOW TO DIFFERENTIATE USING LINGUISTIC FRAMES

	Steps to Use the Scaffold	Example
BRIDGING Light or No Support	Engage without linguistic frames. Listen closely to language choices. Only as needed, provide frames or word banks that elevate and extend students' use of academic language to express what they have already communicated in their own words.	In a language arts task to justify inferences with text evidence, a teacher listens to student conversations. She notices that students make claims and read text evidence but don't often explain the evidence. She provides frames and encourages this next-level skill: When the author wrote "_____," this shows that _____. The quote "_____" reveals that _____.
EXPANDING Moderate Support	1. Post *multiple* response frames that are appropriate for the communication task. 2. Introduce the frames and read them together. 3. Listen as students talk with peers, and provide modeling or feedback as needed. 4. When you hear students communicate effectively without using the frames, create new frames to validate and illuminate these additional possibilities for language use.	In a language arts task to justify inferences with text evidence, a teacher posts four frame options for students: One example from the text that demonstrates this is _____. Here on page ____ the author wrote "_____." This shows that _____. I know this because _____.
EMERGING Substantial Support	1. Write one linguistic frame. 2. Read it aloud while pointing to each word. 3. Model one correct response orally and write it under the linguistic frame. 4. Guide students in chorally reading the frame and the model. 5. Structure think-pair-share to have students each create and share their own sentence using the frame. 6. If needed, provide a word bank or bank of phrases students can use to complete the frame.	In an explicit language lesson with emerging ELs, the teacher says, "Today we are going to learn to ask permission in the classroom using the question frame 'May I please _____?' Let's read it together. One question we ask in the classroom [hold up a dull pencil] is 'May I please sharpen my pencil?' Let's read the question together." Students read and say chorally with the teacher, "May I please sharpen my pencil?" Then, the teacher says, "Now you make a request to a partner using the frame 'May I please _____?'"

6.2 WORD BANKS

WHAT AND WHY?

A word bank is a list of two or more words a teacher posts for students to use as they engage in peer conversations or writing. An effective word bank includes words students understand but rarely use that will help them use precise vocabulary relevant to the task.

WORD BANK EXAMPLE: When students are justifying claims with text evidence, they often need to reference the text specifically. A teacher created the following word bank over time by adding new vocabulary each time students read a new text type or used new words to reference parts of the text. Students reference this word bank when answering questions like "How do you know?" and "What is your evidence?"

Nouns to Reference a Text	
text	poem
passage	stanza
story	line
paragraph	

For substantial support, provide a specific linguistic frame students can use with the word bank. For example, the following frame begins with a blank that students can fill in with a word from the word bank above: In the _____, the author wrote _____. This shows me that _____.

TIPS TO BE STRATEGIC

BUILD ON STUDENT WORD CHOICE: First, structure the peer conversation task without a word bank and listen to the word choices students make. Write one or more of the effective word choices you hear students make on the board. This is the beginning of your word bank. Next, add two to five words to the bank that are relevant to this task and help students be more precise with academic language. Teach the words to students and repeat the peer conversation task, encouraging them to use at least one new word from the bank.

EXAMPLES OF HOW TO DIFFERENTIATE USING WORD BANKS

	Steps to Use the Scaffold	Example
BRIDGING Light Support	1. Have students use digital thesaurus tools to create a word bank to replace an overused word (e.g., *sad*). 2. Encourage students to use more precise words to communicate nuance, and be sure they justify their choices.	Students use technology to look up synonyms and create a word bank that shows a nuanced range of emotion: *depressed, sorrowful, unhappy, mournful, pensive, melancholy.* See Chapter 7, "Teach Word Relationships: Organize Words by Meaning" (p. 166), to turn this scaffold into a dynamic collaboration task.
EXPANDING Moderate Support	1. Provide a written word bank. Make sure the words represent a wide range of possible responses, and expand on vocabulary students already use on their own. 2. As students discuss, when you hear a strong word choice, add student words to the word bank to validate and illuminate new possibilities.	In a language arts task to justify inferences about characters with text evidence, the teacher posts a word bank of words that might be used to describe a character: *kind, brave, thoughtful, energetic, wise, selfish,* etc.
EMERGING Substantial Support	1. Provide one linguistic frame along with a word bank of words that complete the frame. Draw a picture next to each word. 2. Teach each word in the word bank with a picture, action, and direct instruction. 3. Model one correct response. Engage students in chorally reading the frame and the model response.	Helping emerging ELs discuss how a character feels, the teacher posts a frame: "Enrique feels_____" She introduces a word bank of adjectives describing feeling (*angry, sad, surprised, happy, excited*) by drawing and acting out the words, then engaging students in acting out the words and naming the emotion their peers act out. She models how to choose a word and use it with the frame, then has students practice with partners to explain how they think Enrique feels. She then adds to the frame—"Enrique feels _____because _____" —and has students explain their responses.

6.3 WORD BANK TABLE

WHAT AND WHY?

A word bank table is like a word bank but includes at least two lists of words categorized into a table. Use a table in the context of meaningful academic communication to co-create a word bank involving different categories or words.

EXAMPLE 1: WORD BANK TABLE WITH CATEGORIES

In a geology inquiry, students are analyzing different rocks by writing specific observations in their science journals. The teacher notices that descriptions of most rocks are the same, as students lack precise vocabulary to explain nuanced differences. She introduces categories of adjectives (e.g., color, shape, texture) and uses pair-share to engage students in starting the following word bank with their own prior knowledge. Then she uses classroom objects to teach new words she adds to the bank. Students then use the words to revise their rock descriptions.

Adjectives to Describe Rocks

Color	Shape	Texture
gray	round	rough
black	flat	bumpy
white	jagged	smooth
pink	uneven	
pinkish		
grayish		

EXAMPLE 2: WORD BANK TABLE ORGANIZED BY PARTS OF SPEECH

Words for Writing About Eagles Organized for Substantial Support

Adjectives (Describing Words)	Parts of Eagles	Actions
massive	wings	fly
large	wingspans	soar
small	feathers	search
tiny	talons	hunt
sharp	eyes	dive
soft		capture
powerful		keep warm
		build

Color-Coded Linguistic Frames and Examples for Writing About Eagles

Eagles use their (adjective) (part) to (action).

Eagles use their sharp talons to capture fish in the river.

Eagles use their soft feathers to keep warm on cool nights.

EXAMPLES OF HOW TO DIFFERENTIATE USING WORD BANK TABLES

	Steps to Use the Scaffold
BRIDGING Light Support	1. Give each pair or small group a blank word bank table with only the categories listed (e.g., color, shape, texture). 2. Use Color-Coded Writing (p. 80) to have pairs or small groups collaborate to fill the table with as many words as they know. Encourage use of digital tools for research. 3. Do a Gallery Walk (p. 80) to have students compare tables and generate new words to add to their tables. 4. Teach additional words, if needed, to expand word choices in the table. 5. Encourage students to use words from the table, or add new words, as they collaborate in the rock analysis task.
EXPANDING Moderate Support	1. Have students collaborate in pairs to compare two different rocks. Listen for the words they use to describe rocks. 2. Write a list of the words you heard students use, and then demonstrate how you can organize those words into categories (e.g., color, shape, texture) to start a word bank table. 3. Explain the purpose of the table and use think-pair-share to engage students in generating additional words for the table. 4. Teach additional words, if needed, to expand word choices in the table. 5. Encourage students to use words from the table as they collaborate in the rock analysis task. Also encourage students to notice and celebrate when they use other specific words to add to the table.
EMERGING Substantial Support	1. Create a word bank table one category at a time. Introduce the words with modeling, images, and actions. For example, start with texture and give students items of different textures to feel as they learn each new adjective. 2. Provide a linguistic frame that has one blank students can complete using one word from the table (e.g., This rock is _____). Read it aloud, guide students in reading it chorally, and model choosing a word from the table to complete the frame. 3. Use color-coding to connect the word bank table to your linguistic frame, as appropriate. For example, make adjectives orange and make the blank for an adjective in the frame orange.

6.4 SENTENCE CHART

WHAT AND WHY?

A sentence chart is similar to a word bank table, with one important difference: it includes all of the vocabulary students need in sequence to create a complete sentence. A sentence chart is useful for supporting emergent ELs with vocabulary for conversation and writing tasks and is also a great visual to teach advanced ELs and fluent English speakers a specific sentence structure.

EXAMPLE 1: A SENTENCE CHART TO RETELL CHARACTER ACTIONS

A primary teacher read aloud the traditional story of "The Three Little Pigs" and *The True Story of the Three Little Pigs* by Jon Scieszka and engaged students in think-pair-share retellings of key details each time. After reading both texts, she created the following chart as a scaffold for a new task to have students describe what the wolf did from their own point of view. The chart includes some vocabulary from the texts (e.g., *big bad*, *misunderstood*, *blew down*) and also words the teacher taught students or students had learned previously. Students use the chart first in a think-pair-share conversation, then to write sentences about the wolf. As an extension to support emerging ELs and emerging readers, students collaborate using the Syntax Surgery strategy (p. 164) to cut up, exchange, and then resequence the sentences.

STARTER	ADJECTIVE	NOUN	VERB	WHAT? WHEN? WHY? WHERE? HOW?
The One	big bad misunderstood hungry curious	wolf canine	blew down destroyed terrified	the house of straw the three pigs

EXAMPLE 2: A SENTENCE CHART TO DESCRIBE THE CENTRAL IDEAS OF AN EXPOSITORY TEXT ABOUT THE WORLD'S LARGEST EARTHQUAKE

To help her students learn and use precise vocabulary in discussing and writing about a text on the world's largest earthquake, a sixth-grade teacher created the following sentence chart with students in three stages:

STARTER	ADJECTIVE	NOUN	VERB	WHAT? WHEN? WHY? WHERE? HOW?
A	destructive	earthquake	wrecked	thousands of buildings
One	harmful	foreshock	shook	frightened people throughout Chile
The	surprising	aftershock	collapsed	
Many	world's largest	earthquakes	frightened	about 2 million people homeless
Several	magnitude 9.5	foreshocks	destroyed	
	Chilean	aftershocks	left	powerful tsunamis
			generated	

1. **BUILD BACKGROUND:** Before reading an article about the world's largest earthquake, students used the text title, headings, and images to predict with partners what they thought they would learn in the text. The teacher listened for nouns and verbs students used and started the chart with those words.

2. **READ FOR MEANING:** After students read the text, they discussed key details with partners, and the teacher again listened for words and phrases and added them to the chart.

3. **REREAD FOR WORD CHOICE:** The teacher then introduced the chart as a support to use strong word choice when talking and writing about the earthquake. She projected the text the students had read and said it was also a great resource for precise vocabulary. She modeled and then engaged students in rereading the text to highlight precise verbs the author used to describe the impact of the earthquake. Students highlighted and discussed with partners the verbs they found to describe the earthquake's impact (e.g., *collapsed*, *frightened*, *left*). The teacher added these words to the chart. The teacher then invited students to reread for other precise words or specific details to add to the chart, and students collaborated to highlight and share examples.

4. **USE THE CHART TO WRITE A SENTENCE:** The teacher modeled creating a sentence from the chart and then structured think-write-pair-share to have students each create and share their own sentence. She challenged students (with expanding and higher proficiency) to also try writing a sentence using at least one word from the chart but a different sentence structure. She shared the examples to demonstrate that students could use the chart in two ways: (1) to write a specific type of sentence or (2) to find strong words for other sentences they want to write.

5. **USE THE CHART AS A RESOURCE FOR RELEVANT WRITING:** In a new writing task, the teacher had students collaborate in pairs to create a report on the world's largest earthquake in a multimedia format (e.g., slide show, podcast) for other students. Partners first collaborated using Color-Coded Writing (p. 80) to write the most essential ideas. She posted the chart as a resource and asked students to use in their writing a minimum of three specific words from the chart and a variety of sentence structures (not just the one in the chart).

EXAMPLE 3: A SENTENCE CHART TO TEACH EMBEDDED CLAUSE

After reading their first drafts about earthquakes, the teacher noticed many students used run-ons and a lack of sentence variety. She generated the following chart to teach students one new way to combine multiple ideas into a sentence. She had them use it to create sentences orally and then to revise one sentence in their draft. Partners then critically evaluated how the revised sentence affected their communication, and students had the option to use it or not use it in their final draft.

SUBJECT	, EMBEDDED CLAUSE,	VERB	WHO? WHAT? WHEN? WHERE? WHY?
An earthquake The Valdivia earthquake	, near Valdivia, Chile, , a 9.5-magnitude terror, , the largest recorded quake,	destroyed generated	thousands of buildings in Chile in 1960. tsunamis that killed people as far away as the Philippines.

EXAMPLES OF HOW TO
DIFFERENTIATE USING SENTENCE CHARTS

	Steps to Use the Scaffold
BRIDGING Light Support	For advanced ELs and fluent English speakers, the primary benefit of this scaffold is to enhance word choice. The primary risk is that it limits students to one sentence structure, a problem for students who need sentence variety. To encourage sentence variety, only use a sentence chart to teach a new sentence structure that students don't already use in their speaking and writing. For example, use the previous embedded clause example. Engage students in generating the chart content with you from their prior knowledge and via rereading a text for word choice.
EXPANDING Moderate Support	Use this strategy when it will expand students' word choice or to teach a specific way of adding detail to sentences (e.g., adjectives before nouns; expanding a sentence with *what*, *when*, *where*, or *why*). Vary the sentence structures you use with this strategy to ensure students understand there are multiple ways to create sentences. First post the chart and a few words in each column. Next engage students in peer conversations to generate more words for the chart. Then, when relevant, engage students in rereading for specific word choice to add to the chart.
EMERGING Substantial Support	Try this strategy first with a familiar context and topic (e.g., describe student actions). Create a sentence chart with a simple sentence structure (e.g., noun, verb). Fill it with familiar vocabulary (e.g., nouns are students' names, and verbs are actions students love to do) and model how to choose a word from each column to create a sentence. Structure think-pair-share to have students create sentences orally from the chart. Build from this success to add one new column to the chart (e.g., adjectives or "What?"/"When?"/"Where?"), and engage students in using the new addition to create more detailed sentences. In a different lesson, build from the familiar context to an academic context using the same familiar chart structure with new words for an academic task (e.g., use text evidence and illustrations to describe character actions).

6.5 GRAPHIC ORGANIZERS

WHAT AND WHY?

A graphic organizer, also known as a conceptual organizer, helps us organize ideas visually. We use graphic organizers to help students organize ideas for writing and to help students analyze ideas within a text or across texts. Used in tandem with linguistic scaffolds, peer conversations, and writing, graphic organizers help us teach and scaffold the language of different thinking processes.

EXAMPLES OF GRAPHIC ORGANIZERS

The following graphic organizers are examples of ones you may use in your classroom for different purposes, not an exhaustive list. Please use the organizers you find most beneficial to help students organize their high-level thinking and communicate with power.

1. A SEMANTIC WEB TO GENERATE RELATED IDEAS

A group of students uses the following web to map what they know about cherries. This web includes only adjectives to describe a central word. Sometimes a web is more complex with multiple words branching from each new word or idea. Sketch a web as you brainstorm, and let the ideas drive your design.

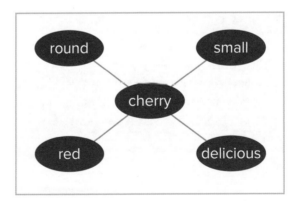

2. A FLOW CHART TO SEQUENCE

After reading a narrative, students draw or write events in a flow chart to support their retelling of a story. Before writing a narrative, students use a flow chart to plan their ideas. In science class, the teacher writes the steps of a science experiment in a flow chart to scaffold multistep directions. In history, a teacher uses a flow chart to help students map cause and effect across a linear chain of events.

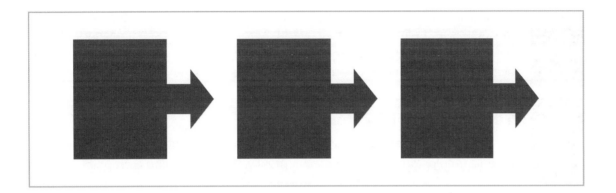

3. MULTIPLE FLOW CHARTS TO SHOW CAUSE AND EFFECT

To build background with this graphic organizer and language for talking about cause and effect, a sixth-grade teacher introduced these concepts with a familiar topic: homework. The teacher first had students discuss with partners some possible causes and effects of not turning in homework. As students shared, then reported to the class, he sketched the following organizer to include their ideas.

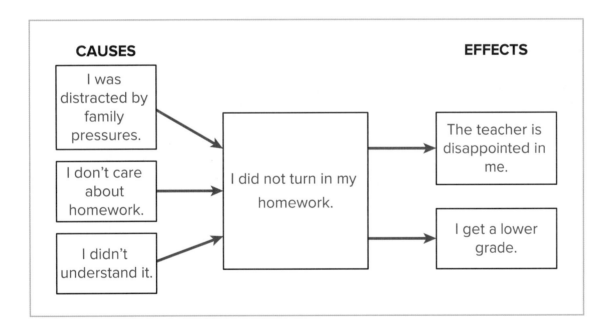

He then taught students academic words and sentence structures for communicating cause-and-effect relationships and had students discuss their ideas a second time using at least one of the following academic structures:

_____. As a result, _____.

Since _____, _____.

Building from this shared experience, the teacher then had students use a similar organizer and language to communicate ideas in an academic task (e.g., the effects of changing a

Flip-to Tip:
Flip to the Appendix (p. 284) for reproducible graphic organizers you can use to facilitate conversations, teach vocabulary, and help students organize ideas as they read closely and write with text evidence.

variable in a science experiment, the causes and effects of a historical event, the causes and effects of a story event). Across the year, each time students communicated cause and effect, they added to their list of linguistic frames and academic vocabulary for describing cause and effect.

TIPS TO BE STRATEGIC

CHOOSE AN ORGANIZER BASED ON THE TASK AND STUDENTS: A graphic organizer helps organize ideas conceptually. When choosing a graphic organizer, reflect, "What thinking process does the task demand? How do I want students to organize and communicate ideas? Which organizer best supports how I approach this task? Which best supports how my students approach this task?"

ALWAYS STRUCTURE DISCUSSIONS: Whenever you use a graphic organizer with students, don't just fill it out or have them fill it out silently. Have students collaborate to build the content of the organizer and/or engage in discussions after completing the organizer to explain the information. Talking about a completed organizer is essential for helping students build academic language for understanding and communicating lesson concepts. When possible, have students also write from the graphic organizer.

TEACH LANGUAGE FOR COMMUNICATING IDEAS: In addition to structuring discussions about completed organizers, provide linguistic frames and/or word banks to help students use the language that goes with the thinking of the organizer. For example, if you want students to explain ideas in a Venn diagram, expect students to use language to compare (e.g., *both*, *and*) and contrast (e.g., *however*, *but*, *although*). Provide linguistic frames or word banks as appropriate to make your language expectations visible and help students build on the language they know to use language in more sophisticated and effective ways.

EXAMPLES TO DIFFERENTIATE USING A GRAPHIC ORGANIZER

	Steps to Use the Scaffold
BRIDGING Light Support	Provide students with a blank organizer for the task, or invite them to draw or choose the organizer that best supports their approach. Have students either collaborate to complete the organizer or create it independently and then discuss their completed organizers after the independent task. Check for understanding as students engage, and prompt or reteach as needed.
EXPANDING Moderate Support	Provide students with a blank organizer for the task. Structure think-pair-share to have students discuss how they will use the organizer and listen to check for understanding. If students need support, follow the directions below for substantial support. If not, have them begin the task with a partner or independently. When all have finished their organizers, structure peer conversations to have students communicate the ideas in the organizers. Provide a range of response frames, as appropriate, to help students use academic language relevant to the concept (e.g., *contrast*) to connect ideas.
EMERGING Substantial Support	First teach students to use the organizer in a familiar context. Model how to complete an organizer with the gradual release process as follows: 1. I DO: Model filling out part of the organizer in front of students. Have students take notes on their own copy. 2. WE DO TOGETHER: Structure think-pair-share to have students discuss ideas for the next part of the organizer. Support the discussion with models, linguistic frames, and word banks as needed. Write some of the student ideas in your class model and have students take notes on their own copy. 3. WE DO: Use think-pair-write to have students discuss the next part of the organizer with partners and then write their ideas in their own organizers. 4. YOU DO: If students demonstrate comprehension, continue having students work in partners or individually to complete the organizer. If not, model and guide until they do. 5. DISCUSS: After students complete the organizers, structure a peer conversation to have students explain the content in the organizer. Provide one or two linguistic frames, model, and guide student success using the language to explain ideas in the organizer.

REFLECT ON CHAPTER 6

- Which tasks in your everyday teaching present the greatest linguistic challenges for ELs in your class? Which aspects of language are your top priorities to scaffold or support?

- How do you approach designing language scaffolds for a task? How is your approach similar to or different from the four-step process described on pages 137–139?

- Which of the strategies in this chapter are most relevant to your teaching priorities and students' language assets and learning needs?

- What is one familiar strategy you want to improve upon or one new strategy you want to try next week?

CHAPTER 7

TEACH LANGUAGE BEYOND A TASK

"To effectively help all children develop competence with the registers and genres that are powerful for learning in school, teachers need to recognize, build on and expand the language resources students bring to school to help them develop new ways of using language to think about the world."

—Mary J. Schleppegrell (2004, p. 156)

WHAT AND WHY?

In addition to providing linguistic scaffolds during a task, as emphasized in the previous chapter, it is valuable to provide designated language lessons that help students understand how English works and strengthen their use of academic language. Such designated language lessons are most powerful when they focus on meaningful communication and intentionally connect to the language students need to thrive in core literacy.

WHAT FEATURES OF LANGUAGE DO I TEACH?

With the old-school view of language, we might seek a grammar book to answer this question. The clean scope and sequence of lessons and activity pages is enticing. It feels familiar, if we learned a second language this way. We know we need to teach language, and this isolated workbook looks like language, has specific goals, and gives students something to do.

Be advised—the isolated grammar or vocabulary approach to teaching language will not close opportunity gaps for ELs. It will not prepare students for the academic language demands of your core literacy expectations. It will not empower students with effective language choices in their writing.

There is value in explicit language teaching, of course, but not as an isolated subject or scope and sequence disconnected from the listening, speaking, reading, writing, and content learning we expect our students to engage with every day. We must teach and support language connected to core content. The mini-lessons in this section help teach word-, sentence-, or text-level features of academic language connected to the content you teach. See Figure 7.1 for examples of specific aspects of language that could be the focus of a language mini-lesson.

FIGURE 7.1

ACADEMIC LANGUAGE EXAMPLES

Word	Sentence	Text
• High-leverage Tier II vocabulary (e.g., *impact, result, transfer, persistent*) • Words to link ideas (e.g., *so, since, while*) • Use of informal or formal language • Affixes and suffixes	• Subordinate clauses (e.g., *While _____, _____*) • Embedded clauses, *such as this*, to include an example • Dense text involving "nominalization" where concepts become nouns or noun phrases (e.g., *Extensive automobile use causes pollution*)	• Text organization structures (e.g., *cause and effect, problem and solution, compare and contrast*) • "They say/I say" argument structure (e.g., *Advertisements claim chewing sugar-free gum helps fight tooth decay. These claims, however, are misleading. In fact, . . .*)

- Flip-to Tip:
Flip to pages 95–100 to learn more about using formative data to choose priorities for language instruction.

- Flip-to Tip:
For examples of mini-lessons in language that support content learning goals, flip to the heading "Teach Language Beyond a Task" on pages 190, 201, 213, 229, 241, 252, 264, and 281.

Use the mini-lesson routines in this section in the context of reflective teaching to teach the aspects of language students most need to thrive with your meaningful content tasks.

Choose not just any random aspect of language to teach, but a specific aspect of language that you know students need for a task in your class or that you observed they struggled to understand or use in the context of your core tasks. For example, if you want students to compare two texts, they need language to articulate comparisons. At the sentence level, you notice students only use *but* when contrasting ideas. You decide to teach a mini-lesson in complex sentence structures to contrast ideas (*While _____, _____. Although _____, _____*).

STRATEGIES TO TEACH LANGUAGE IN THIS CHAPTER

NOTES

_____

_____

_____

_____

_____

_____

_____

_____

_____

_____

_____

_____

7.1 TEACH LANGUAGE FROM LIFE EXPERIENCE

WHAT AND WHY?

The best way to learn something new is to start with what you know. When you want to teach students an aspect of English grammar that is new, use topics and contexts that are meaningful and interesting to students. This is a simple mini-lesson strategy you can use anytime. Use this strategy to build background for language students need to succeed with a task (past-tense verbs for retelling, cause-and-effect language to explain effects of a historical event, etc.) or to address a specific need you observed after engaging students in speaking and writing tasks.

STRATEGY AT A GLANCE

1. **PREPARE:** Choose one specific aspect of grammar or word choice needed for success with your content task(s). Explain the goal and purpose.

2. **MODEL:** Model language in a familiar context.

3. **ENGAGE:** Structure conversations for students to use the language.

4. **OBSERVE:** Listen to student language use.

5. **EXTEND:** Extend language learning to an academic context connected to your core.

STRATEGY LESSON EXAMPLE: TEACH FUTURE VERB TENSE

1. **EXPLAIN GOAL AND PURPOSE. MODEL LANGUAGE IN A FAMILIAR CONTEXT**

   As you explain the agenda for the day, write a sentence starter to emphasize your verb uses: "Today we will _____." Underline *will* and explain that this is the future tense and we use it to talk about what will happen next or in the future. The future tense helps you make predictions or talk about your plans.

2. **ENGAGE STUDENTS IN CONVERSATIONS TO USE THE LANGUAGE**

   Guide practice by structuring think-pair-share to have students using the future tense to discuss the question, "What will you do after school today?"

   - For substantial support, provide the frame "After school, I will _____" and model how to use it in speaking and writing.

   - For moderate support, provide the frame "After school, I _____" and listen to see if students use the future tense on their own.

   - For no support and a formative assessment, have students talk without a response frame.

3. **OBSERVE TO LISTEN TO STUDENT LANGUAGE USE**

   As students engage, listen for the verb phrases students use and write all examples that model the future tense in a list. For example, a list from this class discussion might include phrases such as the following:

   > will run

   > will play basketball

   > will talk with my friends

   Underline the verbs (*will run*, *will play*, etc.) and explain that these are all examples of future tense. When we want to talk or write about the future, we use *will* before the verb.

4. **EXTEND LEARNING TO CORE ACADEMIC CONTEXT**

   Example: Next connect learning from this familiar context to the academic context of making predictions. Write an example of a prediction on the board and underline the verbs (*I predict Ferdinand will smell flowers all day*). Show how we use the same tense when making predictions. Have students make predictions in the classroom, and listen again for use of verb tenses. Generate a list of verb phrases you hear in students' predictions (*will smell*, *will fight*, *will solve*, etc.). Post these as models to reinforce the learning and also connect directly to the previous lesson. Provide one-on-one feedback, as appropriate, to help students use the future tense in the context of making a prediction.

TIPS TO BE STRATEGIC

FOCUS ON MEANINGFUL COMMUNICATION FIRST AND FOREMOST: Even when explicitly teaching a grammatical structure, always teach it in a meaningful context. Structure tasks that have students practice the structure in the context of meaningful communication. Extend learning to help students apply what they have learned to enhance how they communicate in a core lesson task.

CHOOSE YOUR LESSON OBJECTIVES RELEVANT TO HOW STUDENTS NEED TO USE LANGUAGE IN YOUR CORE LESSON TASKS: Don't teach English grammar for the sake of teaching grammar. Teach a specific aspect of grammar that you notice students may be ready to learn that they can also apply beyond this lesson to your core lesson tasks. For example, if students are retelling stories and some struggle with past-tense verbs, teach a targeted lesson in past-tense verbs. Build from that lesson to help the students apply their learning to story retelling.

USE A GRAPHIC ORGANIZER AND LINGUISTIC SCAFFOLDS: Use language scaffolds from Chapter 6, as appropriate, to model and guide students in understanding and using the language you teach. Use the same scaffolds (e.g., linguistic frames and graphic organizers) when you extend learning to help students see the clear connection in language use across the two different contexts and tasks.

7.2 TEACH LANGUAGE FROM A TEXT

WHAT AND WHY?

Texts students read and write are excellent resources for language teaching. Use exemplars of student writing to model effective language choices you want students to make in their writing. Use academic texts students have read to model one or more specific uses of word choice, grammar, or text organization they will encounter in texts and can use in their own academic communication.

STRATEGY AT A GLANCE

1. **PREPARE:** Choose one specific aspect of language to teach for a text. Choose a priority that is essential for success with your reading or writing tasks. Explain the goal and purpose.

2. **MODEL IN THE TEXT:** Highlight the target language in the text.

3. **MODEL BEYOND THE TEXT:** For a sentence-level lesson, write a response frame on the board to emphasize the pattern used in the text. For a word-choice lesson, write the words found in the text. For a text-organization lesson, model a graphic organizer that makes the same organization visual.

4. **ENGAGE:** Guide practice by structuring a conversation, collaborative writing, or revision task for students to use the language.

5. **OBSERVE:** Listen to student language use.

6. **EXTEND:** Guide students in applying their learning to core speaking and/or writing tasks in a new context.

SAMPLE LESSON—Teach Phrases to Build Cohesion Between Evidence and Explanation

1. **PREPARE:** A seventh-grade teacher notices that student arguments with text evidence are choppy and lack cohesion. She chooses to teach students some phrases and grammatical structures they can use to connect their text evidence to their explanations.

She explains the goal and purpose of her lesson:

Words like and connect ideas within one sentence. Strong writers also use words and phrases to connect ideas between sentences. We call this "cohesion."

Cohesion helps make writing flow, and helps readers understand your thinking. Let's look at one example of cohesion you can also use when you explain text evidence in your writing.

2. **MODEL IN THE TEXT:** Highlight the target language in the text.

   In the following exemplar, the author does a great job explaining the text evidence she uses to support her argument. Let's look at the phrases she uses to explain her thinking:

   > Rhina P. Espaillat's message in "Bilingual/Bilingüe" is that being bilingual strengthens her instead of weakening her. The narrator shows her father's fear in the second stanza "that words might cut in two his daughter's heart (el corazón) and lock the alien part." This means her father believes Spanish and English are two different cultures and your heart should only belong to one. The narrator then teaches herself Spanish at night without her father's consent. When she writes "And still the heart was one," she is telling her father that being bilingual didn't break her, but made her stronger.

   Look at the phrases I've highlighted in this exemplar. These are great phrases that we can also use when we want to make an argument that is cohesive, or connected.

3. **MODEL BEYOND THE TEXT:**

   The teacher writes the following phrase and frame on the board.

   This means that . . .

   When the author writes _____, she is telling us that _____.

4. **ENGAGE:** Structure conversations or a revision task for students to use the language. The teacher gives students an example of a three-sentence argument that lacks cohesion, and has them collaborate in partners to make one revision to add cohesion.

5. **OBSERVE:** Listen to their language use as students collaborate, and watch to see how they apply learning in this task.

6. **EXTEND TO APPLY TO CORE TASKS:** Soon after this lesson, engage students in the close reading routine to make and justify a claim on a new topic and text. Before their discussions and writing, revisit the concept of cohesion and post the frames from this lesson. Listen and watch for their use of these and other words or phrases to connect their ideas. Generate additional words and phrases from their strong examples and provide targeted feedback as needed specific to this goal.

Note: This is a great follow-up to the exemplar lesson on page 128. Use the same exemplar again for this language lesson.

In addition to using this routine with student writing, use it with any academic text students have read to teach an aspect of word choice, sentence structure, or text organization that will enhance their comprehension of the text and/or their use of language in speaking and writing.

7.3 SYNTAX (OR PARAGRAPH) SURGERY

WHAT AND WHY?

Syntax surgery engages students in reconstructing cut-up sentences or paragraphs to create meaningful communication. Use syntax surgery to reinforce a specific sentence structure you have taught, support one-to-one correspondence for emerging readers, and/or engage students as active problem solvers to make meaning. Use paragraph surgery to deepen students' understanding of text organization and engage peers in collaborative problem solving to figure out the meaning of an academic text.

WHO BENEFITS?

Emerging English learners and emerging readers benefit from syntax surgery with simple and complex sentences. All students benefit from syntax surgery to reconstruct a grammatically dense academic sentence from a content text.

THREE WAYS TO USE SYNTAX SURGERY

1. **RECONSTRUCT STUDENT SENTENCES:** Use syntax surgery as a natural extension to any short writing task in which students write a sentence such as Color-Coded Writing (p. 80) or think-write-pair-share (p. 54). Have students cut and trade sentences for a puzzle that also reinforces the focus of the lesson. This extension is especially valuable after a direct instruction lesson in language, such as the example shown on page 148.

Three students collaborated to write the sentence shown in a language development lesson on comparisons. Their task, connected to a content unit on transportation, was to describe a similarity between two modes of transportation. Each student trio first co-wrote a sentence using the Color-Coded Writing strategy (p. 80), then cut up their sentences and traded them with other groups to reconstruct using syntax surgery.

2. **RECONSTRUCT AN ACADEMICALLY DENSE SENTENCE FROM A CONTENT TEXT:** For a great meaning-making activity, choose a complex,

meaning-rich sentence from a text students are reading, type it, and cut up one copy for each pair of students. Have them collaborate to reorganize the words in any way that makes sense and justify their constructions to each other.

For example, a third-grade teacher chooses an academically dense, meaning-rich sentence from a text students read on hurricanes. She gives each partner a copy of the cut-up sentence in words (most challenging) or phrases (easier). For example, she chooses the following phrases and gives them to each pair to reconstruct:

and presses

in the atmosphere

the earth

that surrounds

envelope of air

on the surface

they take place

Like all storms,

She teaches/revisits the meaning of any unfamiliar words and then has partners collaborate to reconstruct the sentence. Try this task before looking at the full sentence below.

Using all the words to re-create the same sentence is one challenge. For deeper engagement with the content vocabulary and academic thinking, also encourage students to create other meaningful sentences with the words. Do this activity before students read as an anticipation task or after reading as an extension for language learning.

3. RECONSTRUCT A PARAGRAPH: Use the same strategy to have students reconstruct a paragraph. Use the easiest approach (sequence the complete sentences to create a logical sentence) when you want to emphasize text-level organization such as the integration of claim, evidence, and explanation with students new to the concept. Use a more challenging approach (reconstruct a paragraph that is cut into words and phrases) when you want students to engage in extended problem solving with close attention to both text organization and syntax.

TIPS TO BE STRATEGIC

FOSTER ACADEMIC CONVERSATIONS: If partners do the task silently, try one or both of the following strategies: (1) Make the task more challenging to merit a collaborative discussion or (2) divide up pieces and give each partner half to each contribute, one at a time, to the reconstruction.

Sentence in third-grade example: Like all storms, they take place in the atmosphere, the envelope of air that surrounds the earth and presses on the surface. (Lauber, 1996)

WHAT AND WHY?

Students need multiple exposures to new vocabulary to learn the words deeply and use their own speaking and writing (Beck, McKeown, & Kucan, 2002; Gersten et al., 2007). Beyond teaching words in isolation, we need to help students understand how words are connected and related to one another. The three strategies on this page are powerful, low-prep routines you can use weekly to engage students in going deeper with the high-priority academic words you teach.

HOW?

First, use the strategies on pages 114–125 to teach high-utility academic vocabulary that is relevant to your content tasks and texts. Deepen learning beyond those lessons by engaging students in using one or more of the words you taught in any of the following tasks:

1. COMPARE AND CONTRAST

Give students two words to compare and structure think-pair-share or think-write-pair-share to have students describe how they are alike and different. You can vary the complexity of this task with the words you pair together. This is easiest with concrete words (e.g., *heading* and *title*) and most conceptually challenging with abstract words (e.g., *claim* and *support*). To engage students in analyzing nuanced differences in word meaning, have them compare words with very similar meanings (e.g., *edit* and *revise*, *introduce* and *begin*).

Examples of linguistic frames you may provide for additional support:

- *They both have to do with _____ _____.*
- *With one, _____.*
- *With the other, _____.*

A creative variation is to have students compare a new concept word you have taught with something tangible (e.g., "How is inference like a window?"). Such a task invites creative thinking and metaphors, both powerful to foster new connections in the brain to deepen learning.

2. ORGANIZE WORDS BY MEANING

Use this strategy to engage students in collaborating to analyze how similar words are related in meaning. Start with at least one word you have taught and want to further teach. Choose three or more words that have similar, related, or opposite meanings. For example, after teaching *courageous*, have each pair or small group write the following words on separate self-stick notes: *brave*, *scared*, *timid*, *courageous*, *bold*. Have students collaborate to organize the words physically in any way they choose (line, circle, web, etc.) to represent visually how the words are related.

This strategy often elicits great collaborative conversations involving claims, clarifying questions, and debate. Use the fishbowl strategy (p. 60) to watch a group of students engage in this task and analyze their collaborative conversation moves (p. 70).

After each pair (or group) organizes the words, have students compare their approaches. You can do this as a whole group by inviting different pairs to explain and show (e.g., using a document camera) how they organized the words, or structure a gallery walk (p. 80) to have students analyze the different approaches visually.

3. WORD FAMILIES

After teaching a new word, teach students the different forms of the word using the Word Family Chart on page 288 in the Appendix. For example, after teaching the words *inference* and *courageous*, write the different forms of each word on the chart, as shown in Figure 7.2.

FIGURE 7.2

WORD FAMILY CHART: EXAMPLE

Noun	Verb	Adjective	Adverb
inference	infer	inferential	
courage		courageous	courageously

Say and write sentences to model using the different forms of the word, then engage students in using the different forms of the word in sentences. Highlight the different ways these words are used in your task directions (e.g., "Make an inference") and student conversations (e.g., "I infer that _____"). Create sentences using each form of the word, and then omit each word and have students figure out the correct word form for each sentence. For example, a sixth-grade teacher wrote the following cloze sentences about the novel *Holes* to use forms of the word *courage*:

- Stanley Yelnats has a lot of _____ to steal the truck keys.
- I'd love to have a _____ friend like Stanley Yelnats.
- Stanley _____ drove off into the desert to save his friend.

For a student-directed approach, have students identify the different forms of a new word on the chart and then collaborate to create cloze sentences for each form. Have groups trade sentences and collaborate to complete them.

REFLECT ON CHAPTER 7

- Which aspects of language are your top priorities to teach with language mini-lessons? Choose one goal and one strategy from this chapter to try to address that goal.

- Choose an academic text that students read in your classroom. Notice how the text is structured at the text level, and notice sentence-level grammar and word choice. What is one aspect of language use in the text you'd especially like to help all students understand and use in their academic communication? How might you use Strategy 7.2 to teach this goal?

- In what ways do you help students have multiple exposures to learn and use new vocabulary? What is one new word relationship strategy you want to add to your routines?

SECTION IV

APPLY STRATEGIES TO DIFFERENTIATE ACADEMIC LITERACY

Section IV helps you apply the six essentials for excellence with English learners to your everyday literacy teaching to help ELs, and all students, excel with core literacy goals.

IV. Apply

iStock.com/monkeybusinessImages

CHAPTER 8
MAKE EL EXCELLENCE ROUTINE

"We need talented, committed teachers, teachers who will stand up for the goals of equal and high quality education."

—Sonia Nieto (quoted in Ferlazzo, 2016)

We have learned the essential mindsets and strategies for EL excellence. Now let's make them central to our everyday teaching. This section shows you how to easily integrate the essentials into a four-step routine for engaging students in closely reading, discussing, and writing about texts. In this chapter, I introduce the routine. In the following chapters, I help you go deep within each step of the routine to help you integrate the six EL essentials (Value, Expect, Engage, Observe, Support, Reflect) to teach your highest-priority literacy goals.

The routine I emphasize is one you likely already use, and this is intentional. My goal is to show you how you can easily apply the essentials for EL excellence to what you already teach. Do you engage students in making predictions or asking questions before reading? Do you have them read to understand texts? Do you expect students to read closely to analyze and make inferences? Do you want students to write with text evidence? If you answered yes to any of these questions, this routine will be familiar and relevant to what you already do every day.

Here are the four steps of what students do during the close reading routine:

1. **BEFORE READING:** Anticipate
2. **DURING READING:** Read to Understand
3. **DURING READING:** Reread to Analyze and Infer
4. **AFTER READING:** Collaborate to Write With Text Evidence

See Figure 8.1 for a visual of the routine at a glance.

Use these four steps to actively engage ELs (and all students) in reading to understand and analyze complex grade-level texts. Whether the text is long or short, informative or narrative, or part of a textbook, newspaper, primary source, or multimedia, this is a go-to sequence for engaging students in analyzing texts academically.

Use this routine when you want to focus deeply on a text. Use it for texts worthy of rereading for nuance, analysis, and deeper levels of comprehension. This is a routine for closely reading shared texts, meaning the texts that you read with *all* students in a class

FIGURE 8.1

FOUR-STEP ROUTINE FOR CLOSE READING OF COMPLEX TEXTS

| Anticipate | Read to Understand | Reread to Analyze and Infer | Write With Text Evidence |

regardless of their reading level. Typical examples of shared texts include anthology experts, novels, texts printed and copied for all students, and digital texts that students can access online. We can also closely read shared "texts" that are off the page like TED Talks, spoken word, multimedia presentations, podcasts, and more.

THERE IS MORE TO READING THAN CLOSE READING

Before we dig into these four steps for close reading, let me make a very important point. Close reading of shared texts is only one part of strong literacy instruction. My emphasis on close reading in this book does not mean I recommend that the close reading of grade-level texts be the *only* reading your students get to do. It is important that ELs and all students in your classroom also have opportunities to read texts at their instructional level (guided reading, reciprocal teaching with leveled readers, literature circles, etc.), read texts they choose for pleasure, and get targeted instruction in foundational reading skills they need to be fluent readers.

WHY EMPHASIZE CLOSE READING IN THIS BOOK?

Of all the aspects of academic literacy I could emphasize in this section, I chose close reading for five important reasons:

1. **It's hard.** It's challenging to lead close reading of grade-level texts in any classroom where students have diverse reading levels and levels of English proficiency.

2. **It's important for learning language.** Reading, discussing, and writing about grade-level texts are all essential activities for building grade-level academic language and literacy. Rigorous texts use language in ways we never use in classroom talk, and students need to learn that language to be able to read and write academic texts.

3. **It builds student capacity with academic argument.** Making claims and justifying thinking with text evidence is a high-priority capacity for career and college readiness. We build all the essential subskills of this rigorous goal via the close reading routine in tandem with reflective teaching and strategic supports.

4. **Many ELs don't get the opportunity.** Many ELs have no opportunities to engage with grade-level texts or higher-level analysis tasks. Traditionally, in the spirit of differentiation, many ELs are given watered-down texts or pulled out of academic literacy opportunities to learn "language" as something isolated from academic literacy. ELs need opportunities to engage in core academic literacy to build the language for core academic literacy.

5. **It's a learning opportunity for all of us.** Engaging all students in linguistically diverse classrooms in reading, analyzing, discussing, and writing about rigorous texts is not easy. This makes it a high-priority goal for professional learning and professional collaboration among teachers.

FOUR STEPS, FOUR CONVERSATION TASKS

Each step of this close reading routine is the perfect opportunity for a peer conversation. Use this routine to apply the conversation strategies from Chapter 3 in daily action. Rather than calling on individual students or expecting students to answer written questions alone, facilitate peer discussions for each step of the routine. See Figure 8.2 for examples of questions to drive peer conversations at each step of the routine.

Every time you engage students in closely reading a grade-level text, whether as a whole class or in a small group, plan to have peers discuss at least one question at each of the first three steps: (1) Anticipate, (2) Read to Understand, and (3) Reread to Analyze and Infer. When time allows, ideally with at least one text per week, have students also use their ideas from the analysis conversation to (4) Collaborate to Write With Text Evidence.

The questions in Figure 8.2 are a starting point and general enough to apply to many text types. Plan to use the many resources in Chapters 9–11 to adapt and vary the questions according to your literacy goals. For example, if your students are reading narrative texts and you want them to analyze and discuss theme, ask questions about theme for the third step of the routine. Flip to 11.4, "Make and Justify Claims About Theme and Author's Message" (p. 266), for a wealth of resources to teach this skill including discussion prompts, linguistic frames, word banks, differentiation charts, and more.

WHY ROUTINE?

Routines make your planning easier and help you shift from teacher-directed to student-directed learning over time. Often, when you first establish routines, you model, guide, and use substantial supports to ensure every student can successfully engage. You then build on those successes the next time you use the routine to reduce the modeling and supports and foster increasing levels of student independence. When students struggle with part of

FIGURE 8.2

FOUR CONVERSATION TASKS FOR COLLABORATIVE CLOSE READING

Step	1. Anticipate	2. Read to Understand	3. Reread to Analyze and Infer	4. Collaborate to Write With Text Evidence
Sample Questions for Peer Conversations	Based on the title, headings, and/or images, what do we expect this text to be about? What questions do we expect this text to answer?	What's the gist? What doesn't make sense? How do our predictions compare to the actual text?	What can we infer, conclude, or interpret beyond the literal? Discuss open-ended questions aligned to literacy or content standards.	What is our claim? Which evidence is most relevant to the claim? How will we explain the connection between our evidence and the claim?

the routine, you have multiple opportunities to address that challenge: in the moment, as a targeted lesson, and the next time you lead the routine.

Without routines, we can get stuck in the first step of modeling, guiding, and using substantial supports. This is a life sentence of low-level learning for ELs and also very frustrating for teachers. With routines, students spend more brainpower on self-reflection and learning than on the question, "What does the teacher want me to do?"

Routines especially benefit ELs as once students know the routine, a teacher spends less time explaining the directions of tasks and creates more time for students to do the heavy lifting of critical thinking, analysis, and using academic language.

Routines help us raise rigor and release responsibility over time. Any teacher working with students whose language, literacy, or collaboration skills are currently below grade level knows that the famed gradual release model of shifting from explicit modeling to student-directed learning doesn't always happen in one lesson. It's more helpful to think of the gradual release of responsibility across multiple lessons and learning opportunities.

"Tasks in the classroom need to be both predictable and variable to a degree. There must be a level of continuity, predictability and familiarity in order to provide a sense of security. At the same time there must be variability in order to provide interest, expectation and challenge."

—Leo van Lier (2007, p. 60)

VARIETY IS THE SPICE OF LIFE

If you are like me, you both love and hate routines. The last thing anyone wants is to do the same thing every day. Boring! Luckily, close reading with the close reading routine is *never* the same. Why? Every text we read is different because the text *is* the main focus.

Think of the routine as a frame for a work of art. Our focus is the art. The frame just enhances our viewing experience.

In an art museum, the fact that most frames have similar features (e.g., four sides, rectangular shape) doesn't bore us. It actually helps us focus on what we really want to see: art.

Art is rich and varied. The texts we read in our classrooms should be rich and varied as well. Thanks to the infinite variety of texts we can read and of interpretations and perspectives students bring to those texts, close reading is always a unique experience.

Also, we can vary our routine, just as framers can vary how they frame a piece of art. With framing art, a framer might vary the color, material, thickness, or style of a frame, but none of these variations changes the basic purpose and structure of the frame. In the same way, as you keep the basic structure of the close reading routine, you can always change any of the following features:

- Questions you ask
- Supports you provide
- Peer collaboration structures you use
- Whether to have students write (Step 4) or end with the discussion (Step 3)

The chapters in this section are dedicated to such variety. They help you go deep with any aspect of the routine you want to emphasize to help students excel with a specific literacy skill. They include a menu of tools you can use or lose to personalize teaching for each student.

GETTING STARTED: The best way to use this section is to try the close reading routine with your students and watch as they engage to notice what strengths they bring and what they are ready to learn.

INTRODUCING THE CLOSE READING ROUTINE

You can introduce the routine with any text or comprehension focus. I like to begin with a narrative text and the comprehension focus of making inferences about a character. This is a great place to start as narratives often are easier to access than information text, and many of the good narratives at our fingertips are full of details that *show rather than tell us* about characters. This translates to a very rich opportunity to teach making and justifying inferences with text evidence.

I am intentionally starting with a focus that I believe will be easiest for students so I can put more attention into the routine than the complexity of the comprehension task. I then build on early successes to both remove supports *and* increase the rigor of texts and comprehension tasks over time. I also notice how students struggle, and I use those data to adjust my teaching within the task and to prioritize goals for follow-up lessons.

Let's dig in to the basic routine. Begin with the grouping configuration (small group or whole class) that you most frequently use when reading a shared text with students. Give every student in the group a copy of the same text.

1. **Anticipate:** Before reading, have partners scan the title, headings, and/or images to think about, then discuss, "What do we predict this text is about?"

2. **Read to Understand:** After reading, have partners discuss, "What is the gist of this text? How does it compare to your prediction?"

3. **Reread to Analyze and Infer:** Have students reread to prepare to discuss an open-ended comprehension question relevant to your teaching goals. For example, if students are learning to identify and discuss theme, the question could be "What can you infer about the characters in the story?" Students reread with this question in mind, annotate to underline clues that can help them answer it, and then discuss the question with a partner.

4. **Collaborate to Write With Text Evidence:** Use Color-Coded Writing (p. 80) to have students collaborate to write a short (three- to five-sentence) response to the question they have just discussed. For example, "What can you infer about one character in the story? Justify your thinking with evidence from the text."

WHAT ABOUT MODELING, SCAFFOLDS, AND SUPPORTS?

If you structured all the tasks listed above without any modeling, scaffolds, or supports, how would your students engage and participate? Would they discuss the questions? Would they understand the tasks? Would they engage in collaborative conversations? Would they annotate the text and use evidence to support their thinking? Would they collaborate productively together to write with text evidence?

If you answered no to any of these questions, then this guide is for you! Every next chapter in this guide goes deep with instructional resources to help teach these subskills strategically so that your ELs, and all students, thrive.

APPLY ESSENTIALS TO MEET SPECIFIC LITERACY GOALS

Establishing a routine is the first step. The next step, and the focus of every chapter in this section, is addressing students' needs to thrive with each step of the routine across a wide variety of instructional contexts and texts to meet specific literacy goals.

Flip back to the table of contents for this section on page 171. Notice that each chapter represents one of the four steps of the close reading routine. Each includes two or more different literacy skills you might choose as your focus. Vary your focus based on your ever-changing literacy goals and texts.

Collaborating to write, the fourth step of the close reading routine, does not need a separate chapter. All of the essentials students need to build up ideas for writing with text evidence are embedded in the close reading, annotation, and conversation tasks in Chapter 11. To extend any of these tasks from talk to collaborative writing, use one of the "Collaborate to Write Strategies" (3.12, p. 80) to have students collaborate to write their analysis of the text.

WHERE DO I BEGIN?

The chapters in Section IV are designed not to be read from cover to cover but to be your flip-to companion when you want to enhance your students' close reading skills or go deep with a specific literacy goal. With so many choices, where do you begin?

There are two great ways to choose your focus:

1. **Begin With Formative Data.** Notice where students struggle in the close reading routine, and choose one step to teach deeply. Choose one chapter and subskill in that chapter to begin addressing students' needs.

2. **Begin With Your Standards or Curriculum Goals.** What reading comprehension strategies in your standards or curriculum are your top priority to teach right now? What types of close reading subskills do students most need to thrive with relevant reading and text-based writing in your core classroom? Choose a priority and flip to the chapter that best meets your goals.

TIPS TO BEGIN
WITH FORMATIVE DATA

As a formative assessment, engage your students in the close reading routine described on page 177. Use the minimum amount of scaffolds needed for your students to productively engage, and watch students to gather formative data about their needs. Make a list of your top priorities to address, and then flip to the chapter in Section IV that is your very top priority to address.

If students struggle to even begin the formative assessment task, use these three sections as your entry point to introduce the routine one step at a time:

9.1   Make Predictions

10.1   Identify Main Ideas

11.3   Make Inferences About Characters

For the fourth step of the routine, add the optional writing step by using the Color-Coded Writing strategy (p. 80). In this strategy, students apply the ideas they have built up together through close reading discussions to write a short paragraph including a claim, evidence, and an explanation.

Data we gather by observing students are layered like an onion. The first time we watch students in the close reading routine, we notice some general aspects of their successes and challenges such as where they engage and where they get stuck. When we start teaching specific goals within the routine (e.g., predictions), we also want to gather data specific to the success criteria for that goal. To gather formative data specific to a goal, flip to the chapter of the skill you want to emphasize (e.g., predictions). Under the heading "Observe," you'll find questions to help you gather observation data specific to that literacy goal.

> **Flip-to Tip:**
> Notice that the color-coding for engagement tasks (purple) and support strategies (orange) reminds the reader that this content directly connects to the flip-to chapters of engagement strategies (purple) and support strategies (orange). Use the color-coding as an easy reference to refer back to a connected chapter anytime you want to build background in a strategy or vary the strategies you use.

WHAT WILL I FIND IN EACH CHAPTER?

Each chapter in Section IV helps you address a high-priority goal that is part of a high-priority close reading routine. Within each chapter, I organized the content to be flip-to friendly and help you integrate the six essentials for everyday excellence to your teaching.

As I outlined in Chapter 1, for every literacy goal in Section IV, you'll find the content described in Figure 8.3.

Value is the only essential verb that doesn't have unique content in each chapter. This is intentional as the value mindsets are foundational to everyday excellence no matter what literacy skill we teach. Reread Chapter 2 to integrate value mindsets into your everyday teaching.

FIGURE 8.3

ESSENTIAL SECTION IV CONTENT TO HELP YOU TEACH FOR EL EXCELLENCE

HEADING	RESOURCES TO HELP YOU TEACH FOR EL EXCELLENCE
EXPECT	A purpose statement that helps you explain why the skill matters Literacy goals and aligned language needed for success
ENGAGE	Tasks to actively engage students in learning the goal and/or demonstrating what they know and can do Collaborative conversations central to every task
OBSERVE	Questions to focus your observations of students to help you gather formative data to personalize teaching
SUPPORT	An if–then personalization chart to help you differentiate teaching based on students' needs A detailed menu of strategies and supports to choose or lose according to what your students need
REFLECT	Questions to help you reflect and refine teaching based on impact

BE IN CONTINUOUS INQUIRY ABOUT YOUR IMPACT

As you teach any skill in any chapter in Section IV, may the headings and flow of the content make it easy for you to start with high expectations, actively engage all students, personalize supports, and teach for impact. These are high-priority literacy goals to teach across multiple contexts with different texts—so you have many opportunities to engage, observe, support, and reflect to refine your approach as students continue to learn with increasingly higher levels of success and self-direction.

Flip back to the front inside cover of this guide to remember the essentials for EL excellence. Use the reflection questions in your own daily teaching, and in collaboration with colleagues, to support your continuous journey to help ELs and every learner thrive.

CHAPTER 9

ANTICIPATE

"We need to be astonished by our kids' curiosity . . . We need to focus on their thinking, revel in their wonder, teach strategies for understanding, foster deep conversation, and support them to turn information into knowledge."

—Stephanie Harvey (2011, p. 126)

WHAT AND WHY?

An effective anticipation task helps generate student curiosity and interest in a text. It also helps students use their prior knowledge related to the text topic. The best anticipation tasks are quick and engage every student via conversation structures or action strategies.

Anticipation is the first step for reading any new text and the first step of the close reading routine.

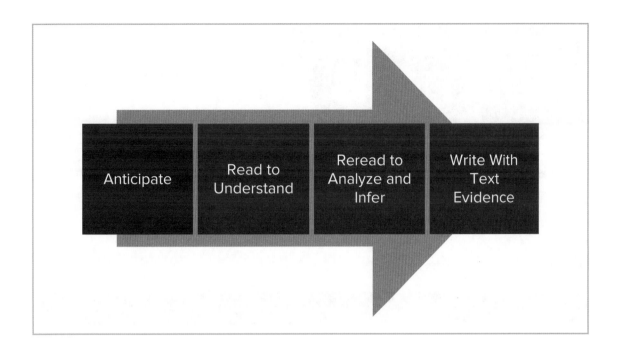

LITERACY GOALS IN THIS CHAPTER

9.1 Make Predictions

9.2 Ask Questions Before Reading

NOTES

_____

_____

_____

_____

_____

_____

_____

_____

_____

_____

_____

9.1 MAKE PREDICTIONS

PURPOSE: We make predictions to feed our natural curiosity about what we are about to read. We use text features to preview the possible structure or topics in a text so it is easier to read.

EXPECT

What students will know or be able to do:

	LITERACY GOALS	LANGUAGE FOR SUCCESS
Predict	I can predict what the text will be about or what will happen next.	I can engage in collaborative conversations about predictions using complete sentences and present and future verb tenses.
Support	I can explain the prediction using prior knowledge or text evidence (e.g., from the title, headings, pictures, or text).	I can justify predictions using precise vocabulary to reference the text—*title*, *heading*, *illustration*, *photo*, and *diagram*.

ENGAGE

What students do to learn and demonstrate current understandings with predictions: Plan these tasks into your lessons, and use them for formative assessment before, during, and after teaching predictions:

1. **PREVIEW TEXT:** Preview (title, images, headings, etc.) to predict what the text will be about. *Variation: stop in the middle of a longer text to predict what will happen next.*

2. **DISCUSS PREDICTIONS:** Discuss with a partner or small group, "What do you predict the text will be about?" *Variation: when stopping in the middle of a longer text, discuss, "What do you predict will happen next?"*

OBSERVE

Literacy goals:

- Is the prediction logical based on the text clues and students' prior knowledge?
- Does the student explain the prediction using evidence (e.g., title, images, or text clues) or an explanation?

Language use:

- Is the spoken or written prediction communicated in a way that is easy to understand?
- What effective uses of grammar and word choice does the student use?

- If there are errors, do they interfere with communication?
- What aspects of language use, if any, are a priority to support or teach?

SUPPORT

Use what you learned from observing students to prioritize what you will teach and support to help them thrive with making predictions and discussing predictions in collaborative conversations with peers.

PERSONALIZATION CHART

IF STUDENT PREDICTIONS	THEN
Are invisible: • Students are silent in peer conversations. • Students leave the page blank. • Students are focused on something else during the task.	Reflect: • Is the text I'm using engaging—do the clues provoke natural curiosity for predictions? • Do students understand *why* it is valuable to learn this skill? • Do they understand *how* to do the task (in any language)? • Do they have the language to communicate their thinking with this task? Use "build background" strategies to connect to students' prior knowledge, teach concepts, and model making predictions. Use "scaffold language" strategies in this chapter as appropriate to engage learners at the optimal level of challenge and support.
Are illogical or not justified: • The prediction doesn't make sense based on the clues and student experiences.	Reflect: • Is the prediction logical from the students' point of view and background experiences? • Is explaining the prediction a priority in this lesson, or is the primary goal to pique student curiosity about the text to start reading? When justifying the thinking behind a prediction is a priority, structure peer conversation tasks using linguistic frames that encourage students to support their thinking (p. 70). Listen to understand diverse perspectives, not a specific prediction you consider "correct." Have students revisit predictions during and after reading to reflect and change them based on new clues.

CONTINUED ⟳

CONTINUED ➔

IF STUDENT PREDICTIONS	THEN
Are explained only in the present tense	Teach a language mini-lesson on future tense (p. 190).
Include language errors	Reflect: • Do they interfere with communication? • Are they the natural part of risk taking for communication? • Which are priorities to address in the moment? • Which are priorities for follow-up language lessons? Learn from errors that interfere with communication to prioritize goals for follow-up language development. Use "teach language beyond a task" strategies (Chapter 7) to address priority needs.

CHOOSE SUPPORTS STRATEGICALLY

This section offers you a menu of support options to choose or lose based on your students' ever-evolving needs. There are *way* too many options here to put into one lesson. Be strategic in choosing the supports that are most relevant to what your students need right now to build on what they already can do to excel in new ways.

To find the optimal level of supports, reflect critically on each option. For example, ask yourself, "Will this support help my students extend beyond what they can do on their own, or stagnate their growth or self-direction?"

Remember, differentiation is messy. Don't wait for perfection! Choose the supports you anticipate are the best fit right now, and then watch and listen to students as they engage to reflect and adapt your approach.

Use the headings in this section to choose supports based on why and when you use them before, during, or beyond engaging students with making and discussing predictions:

Build Background

Scaffold Language During a Task

Teach Language Beyond a Task

These headings share titles with Chapter 5, 6, and 7, respectively—a reminder that strategies here are examples of strategies introduced in those prior chapters now applied to this very specific context of helping students make and discuss predictions about texts.

BUILD BACKGROUND

TEACH *PREDICT* WITH THE FRAYER MODEL

Use the Frayer Model strategy on p. 114 to explicitly teach the word *predict*, or use the collaborative approach on p. 118 to engage students in collaborating to deepen their understanding of the word.

TEACH *PREDICT* WITH THE COGNATE

If you have ELs with expertise in Spanish, French, Italian, Catalan, or Romanian, use the cognate from that language to teach *predict*. For example, write the cognate *predecir* under the word *predict*. Ask students to compare the words and notice the similarities and differences. Circle *pre* in both words and help students learn the meaning of the prefix. Underline the root in both words, *decir* and *dict*, and have students discuss what the meaning might be. Spanish speakers have an advantage figuring out the meaning of *dict* as *decir* is a common Spanish word. Flip to page 124 for more on using cognates.

For connected word study, consider engaging students in one of the following tasks using digital (or print) tools:

- Find other English words with the Latin root *dict* (e.g., *dictionary*, *diction*, *dictate*) and collaborate to explain what the word has to do with *say*.

- Find other English (or Spanish) words with the prefix *pre* and collaborate to explain what the word has to do with *before*.

BUILD BACKGROUND FROM MULTIMEDIA TO TEXT

Build on students' natural ability to make predictions by having them first make a prediction from a short video, a sequence of pictures, an engaging picture book such as *The Mysteries of Harris Burdick* by Chris Van Allsburg, or any enticing cover of a picture book. When needed, label the nouns in the picture to create a word bank students can use to explain their thinking about the picture. Then have them apply that knowledge to do a similar task to make a prediction based on a text on a familiar topic. Use the same visuals and linguistic supports across both lessons to help students connect the concept of predictions from one context to the next.

BUILD BACKGROUND FROM FAMILIAR TO ACADEMIC

Begin teaching students to make predictions about texts on familiar topics that connect to students' background knowledge and expertise beyond school. Build from these successes to have students make predictions about texts that introduce new topics and ideas.

SCAFFOLD LANGUAGE DURING A TASK

LINGUISTIC FRAMES

BE STRATEGIC: Listen to the sentence structures students use to make predictions. Create frames from the effective structures they use. Then add one or more frames, as appropriate, to help stretch students to use more complexity or variety as they communicate predictions.

Sample Linguistic Frames From Simple to Complex

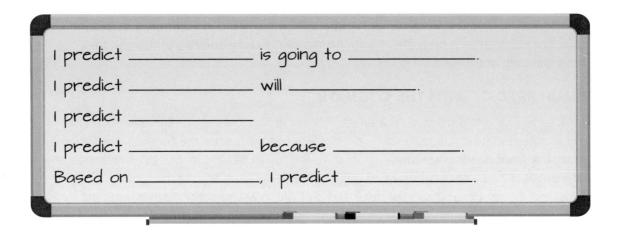

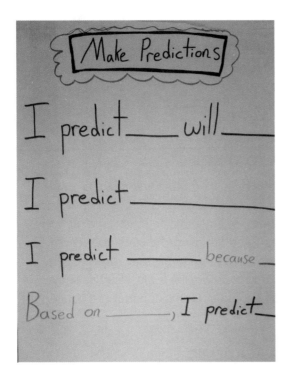

An example of frames provided for a core literacy class involving ELs at a range of levels and fluent English speakers.

Draw and label pictures for the word bank to provide additional support, especially for emerging ELs.

WORD BANK

BE STRATEGIC: Listen to the word choices students make to talk about the clues they use to make predictions. Begin a word bank with their effective choices. Add new words to the bank and teach them to students, and encourage them to use these words as they explain their predictions.

Sample Word Bank of Text Clues for Making Predictions

title	picture
heading	photo
illustration	

Differentiate Linguistic Supports: One Example

BRIDGING	**Light or No Support**	Have students preview the text independently and then discuss their predictions with peers. Encourage students to justify their thinking by explaining the clues they used to make their prediction, and negotiate ideas if they disagree. Only provide linguistic frames if they stretch students to incorporate variety and precision into how they communicate their ideas.
EXPANDING	**Moderate Support**	Have students perform the same task as above but provide a variety of linguistic frames that encourage students to explain their predictions. For example: I predict _____ because _____. Based on _____, I predict _____. Provide a word bank of nouns students can use to get specific about the parts of the text they use to make their prediction: title heading illustration photo Model the use of the frame and word bank without sharing your prediction (and stealing students' thunder): "Based on the illustrations, I predict this article will be about . . ."
EMERGING	**Substantial Support**	Teach predictions with an enticing picture. Build vocabulary for the task by labeling the picture, creating a short word bank, and engaging students in saying and acting out the words. Provide one linguistic frame (e.g., "I predict the cat will _____"). Model using the linguistic frame and word bank to make a prediction. Guide students in repeating your model and then invite them to make a new prediction or choose between two possible predictions (e.g., "Will the cat fly or swim?"). Connect from this lesson to predict with text. Build and connect to the concept in students' primary language when possible.

TEACH LANGUAGE BEYOND A TASK

In addition to providing linguistic scaffolds *during* a task, it is valuable to provide designated language lessons that help students advance their use of academic English. Such designated English language development (ELD) lessons are most powerful when they intentionally connect to the language students need to thrive in core literacy.

One specific language objective to teach beyond predictions that also helps students communicate predictions is future verb tense.

> *BE STRATEGIC*
>
> **ENGAGE:** Have students make predictions without a sentence frame or only with the starter "I predict."
>
> **OBSERVE:** Notice the verbs students use to finish the sentence. Do they use future tense ("I predict Ferdinand will . . . ," "I predict the text will be about . . .")?
>
> **SUPPORT:** If students do not use future tense, or if you notice students struggle with future tense in other aspects of communication, use the following lesson:

EXPLICIT LANGUAGE TEACHING: FROM PERSONAL EXPERIENCE

TEACH FUTURE VERB TENSE: For ELs new to using the future tense in English, teach the future verb tense in a familiar context. Use the "Teach Language From Life Experience" routine detailed on page 160. Here is an example of how to use this routine to teach future verb tense:

1. MODEL LANGUAGE IN A FAMILIAR CONTEXT

   Example: As you explain the agenda for the day, write a sentence starter to emphasize your verb uses: "Today we will _____." Underline *will* and explain that this is the future tense and we use it to talk about what will happen next or in the future.

2. ENGAGE STUDENTS IN CONVERSATIONS TO USE THE LANGUAGE

   Example: Guide practice by structuring think-pair-share to have students using the future tense to discuss the question, "What will you do after school today?"

   - For substantial support, provide the frame "After school, I will _____" and model how to use it in speaking and writing.

   - For moderate support, provide the frame "After school, I _____" and listen to see if students use the future tense on their own.

   - For no support and a formative assessment, have students talk without a response frame.

3. **OBSERVE TO LISTEN TO STUDENT LANGUAGE USE**

   Example: As students engage, listen for the verb phrases students use and write all examples that model the future tense in a list. For example, a list from this class discussion might include phrases such as the following:

   will run

   will play basketball

   will talk with my friends

   Underline the verbs (*will run*, *will play*, etc.) and explain that these are all examples of future tense. When we want to talk or write about the future, we use *will* before the verb.

4. **EXTEND LEARNING TO A NEW CONTEXT**

   Next connect learning from this familiar context to the context of making predictions. Write an example of a prediction on the board and underline the verbs ("I predict Ferdinand will smell flowers all day"). Show how we use the same tense when making predictions. Have students make predictions in the classroom, and listen again for use of verb tenses. Generate a list of verb phrases you hear in students' predictions (*will smell, will fight, will solve*, etc.). Post these as models to reinforce the learning and also connect directly to the previous lesson. Provide one-on-one feedback, as appropriate, to help students use the future tense in the context of making a prediction.

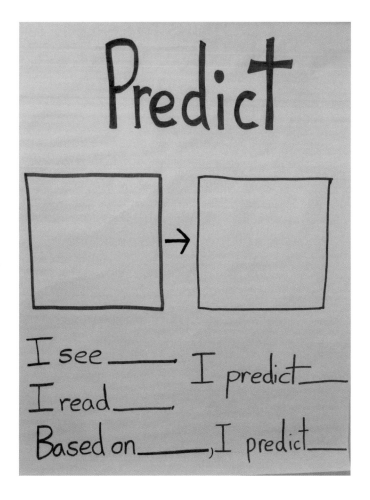

For substantial support through all steps of this lesson, use a graphic organizer to clearly distinguish present (clues in the text) from future (prediction).

Color-coding is visual support you can always use to make explicit connections across the different linguistic scaffolds. For example, notice how I use color-coding in my photos of sentence frames, word banks, and the graphic organizer in this section: green consistently represents what we talk about in the present tense (text clues), and blue consistently refers to what we talk about in the future tense ("I predict . . .").

QUESTIONS TO REFLECT AND ADAPT TEACHING

Watch students as they make predictions and reflect on their strengths and priorities for learning.

Reflect:

- Do students understand the concept of predictions? Do they use text clues to build natural curiosity about the text?

- What language strengths do they use to communicate their ideas? Is their thinking and curiosity driving their predictions? Or are they just going through the motions to follow my scaffolds?

- How do the scaffolds I use impact student engagement and learning? Do they advance or hinder student participation? Advance or hinder learning? Advance or hinder critical thinking? Advance or hinder language use?

- What shifts will I make in my teaching and scaffolds to build on the strengths I see in my students and to help them thrive with my rigorous expectations?

QUICK GUIDE TO ADAPT SUPPORTS ACCORDING TO NEED

If . . .	Then . . .
Students struggle unproductively or are off task	⌃ Increase supports
Some students don't participate	⌃ Increase supports
Students struggle with a specific aspect of a task	⌃ Increase supports
Students actively engage in learning through challenge	*Keep this sweet spot!*
Students (above emerging EL) only copy your model	⌄ Decrease supports
Student responses are predictable or canned	⌄ Decrease supports
Students don't get to struggle, think, or problem-solve	⌄ Decrease supports
You want to assess how students approach a task	⌄ Decrease supports

NOTES

_____

_____

_____

_____

_____

_____

_____

_____

_____

9.2 ASK QUESTIONS BEFORE READING

PURPOSE: Asking questions fuels our curiosity about what we read. The skill of asking questions and reading to find the answers empowers us to research anything we want to learn.

EXPECT

What students will be able to know or do:

	LITERACY GOALS	LANGUAGE FOR SUCCESS
Ask Questions	I can ask my own questions about content topics and texts.	I can ask questions in conversations and writing about academic topics and texts. I can understand and use a variety of effective sentence structures to ask meaningful questions (e.g., "What is . . . ?" "Did they . . . ?" "Why didn't . . . ?").

ENGAGE

What students do to learn and demonstrate current understandings with asking questions about texts: Make this sequence routine each time students read a new text, and use each engagement task as a formative assessment before, during, and after teaching the skill of asking questions:

What students do *before* reading:

1. **PREVIEW TEXT:** Preview the title, cover, headings, and visuals (images, illustrations, or graphics) in a text. Think of questions you anticipate the text may answer.

2. **DISCUSS QUESTIONS:** Collaborate with a partner or small group to generate a list of questions. Discuss, "What questions do we think this text will answer? What other questions do we want to know about this topic?" *Collaborate to write a list of questions using the Think-Write-Pair-Share (p. 54), Color-Coded Writing (p. 80), or Digital Collaboration (p. 81) strategy.*

What students do *during* reading:

3. **READ** to understand the text, then reread to see which questions the text answered, which it did not, and what new information you learned.

What students do *after* reading:

4. **DISCUSS:** With partners (or small groups), students revisit the list of questions you created together and discuss, "Which questions did the text answer? What else did the text teach us that we didn't ask about? What questions do we still want answered? What new questions on this topic do we now have?"

OBSERVE

What teachers watch and listen for as students engage:

Literacy goals:

- Do students ask questions that are relevant to the topic, title, and clues in the text?
- What types of questions do students ask? Are they open-ended questions requiring explanation, factual questions that can be answered with a word or a phrase, or yes/no questions?
- Do their questions seem fueled by their curiosity, or are students going through the motions of this task?

Language use:

- Do students communicate their own curiosity in questions that others understand?
- Do students use effective syntax for asking questions in English?
    - If yes, create exemplars and/or response frames from their language choices. Add to these, as appropriate to the task, to invite additional types of questions.
    - If no, write the specific awkward phrases you notice. Also write how you would ask the question. Use these notes to create linguistic frames and/or to teach a language mini-lesson in question syntax.

Collaborative conversations:

- Are students each just sharing a question, or are they discussing their questions in an extended conversation?

SUPPORT

Use what you learned from observing students to prioritize what you will teach and support to help them thrive with asking questions about texts in peer conversations or writing.

PERSONALIZATION CHART

IF STUDENT QUESTIONS	THEN
Are invisible: • Students are silent in peer conversations. • Students don't write a question. • Students are focused on something else during the task.	Reflect: • Is the text I'm using engaging for this task? • Do students understand *why* it is valuable to learn this skill? • Do they understand *how* to ask questions (in any language)? • Do they have the language to ask questions in English? Use "build background" strategies to connect to students' prior knowledge and model asking questions. Use "scaffold language" strategies, as appropriate, to engage learners at the optimal level of challenge and support.
Students ask only a few types of questions (e.g., "What?" "Who?")	Model a variety of question types in speaking and writing. Use the "scaffold language" strategies of providing a word bank of additional question words or linguistic frames to foster increased variety in the types of questions students ask.
Students ask only low-level questions that have yes/no answers or short answers.	Reflect: • Are these questions driven by students' natural curiosity about the topic and text? Use "build background" strategies to model high-level questions. Use the "scaffold language" strategy of providing linguistic frames, as appropriate, to guide students' use of high-level questions.

CHOOSE SUPPORTS STRATEGICALLY

This section offers you a menu of support options to *choose* or *lose* based on your students' ever-evolving needs. There are *way* too many options here to put into one lesson. Be strategic in choosing the supports that are most relevant to what your students need right now to build on what they already can do to excel in new ways.

To find the optimal level of supports, reflect critically on each option. For example, ask yourself, "Will this support help my students extend beyond what they can do on their own, or stagnate their growth or self-direction?"

Remember, differentiation is messy. Don't wait for perfection! Choose the supports you anticipate are the best fit right now, and then watch and listen to students as they engage to reflect and adapt your approach.

Use the headings in this section to choose supports based on why and when you use them before, during, or beyond engaging students in generating their own questions about content topics or texts:

> Build Background
>
> Scaffold Language During a Task
>
> Teach Language Beyond a Task

These headings share titles with Chapters 5, 6, and 7, respectively—a reminder that strategies here are examples of strategies introduced in those prior chapters now applied to this very specific context of helping students ask questions about content topics and texts.

BUILD BACKGROUND

BUILD BACKGROUND IN A FAMILIAR CONTEXT

Build on students' natural curiosity and background experience asking questions by bringing in an interesting photo from your personal life (e.g., of family members, a place you've visited, or a pet). Don't describe what's in the photo; only give students just enough information about the photo to pique their curiosity, then invite them to ask any questions. Have students first generate questions with a partner, then ask their favorite questions to you in front of the class. As students ask questions, listen for the types of questions they ask and the language choices they make.

USE STUDENT QUESTIONS AS LANGUAGE MODELS

As peers discuss during the previous task, silently identify a handful of students who demonstrate success (or give one-on-one feedback to a student who can revise a response to thrive when sharing it with the whole class). Call on the students you preselected and answer their questions in a casual conversation about the picture you shared. Also write each question or the first words of each (e.g., "Who is . . . ?" "Why did . . . ?" "Where was . . . ?"). Use these written models to start a bank of question frames, and then add additional frames to build on these language choices students already make on their own. Post the frames each time you engage students in asking questions, and build on the list as you discover more possible types of questions in classroom discussions and reading.

ANALYZE QUESTIONS IN MENTOR TEXTS

Searching for questions in texts is easy, even for emerging ELs, because the clue is a visual punctuation mark. Have students search for questions in a textbook or other print or online text that includes questions, and write each question on a self-stick note. With emerging ELs, write similar questions on the board (e.g., "What is your _____ _____?") and help students find the pattern, then use it to ask their own questions. From intermediate ELs to fluent speakers, engage table groups in sorting questions they find. As they collaborate to determine how to sort the questions, it may help to discuss, "How are these similar? How are they different? Which might we group together? Why?"

BUILD DIRECTLY ON PRIMARY LANGUAGE SKILLS

How we ask questions varies tremendously by language. While the concept of asking a question transfers across language, the grammar often does not. In Mandarin Chinese, one common question structure uses the same word order as the sentence but adds the word *ma* at the end to make it a question. In Spanish, for example, the word order of a question is different than in English.

SCAFFOLD LANGUAGE DURING A TASK

BE STRATEGIC: To support the language of asking questions, first reflect, "Do students need help with the syntax of asking questions or just ideas for how to begin a question?"

WORD BANK

If students need help getting started, use a word bank of question words.

Why?	How?	Who?	What?	When?	Where?
Does?	Do?	Is?	Are?	Can?	

LINGUISTIC FRAMES

If students struggle with syntax, model effective questions and provide linguistic frames that include at least the verb after the question word. Try asking a few questions specific to the task you expect students to do. Notice the verb tense you use. Use that verb tense in your models and your frames. Note the verb tenses in the following examples. Which are most relevant for your task?

Asking Questions About Texts in Future Tense

I wonder if_____ will_____ .

What will happen if _____?

Asking Questions in Present Tense (e.g., for information text or a narrative)

How is _____ _____?

Why does/is _____ _____?

What does _____ _____?

Asking in Past Tense (e.g., for a historical article, biography, or narrative in past tense)

How did _____ _____?

Why did _____ _____?

What did _____ _____?

MODEL AND LINGUISTIC FRAMES

For additional support, provide a model question with each frame. Underline the words in the model that you use in the frame.

Models and Frames for Asking Questions About Text Images in Present Tense

Model: Where are the penguins going?

Frame: Where are _____?

Model: How do penguins find food?

How do _____ _____ _____?
      (subject)   (verb)

Models and Frames for Asking Hypothetical Questions About a Text

Model: What might happen next? What might Stanley Yelnats do?

Frames: What might _____?

Model: How could the characters solve this problem?

Frame: How could _____?

SENTENCE CHART

If your students need help with syntax and word choice to ask questions on the topic, build a sentence chart of relevant vocabulary and practice asking one type of question. Use this strategy to provide substantial support with one type of question, not when variety is your top goal.

QUESTION WORD	VERB	SUBJECT	VERB
How	do	penguins	find
Why	don't	seals	eat
What		people	sleep
Where			hunt
When			fly
Who			

Choose one word from each column to begin a question. Add additional words or phrases to the end to complete the question, if needed. For example, "How do penguins find food during a storm?" or "Why don't penguins fly?"

As students experience success with this strategy, build the complexity of the chart and/ or vary the sentence structures you use (e.g., question word/subject/verb: "Are penguins hungry in winter?").

LINGUISTIC SCAFFOLDS IN A GRAPHIC ORGANIZER

If your goal is to help students ask different types of questions, model variety and organize your word bank or linguistic frames into categories such as the following example. Use the visual to be specific about the types of questions students are asking and which different types you want them to try.

TYPE OF QUESTION	WORD BANK	SAMPLE QUESTION FRAMES
Open-Ended Question	Why? How?	Why does _____? Why is _____? Why are _____? Why did _____? Why was _____? Why were _____? How does _____? How is _____? How are _____? How did _____? How was _____? How were _____?
Factual Question	Who? What? When? Where?	Who was _____? Who is _____? What is your _____? What happened when _____? When did _____? When will _____? Where is _____? Where was _____ when _____?
Yes/No Question	Do? Does? Is?	Do you like _____? Does _____ have _____? Is _____?

Differentiate Linguistic Supports: One Example

BRIDGING Light or No Support	Have students collaborate to ask higher-level, opened-ended questions about a task. Only provide a word bank of question words if it helps students to incorporate variety or rigor into the types of questions they ask.
EXPANDING Moderate Support	Post multiple response frames to support students with the syntax of asking questions specific to the task. For example, following support the task of asking questions about a historical text based on pictures and headings before reading the text: How did _____ _____? Why did _____ _____? What did _____ _____?
EMERGING Substantial Support	Focus first on one type of question or verb tense for questioning. Model on a familiar topic. Post one to two linguistic frames specific to that focus. Model and guide students in using the frames to generate questions about the topic. Structure multiple opportunities for students to generate questions with a peer in speaking and writing. Build from initial lessons to asking questions in academic contexts. As an alternative, provide question frames that can all be completed with a word bank of words you explicitly teach students to complete the frame. For example: How do wolves _____? Why do wolves _____? Where do wolves _____? What do wolves _____? Verb bank: *eat, survive, live, run, play, climb*, etc. Practice creating new questions chorally and in partners.

TEACH LANGUAGE BEYOND A TASK

In addition to providing linguistic scaffolds *during* a task, it is valuable to provide designated language lessons that help students advance their use of academic English. Such designated ELD lessons are most powerful when they intentionally connect to the language students need to thrive in core literacy.

An important language objective relevant to asking questions is question syntax. All of the previous scaffolds support this goal. To further develop students' language for questioning, teach one or more of the following ELD lessons:

WHAT'S IN THE BAG?

Bring something interesting from home, hidden in a shopping bag. Give students a small clue about what is in the bag, then encourage them to ask questions to get you to describe it.

As needed, provide frames to help students ask questions such as the following:

Does it have (noun)?   Is it (adjective)?

Is it bigger than a _____? Is it smaller than a _____?

Students may start trying to guess what it is (e.g., "Is it a _____?"). Don't answer guess questions until students have asked at least five to ten questions about the clues.

Extend this by having students bring something from home and take turns inviting questions from the class or from partners in the classroom.

COLOR-CODED COLLABORATION

Pair students and give each pair two markers (different colors) and a sentence strip (or strip of paper long enough to write on one line). Have students collaborate to write a question relevant to a book or topic your class is discussing. For shared accountability, each student uses a different-color marker, and both colors must be part of the final product.

SYNTAX SURGERY

Extend color-coded collaboration by having partners cut their question into separate words and then trade it for a question another pair has created together. Every pair now has a new cut-up question to reconstruct. Have partners collaborate to reconstruct the question, and then check with the authors to see if their reconstruction is correct. *Variation: do syntax surgery with cut-up questions from mentor texts. Challenge: scramble multiple cut-up questions together, and have students put them back together.*

QUESTIONS TO REFLECT AND ADAPT TEACHING

Watch students as they generate questions about texts, and reflect on their strengths and priorities for learning.

Reflect:

- What are my goals for student learning (p. 194)? Which aspects of these goals can students now understand and do? Which are goals for growth?

- How do the scaffolds I use impact student engagement and learning? Do they advance or hinder student participation? Advance or hinder learning? Advance or hinder critical thinking? Advance or hinder language use?

- What shifts will I make in my teaching and scaffolds to build on the strengths I see in my students and help them thrive with my rigorous expectations?

Adjust scaffolds and supports continuously to build on strengths and help students realize increasing levels of self-direction and success.

QUICK GUIDE TO ADAPT SUPPORTS ACCORDING TO NEED

If . . .	Then . . .
Students struggle unproductively or are off task	⌃ Increase supports
Some students don't participate	⌃ Increase supports
Students struggle with a specific aspect of a task	⌃ Increase supports
Students actively engage in learning through challenge	*Keep this sweet spot!*
Students (above emerging EL) only copy your model	⌄ Decrease supports
Student responses are predictable or canned	⌄ Decrease supports
Students don't get to struggle, think, or problem-solve	⌄ Decrease supports
You want to assess how students approach a task	⌄ Decrease supports

NOTES

_____

_____

_____

_____

_____

_____

_____

_____

_____

_____

iStock.com/monkeybusinessimages

CHAPTER 10
READ TO UNDERSTAND

"Good readers construct, revise and question the meanings they make as they read."

—Nell K. Duke and P. David Pearson (2008, p. 205)

WHAT AND WHY?

The purpose of the first read is to understand and enjoy the text. With complex texts on unfamiliar topics, reading to understand is a problem-solving process to make meaning. Strategies we use to make meaning include self-monitoring and reading for main ideas. When we encounter confusing words or sections, we use prior knowledge, text features, context clues, or affixes and suffixes to make meaning from complexity.

Reading to understand is the second step of the close reading routine.

EL Excellence Every Day

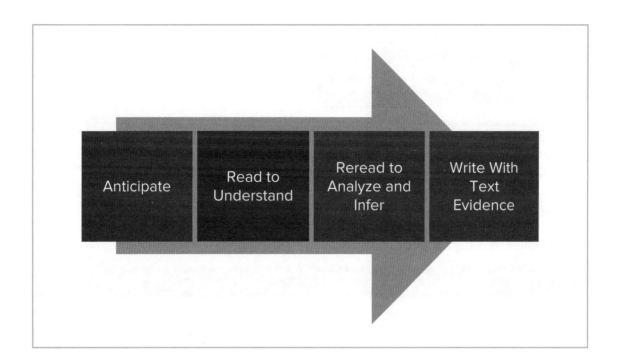

READ TO UNDERSTAND GOALS IN THIS CHAPTER

10.1   Identify Main Ideas

10.2   Self-Monitor and Use Context Clues

10.3   Use Affixes and Roots to Figure Out Unknown Words

10.1 IDENTIFY MAIN IDEAS

PURPOSE: I read for main ideas so I can learn what the authors are saying in any text. With this skill, I can make meaning from any text on any topic to read to learn.

EXPECT

What students will know and be able to do:

	LITERACY GOALS	LANGUAGE FOR SUCCESS
Main Idea	I can read to understand the main idea and key details in academic texts.	I can read to comprehend the main idea and details in academic texts. I can collaborate to discuss the main idea and key details about a text using academic vocabulary relevant to the topic and task. I can paraphrase the main idea of a text to express key concepts in my own words in speaking and writing.

ENGAGE

What students do to learn and demonstrate current understandings of main idea: Make this sequence routine each time students read a new text. Use the engagement tasks for formative assessment before, during, and after teaching main ideas.

What students do:

Have students read a text in preparation for discussing the main idea. This task includes two steps:

1. **READ AND ANNOTATE:** After students preview a text to make predictions, students read for main idea or the "gist" of the text. Students annotate by underlining central ideas or clues about main ideas in the text. *Variation: if the text can't be marked, have students take notes on words and phrases related to the main ideas.*

2. **DISCUSS MAIN IDEA:** Students discuss main idea with a partner or small group. Discuss, "What is the main idea of this text?" (or use an alternate question). *Variations: use Think-Write-Pair-Share to write or Color-Coded Writing to collaborate to compose a main idea sentence.*

Find scaffolds for this task on pages 209–212. When your primary goal is assessment, use the minimal scaffolds needed to ensure students understand and can actively engage in the task. Each time you repeat this routine during reading instruction, adjust scaffolds based on what you observe to strategically support and challenge all students.

OBSERVE

What teachers watch and listen for as students engage: Focus your observation on your top-priority goals. Choose one or more questions from the following to focus your observation:

Literacy goals:

- Do students underline the most important ideas in a text? Or details of minor importance?
- Do they express main idea as the general topic of the text (e.g., pollution) or communicate a more nuanced understanding of the main idea specific to the text (e.g., human pollution is harming sea life)?

Language use:

- Is students' communication of main idea easy to understand?
- Do students quote main idea statements from the text or synthesize and paraphrase text details to express the main idea in their own words?
- If students use their own words, what language choices do they make? What do these reveal about their strengths and needs with language essential for success with this task?

Collaborative conversations:

- Do students deepen their thinking about main ideas through conversation, or just each say one idea and stop talking?

SUPPORT

Use what you learned from observing students to prioritize what you will teach and support to help them thrive with identifying (and discussing and writing about) main ideas in your content texts.

PERSONALIZATION CHART

IF STUDENT RESPONSES	THEN
Are invisible: - Students are silent in peer conversations. - Students leave the page blank. - Students are focused on something else during the task.	Reflect: - Is the text I'm using engaging for this task? - Do students understand *why* it is valuable to learn this skill? - Do they understand *how* to do the task (in any language)? - Do they have the language to communicate their thinking with this task?

CONTINUED

CONTINUED ⟳

IF STUDENT RESPONSES	THEN
Show that students struggle with grade-level complex text	In close reading lessons with complex texts, try the following strategic ways to differentiate without lowering the complexity of the text: • Chunk the text: Focus on one part of the text (e.g., section or paragraph). • Read aloud first: Read the text aloud, without explaining meaning, and then have students reread for this task. • Build background in concepts and vocabulary that aren't taught in the text, but are essential background knowledge for understanding the text. Also build students' reading fluency beyond close reading with daily opportunities to read texts at an instructional level in small groups and student-selected texts for independent reading.
Demonstrate that they don't yet understand the concept of main idea	Use "build background" strategies to connect to students' prior knowledge and experiences, teach concept vocabulary, and model main idea. Use "scaffold language" strategies, as appropriate, to engage learners at the optimal level of challenge and support.
Demonstrate that they have a basic understand of main idea, but could be more specific in their conversations and written responses	Use the "build background" strategy to compare exemplars (5.8, p. 130) with the example on p. 211 in this chapter.
Use familiar or vague language when talking or writing about main idea	Use the "scaffold language" word bank strategy to help students use precise words for main idea and topic of the text. Teach the "Unpack an Exemplar for Word Choice" language mini-lesson on page 213.

CHOOSE SUPPORTS STRATEGICALLY

This section offers you a menu of support options to *choose* or *lose* based on your students' ever-evolving needs. There are *way* too many options here to put into one lesson. Be strategic in choosing the supports that are most relevant to what your students need right now to build on what they already can do to excel in new ways.

To find the optimal level of supports, reflect critically on each option. For example, ask yourself, "Will this support help my students extend beyond what they can do on their own, or stagnate their growth or self-direction?"

Remember, differentiation is messy. Don't wait for perfection! Choose the supports you anticipate are the best fit right now, and then watch and listen to students as they engage to reflect and adapt your approach.

Use the headings in this section to choose supports based on why and when you use them before, during, or beyond engaging students in reading for main ideas and in discussing or writing about main ideas with peers:

Build Background

Scaffold Language During a Task

Teach Language Beyond a Task

These headings share titles with Chapters 5, 6, and 7, respectively—a reminder that strategies here are examples of strategies introduced in those prior chapters now applied to this very specific context of helping students read for main ideas and communicate their thinking about main ideas in conversations and writing.

BUILD BACKGROUND

BUILD CONCEPT VOCABULARY

Write the words **main** and **central** on the board, and engage students in generating examples of when they hear or see these words used in the world. Provide specific models (e.g., *main office, main course, central library*). Now add *idea* after each word and explain the concept of main idea or central idea. Use the modeling strategies that follow to demonstrate the concept of main idea. Engage students in underlining details and discussing main ideas to apply and deepen their learning.

TEACH MAIN IDEA WITH A LIST

Teach the concept of **main idea** and **details** with a simple text: a list. Leave the topic heading blank and challenge partners to collaborate to use the **details** in the list to figure out the topic. For example:

Topic: _____
baseball
soccer
football

Ask, what's the topic? (Sports.) Make other lists to engage students in the same challenge, then have students create specific topic lists and challenge one another to name the topic. Build from this simple list to a more complex list of points in an argument. For example:

Main idea: _____
Homework is boring.

Homework takes kids away from activities and family time.

Homework doesn't always help learning.

What's the main idea? What's the author's main argument about homework?

Build from success with this game to finding the main idea in a paragraph or short text. For a parallel game with a higher linguistic challenge, white out the topic sentence and have partners collaborate to write a topic sentence they think will best introduce the paragraph.

TEACH CENTRAL IDEA WITH THE COGNATE

If English learners (ELs) in your class have expertise in Spanish, French, Italian, Catalan, or Romanian, then teach the cognate for *central idea*. Choose a cognate from the following chart to teach the meaning of *central idea* using the cognate strategy (p. 124).

LANGUAGE	COGNATE
English	central idea
Spanish	idea central
French	idée centrale
Italian	idea centrale

Write *central idea* on the board and the cognate for *central idea* below it. Have students compare the English to the cognate to notice the similarities and differences and to figure out the meaning of the English word.

MODEL READING FOR MAIN IDEAS

Project a section of text and model reading it for main ideas. Use the think-aloud strategy to reflect on which details are main ideas, and demonstrate annotating to underline each choice. Say the main idea and write what you say as an exemplar of a main idea statement. Be specific to say more than just the topic and also include the central ideas about the topic that are expressed in the text. Write your example as an exemplar and underline the start of your sentence ("The main idea of this article is . . .") as a possible linguistic frame students can also use when talking about main idea.

MODEL DISCUSSING MAIN IDEA

Invite a student who is confident in conversation to join you in modeling a partner discussion about main idea. Practice in advance so your co-modeler is ready to disagree and/or build up ideas together. Start the conversation with a nonexample of main idea and model together how to disagree and discuss to build up ideas together.

BUILD FROM FAMILIAR TO ACADEMIC CONTEXTS

First model and practice finding main idea with texts on familiar topics that connect to students' background knowledge and expertise beyond school. Build from these successes to have students figure out the main idea of texts that introduce new topics and ideas.

COMPARE EXEMPLARS TO GET SPECIFIC ABOUT EXPECTATIONS

Engage students in comparing two or three sentences about main ideas on the same topic. Provide exemplars that model a range of complexity such as the following:

A. "This article is about pollution."

B. "The central idea of this text is that pollution is bad."

C. "The main idea of this article is that human pollution is a threat to the health of our planet."

Have students compare the exemplars and discuss with partners, "How are they similar? How are they different? Which is a stronger main idea statement, and why?"

Note for teachers: The progression across these exemplars goes from stating main idea as a general topic to stating main idea as a specific central idea in the text. Notice the progression in word choice and linguistic complexity. Exemplar A is an entry point for emerging ELs and emerging readers. Help students build from this general expression of main idea toward more nuanced understanding and communication of the central ideas in a text.

SCAFFOLD LANGUAGE DURING A TASK

BE STRATEGIC: Listen to student conversations to notice how students build on ideas together. Notice the sentence structures they use. Notice their word choice.

If your goal is to extend students' academic language use, then create frames from the effective structures students use. Then add one or more frames, as appropriate, to help stretch students to use more precise vocabulary and more sentence complexity or variety as appropriate to the task.

If your goal is to help students negotiate and build up ideas together, then model these conversation skills and provide prompts and frames initially to help students use the skills in their discussions.

Conversation Prompts and Linguistic Frame Examples for Main Idea

FOCUS	CONVERSATION PROMPTS	LINGUISTIC FRAMES
Describe Main Idea	What's the **gist** of the article? What is the **main idea**? What is the **central idea**? What is the **paragraph/article/passage mainly about**?	This text is **mostly about** _____. The author is **basically saying** that _____. The **central idea** of this text is that _____. The **main idea** of this text is that _____.

CONTINUED

CONTINUED ⟶

FOCUS	CONVERSATION PROMPTS	LINGUISTIC FRAMES
Negotiate Main Idea	What do you think? Do you agree?	That's one **detail**, but I don't think it's the **main idea**. I think _____. I disagree. I think the text is **mostly about** _____. Yes, the **text** is about (your partner's idea, a topic). I think we can get more specific by saying the **main idea** is _____.
Build Up a Main Idea Together	What can you add to my idea? How might we strengthen our main idea statement together?	You are right—that is one **important idea**. Another really **important idea** in this text is _____. I agree that's part of the **main idea**. We should also include _____. Let's revise this to say that the main idea is _____.

WORD BANK

BE STRATEGIC: Listen to the word choices students make to talk about the clues they use to talk about **main ideas** and **details**. Begin a word bank with their effective choices. Add new words to the bank and teach them to students, and encourage them to use these words as they discuss main ideas and details.

Concept Nouns (and Noun Phrases)

main idea	key idea	supporting details
central idea	details	

Nouns to Reference the Text

text	story	paragraph
article	biography	section
essay	memoir	stanza
passage	poem	line

TEACH LANGUAGE BEYOND A TASK

In addition to providing linguistic scaffolds *during* a task, it is valuable to provide designated language lessons that help students advance their use of academic English. Such designated English language development (ELD) lessons are most powerful when they intentionally connect to the language students need to thrive in core literacy.

UNPACK AN EXEMPLAR FOR WORD CHOICE

Use a model response to teach academic language for talking or writing about main ideas. For example:

Model Response: "The main idea of this article is that human pollution is a threat to the health of our planet."

Write the same sentence with blanks and collaborate to brainstorm other words or phrases that could be used to complete each blank:

"The _____of this _____ is that human pollution is a threat to the health of our planet."

Two word lists you might generate include the following:

main idea	article
central idea	text
key idea	essay

Use these lists to begin classroom word banks for talking about main ideas and referencing the text (e.g., *article*, *text*, *essay*, *poem*).

UNPACK AN EXEMPLAR FOR COMPLEX SENTENCE STRUCTURE

Exemplar of a Main Idea Sentence: "The main idea of this article is that human pollution is a threat to the health of our planet."

Underline the first part of the sentence. Notice that the first part of the sentence introduces the main idea. The second part of the sentence is the main idea and also could stand alone as its own sentence. Engage students in marking their own copy of this sentence or analyzing it on the board with you.

Erase the second part of the model and replace it with a blank for a linguistic frame. Structure think-write-pair-share to have students use this frame to create their own main idea statements about a text. Read and listen to responses to notice if they use this complex sentence structure, or other effective approaches to communicating main idea, effectively.

BUILD THE LANGUAGE OF PARAPHRASING

When discussing main idea, it is common for students to find a topic sentence in a text and read it aloud as the main idea. This requires receptive language in the forms of comprehension and analysis to determine *which* sentence is the main idea, but it doesn't require any productive language skills. Students just read what is in the text. Help students paraphrase by expecting it, modeling it, and structuring opportunities for students to paraphrase ideas from a text in their "own words."

Here are three great collaborative conversation tasks to engage students in building paraphrasing skills:

1. **READ:** Start with a source to paraphrase (e.g., a sentence, proverb, or paragraph relevant to your students and curriculum).

2. **COLLABORATE TO PARAPHRASE:** Have students collaborate with partners to discuss what it means in their own words, then use Color-Coded Writing to create a sentence that paraphrases the central idea(s) in their own words.

3. **COMPARE APPROACHES:** Next have each pair group with another pair and compare their two approaches to paraphrasing. Have the students discuss similarities and differences in word choice and sentence structure. As they discuss, read their responses and identify a range of three to five to share in the next step of this activity.

4. **SYNTHESIZE AS A WHOLE CLASS:** Project or post three to five different approaches that vary in word choice and/or sentence structure. This alone leads to many "ahas" as we often feel like there is only one way to say something when we attempt to paraphrase. It is inspiring to see the many options! Engage students in reflecting with a partner on how the approaches are similar or different. Guide the class in generalizing the tools we can use when we paraphrase (e.g., synonyms, word order).

Great Texts for This Routine

- **INTERNATIONAL PROVERBS:** Look up *dichos* or international proverbs online for models of single sentences of concise wisdom. Then have students contribute their own that they have learned in their families, in texts, or in multimedia. Choose one for the lesson routine above. The next time you do the routine, have each table group or pair of students choose their own proverb to paraphrase and share with the class. This is a win-win for building language *and* honoring students' values and backgrounds.

- **ANY TEXT YOU READ:** Anytime you are reading a text, you can stop, over the text, and have partners paraphrase the gist of what they read. For deeper analysis, have students think-pair-write-share and then compare some of the written approaches to show the diversity of how students paraphrase across the classroom.

QUESTIONS TO REFLECT AND ADAPT TEACHING

Watch students as they annotate and discuss main ideas and reflect on these questions:

- What are my goals for student learning (p. 206)? Which aspects of these goals can students now understand and do? Which are goals for growth?

- How do the scaffolds I use impact student engagement and learning? Do they advance or hinder student participation? Advance or hinder learning? Advance or hinder critical thinking? Advance or hinder language use?

- What shifts will I make in my teaching and scaffolds to build on the strengths I see in my students and to help them thrive with rigorous expectations?

Adjust scaffolds and supports continuously to build on strengths and help students realize increasing levels of self-direction and success.

QUICK GUIDE TO ADAPT SUPPORTS ACCORDING TO NEED

If . . .	Then . . .
Students struggle unproductively or are off task	⌃ Increase supports
Some students don't participate	⌃ Increase supports
Students struggle with a specific aspect of a task	⌃ Increase supports
Students actively engage in learning through challenge	*Keep this sweet spot!*
Students (above emerging EL) only copy your model	⌄ Decrease supports
Student responses are predictable or canned	⌄ Decrease supports
Students don't get to struggle, think, or problem-solve	⌄ Decrease supports
You want to assess how students approach a task	⌄ Decrease supports

---

NOTES

_____

_____

10.2 SELF-MONITOR AND USE CONTEXT CLUES

PURPOSE: We think about our own understanding as we read and figure out what is confusing so it makes sense.

EXPECT

What students will know and be able to do:

	LITERACY GOALS	LANGUAGE FOR SUCCESS
Self-Monitor	I can monitor my understanding as I read. I notice when I don't understand a word or a section of text.	I can read to understand a text and notice when I don't understand.
Use Context Clues	I can use context clues to figure out the meaning of new words or phrases in a text.	I can use words and phrases I do understand in a text to figure out the meaning of words I don't understand.

ENGAGE

Plan these tasks into your routine every time students read a text for literal meaning. Watch students during these tasks as a formative assessment before, during, and after teaching self-monitoring and context clues.

Use a three-step task to engage students:

1. *READ:* Students read a section of complex text used in grade-level instruction or a text at an instructional level used in small-group reading. The ideal text is not so easy that the reader reads it fluently without any need for strategies, and not so complex that the reader gives up trying to make meaning.

2. *ANNOTATE:* As students read, have them underline key ideas and circle unfamiliar words or phrases. Have them write a question mark next to a confusing section and/or a question in the margin.

3. *COLLABORATE IN CONVERSATION:* Have students discuss their initial understandings and confusions.

Find scaffolds for this task on pages 218–221. When your primary goal is assessment, use the minimal scaffolds needed to ensure students understand and can actively engage in the task. Then, as you repeat this routine with new texts, adjust based on what you observe to strategically support and challenge all students.

OBSERVE

What teachers watch and listen for as students read:

Literacy goals:

- When students reach an unfamiliar word or confusing section of text, do they skip it or try to figure it out?
- How do students approach figuring out an unfamiliar word or confusing section of text? Reread? Use context clues? Notice word parts? Use a dictionary or digital device to look it up?

Language:

- When marking the text is an option, create a safe environment for students to circle words they don't understand. Notice how many words students circle. Students need to understand 95 to 98 percent of words for independent success in making meaning from texts (Schmitt, Jiang, & Grabe, 2011). If they circle more than 5 percent of the words, use the tips in the personalization chart below.
- Notice also the words they circle; identify ones that have strong context clues to use for modeling or guiding practice with this strategy.

Conversations:

- Do students collaborate to figure out confusing sections or unfamiliar words in the text? How does the conversation support or interfere with understanding the text?

SUPPORT

Use what you learned from observing students to prioritize what you will teach and support to help them thrive with self-monitoring comprehension and using context clues to figure out the meaning of unfamiliar words.

PERSONALIZATION CHART

IF STUDENTS	THEN
Understand fewer than 95 percent of the words in the text	Use a text closer to the students' reading level to model and guide practice with self-monitoring and using context clues.
	To support access to grade-level complex texts, build background in the topic of the text, pre-teach vocabulary that cannot be figured out in context, and then prioritize a short chunk of the text (e.g., a meaningful, main idea sentence) that has strong context clues to model and guide practice with self-monitoring and context clues.

CONTINUED

CONTINUED ⟳

IF STUDENTS	THEN
Don't understand the concept of context clues	Use "build background" strategies to connect to students' prior knowledge and experiences, teach concept vocabulary, and model using context clues.
Struggle to articulate their thinking to partners when collaborating to figure out a new word	Use the "build background" strategy of modeling with an exemplar (p. 128) to model an effective collaborative conversation for this task. Use the "scaffold language" strategies of conversation prompts and linguistic frames on pages 220–221 of this chapter.

CHOOSE SUPPORTS STRATEGICALLY

This section offers you a menu of support options to *choose* or *lose* based on your students' ever-evolving needs. There are *way* too many options here to put into one lesson. Be strategic in choosing the supports that are most relevant to what your students need right now to build on what they already can do to excel in new ways.

To find the optimal level of supports, reflect critically on each option. For example, ask yourself, "Will this support help my students extend beyond what they can do on their own, or stagnate their growth or self-direction?"

Remember, differentiation is messy. Don't wait for perfection! Choose the supports you anticipate are the best fit right now, and then watch and listen to students as they engage to reflect and adapt your approach.

Use the headings in this section to choose supports based on why and when you use them to help students excel with self-monitoring and using context clues.

> Build Background
>
> Scaffold Language During a Task

These headings share titles with Chapters 5 and 6, respectively—a reminder that strategies here are examples of strategies introduced in those prior chapters now applied to this very specific context of helping students self-monitor and use context clues.

BUILD BACKGROUND

MODEL MONITORING FOR COMPREHENSION AS YOU READ

Model the following steps and strategies as needed to engage students in monitoring their comprehension as they read.

- Stop to reflect and reread when you don't understand. Use think-aloud: "I'm not sure I understand this part. I'm going to read it again." Reread and reflect.

- Annotate confusions. Choose one or more of the following to model and have students use: (1) circle unknown words, (2) write a question mark by a confusing section, and (3) write a specific question in the margin.

MODEL USING CONTEXT CLUES TO FIGURE OUT AN UNKNOWN WORD

Model using context clues to infer what a word or confusing section might mean. Reread a few sentences surrounding the confusion, underline parts that make sense, and use think-aloud to model making an inference about possible meaning: "I don't know what this means, so I'll look for clues to figure this out. From this clue [read clue], I think this might mean . . ."

TEACH CONTEXT WITH THE COGNATE

If you have ELs with academic language fluency with Spanish, French, Italian, Catalan, or Romanian, use the cognate from that language (e.g., *contexto* in Spanish) to teach the word *context* and phrase *context clues* using the cognate strategy (p. 124).

BUILD FROM A SPECIFIC FOCUS TO AN INTEGRATED TASK

Build from a focused read-annotate-discussion task that emphasizes one skill (e.g., circle unknown words) to an integrated task (e.g., discuss main idea and confusions) as students build confidence and success. The following tasks build from a specific focus to an integrated task. Choose the best starting place for your students and build from there:

A. *Identify Unfamiliar Words—Annotate*: Circle words you don't understand. Discuss choices with a partner: "Which words did you circle?" The teacher tallies selected words as students discuss, then guides the class in figuring out words together and/or teaches words that can't be figured out from the text.

B. *Figure Out an Unfamiliar Word Using Context Clues—Annotate*: Circle unfamiliar words. Discuss, "Which word should we figure out together? Which clues in the text can we use to figure out the meaning of the word? What might the word mean? If we cover up the word, what is another word that might make sense here?"

C. *Figure Out Confusions—Annotate*: Circle unfamiliar words and write a question mark or question next to confusing sections. Discuss, "Which aspects of the text are confusing? What do we want to better understand? Which clues can we use to make sense of a confusing part of the text or unfamiliar word?"

D. *Figure Out What We Understand (Gist) and Confusions—Annotate*: Underline main ideas, circle unfamiliar words, and write a question mark or question next to confusing sections. Discuss, "What is the gist of this text? Which words and sections are confusing? What meaning can we make from the confusing parts and unknown words?" (Note that this task synthesizes the skill of reading for main idea, emphasized earlier in this chapter. See pages 206–216 for support with this skill.)

MODEL DISCUSSING CONFUSIONS

Invite a student who is confident in conversation to join you in modeling a partner discussion to talk about confusing parts in the text. Practice in advance so your co-modeler is ready to disagree and/or build up ideas together. Start the conversation with a nonexample of main idea and model together. As a variation, use the fishbowl strategy (p. 60) to model and/or reflect on peer conversations about confusions.

SCAFFOLD LANGUAGE DURING A TASK

CONVERSATION PROMPTS AND LINGUISTIC FRAMES

Self-monitoring while reading is a silent strategy fluent readers use independently. Use peer conversations to make this thinking visible and collaborative and build students' oral language to clarify confusions together.

Recommendation: Start with one focus for the task and scaffolds. As students build fluency conversing with that focus, introduce additional focus areas into your reading routine.

FOCUS	CONVERSATION PROMPTS	POSSIBLE LINGUISTIC FRAMES
Identify Unfamiliar Words	Which words did you circle? Which words are confusing?	I circled _____. Which words did you circle? I don't know what _____ means. What do you think _____ means?
Figure Out a Word With Context Clues	What is one word we want to figure out? Which clues in the text can we use to figure out the meaning of the word? What might the word mean? If we cover up the word, what is another word that might make sense here? Look up the word in an English or multilingual dictionary and compare your assumption of the meaning to the actual definition.	I don't know what _____ means. Let's reread this section to figure it out. One clue that shows me the meaning of the word is _____. I think _____ might mean _____ because _____. Another word that would make sense here is _____.
Figure Out a Word With Word Parts	Which clues within the word (root, prefix, suffix) can help us figure it out? Is there a prefix? What's the prefix? Is there a root word? What's the root? What does the word ending or the way it is used in the sentence tell us about the part of speech?	I don't know what _____ means. Let's look for clues in the word to figure it out. The prefix is _____. I think this prefix means _____. The root of the word is _____. This root means _____. The suffix tells me this word is a (part of speech).

FOCUS	CONVERSATION PROMPTS	POSSIBLE LINGUISTIC FRAMES
Figure Out Confusions	What doesn't make sense? Which parts are confusing? Which words or phrases do I not understand? What do you think this means? Which clues can we use to figure out what this means?	This part is confusing to me. (Read the part of the text.) This might be saying that _____.

QUESTIONS TO REFLECT AND ADAPT TEACHING

Watch students as they self-monitor and use context clues and reflect on these questions:

Reflect:

- What are my goals? Where are students now in relationship to my goals?
- How do the scaffolds I use impact student engagement and learning? Do they advance or hinder student participation? Advance or hinder learning? Advance or hinder critical thinking? Advance or hinder language use?
- What shifts will I make in my teaching and scaffolds to build on the strengths I see in my students and to help them thrive with my rigorous expectations?

QUICK GUIDE TO ADAPT SUPPORTS ACCORDING TO NEED

If . . .	Then . . .
Students struggle unproductively or are off task	⬆ Increase supports
Some students don't participate	⬆ Increase supports
Students struggle with a specific aspect of a task	⬆ Increase supports
Students actively engage in learning through challenge	*Keep this sweet spot!*
Students (above emerging EL) only copy your model	⬇ Decrease supports
Student responses are predictable or canned	⬇ Decrease supports
Students don't get to struggle, think, or problem-solve	⬇ Decrease supports
You want to assess how students approach a task	⬇ Decrease supports

10.3 USE AFFIXES AND ROOTS TO FIGURE OUT UNKNOWN WORDS

PURPOSE: We use affixes and roots to figure out new words, make reading easier, and expand our vocabulary. Sixty percent of English words (and 90 percent of vocabulary in the sciences and technology) have Greek or Latin roots.

EXPECT

What students will know or be able to do:

	LITERACY GOALS	LANGUAGE FOR SUCCESS
Using Roots and Affixes	I use common, grade-appropriate Greek or Latin affixes and roots as clues to the meaning of a word (e.g., *precede*, *recede*, *secede*).	I can understand the most common grade-appropriate prefixes, suffixes, and roots. I can use affixes and roots to figure out the meaning of words. I can use part of the word (prefixes, suffixes, roots) and my prior knowledge to explain the meaning of a word in speaking and writing.

ENGAGE

What students do to learn and demonstrate current understandings with using affixes and roots to figure out unfamiliar words: Plan these tasks into each reading that includes new words with Latin affixes and roots and use them as formative assessment before, during, and after teaching the skill.

Preparation: Provide students with an unfamiliar word that contains familiar affixes or roots. Ideally, choose a word from a text all are reading and provide the sentence with the word. Eventually, engage students in finding these words for you each time they read. Have students then

1. *ANNOTATE* THE WORD: Circle the prefix, underline the root, and/or highlight the suffix.

2. DISCUSS YOUR ANNOTATION: Is there a prefix we recognize? What is it? What does it mean? Is there a root we recognize? What is it? What does it mean? Is there a suffix we recognize? What is it? What does it tell us about this word?

3. COLLABORATE TO USE AFFIXES AND ROOTS TO FIGURE OUT THE WORD MEANING: Which clues within the word (prefix, suffix, root) can help us figure out the meaning? What do you think the word means, and why? Justify your thinking with evidence from the word (prefix, suffix, root).

Find scaffolds for this task on pages 225–229. When your primary goal is assessment, use the minimal scaffolds needed to ensure students understand and can actively engage in the task. Then adjust based on what you observe to strategically support and challenge all students.

OBSERVE

What teachers watch and listen for as students read:

Literacy goals:

- Watch students as they annotate the word. Notice, do students identify a prefix? A root? A suffix?

- Listen as students discuss. Do they use the prefix, root, or suffix to figure out meaning together?

Language use:

- Do ELs with fluency in Spanish, French, or other romance languages notice and use cognates to figure out word parts or the meaning of words?

Collaborative conversations:

- When students get stuck, how do they respond? Do they problem-solve together, use outside resources, or give up?

- If students disagree, how do they work through the disagreement to influence one another's thinking and success with the task?

SUPPORT

Use what you learned from observing students to prioritize what you will teach and support to help them thrive in using (and discussing using) affixes and roots to figure out unknown words.

PERSONALIZATION CHART

IF STUDENTS	THEN
Have limited background knowledge of prefixes or suffixes	Use "build background" strategies in this chapter to teach the concepts and build language for the task(s).
Struggle to use affixes or roots to figure out word meaning	Use the "Model Reading Using Affixes and Roots" lesson on page 227 in this chapter.
Struggle to articulate their thinking to partners when collaborating to figure out a new word	Use the "build background" strategy of modeling with an exemplar (p. 128) to model an effective collaborative conversation for this task. Use the "scaffold language" strategies of conversation prompts and linguistic frames using examples from page 228 of this chapter.

CHOOSE SUPPORTS STRATEGICALLY

This section offers you a menu of support options to *choose* or *lose* based on your students' ever-evolving needs. There are *way* too many options here to put into one lesson. Be strategic in choosing the supports that are most relevant to what your students need right now to build on what they already can do to excel in new ways.

To find the optimal level of supports, reflect critically on each option. For example, ask yourself, "Will this support help my students extend beyond what they can do on their own, or stagnate their growth or self-direction?"

Remember, differentiation is messy. Don't wait for perfection! Choose the supports you anticipate are the best fit right now, and then watch and listen to students as they engage to reflect and adapt your approach.

Use the headings in this section to choose supports based on why and when you use them before, during, or beyond engaging students in using affixes and roots to figure out word meanings in collaboration with peers:

Build Background

Scaffold Language During a Task

Teach Language Beyond a Task

These headings share titles with Chapters 5, 6, and 7, respectively—a reminder that strategies here are examples of strategies introduced in those prior chapters now applied to this very specific context of helping students use affixes and roots to figure out, and discuss, word meanings with peers.

BUILD BACKGROUND

TEACH CONCEPT VOCABULARY

CONCEPT VOCABULARY	PART OF SPEECH	EXPLAIN	EXAMPLE(S)
affix	noun	A part of a word that changes the meaning of the word	Prefix: *pre-, un-* Suffix: *-s, -ing*
prefix	noun	An affix at the beginning of a word that changes the meaning of the word	*pre-* in **pre**dict *un-* in **un**happy
suffix	noun	An affix at the end of a word that changes the meaning or part of speech of the word	*-ful* in hope**ful** *-tion* in predic**tion**
root	noun	The most basic part of a word after you remove prefixes and suffixes	*hope* is the root of **hope**ful *dict* is the root of pre**dict**ion *happy* is the root of un**happy**

TEACH *PREFIX* WITH COMMON PREFIXES

Demonstrate the concept of *prefix* with a common prefix like *un-*. Write words using the prefix that students are likely to know on the board: *unsafe, unhappy, unafraid*. Have students reflect, "How are these words alike?" Underline *un-* and explain this is a prefix, a group of letters at the beginning of a word that influence the meaning of the word. Engage partners in discussing, "What might *un-* mean?" Clarify the meaning of *un-* and then have students apply their understanding of *un-* to figure out new words such as *unaware*, *unbelievable*, and *uncertain*. Repeat this routine with additional common prefixes to build background in the concept of prefixes and the most common English prefixes found in English words. Flip to pages 229–231 for a list of the most common English prefixes and additional lesson ideas.

TEACH *SUFFIX* WITH COMMON SUFFIXES

Write the words *hope*, *hopes*, *hoping*, and *hopeful* on the board. Have students reflect, "How are these words different?" Underline the suffixes *-s*, *-ing*, and *-ful* and explain that a suffix is a morpheme (a single sound spelled with one or more letters) added to the end of a word to change the meaning or form of the word. Flip to pages 231–232 for a lesson to teach the most common English suffixes.

USE COGNATES TO TEACH PREFIXES AND SUFFIXES

When students in your class know a romance language (e.g., Spanish, French, Italian), they have a strong advantage learning affixes and roots. When teaching the concept of prefixes or suffixes, use a cognate chart such as the following to show the similarities between the two languages. Even students who don't speak Spanish will benefit from analyzing this chart to find patterns (and learn Spanish words!).

Compare English and Spanish prefixes. Use cognates to learn new words!

PREFIX ENGLISH	WORD EXAMPLES	PREFIX SPANISH	WORD EXAMPLES
ex-	express export	ex-	expresar exportar
pre-	predict prevent	pre-	predecir prevenir
co-	collaborate coordinate	co-	colaborar coordinar
inter-	international interpret	inter-	internaciónal interpretar
under-	underline underestimate	sub-	subrayar subestimar
re-	review reunite	re-	repasar reunir

Compare English and Spanish suffixes. Use cognates to learn new words!

SUFFIX ENGLISH	WORD EXAMPLES	SUFFIX SPANISH	WORD EXAMPLES
-y	energy biography	-ía	energía biographía
-ic	academic basic	-ico	academico basico
-ly	perfectly secretly	-mente	perfectamente secretamente

SUFFIX ENGLISH	WORD EXAMPLES	SUFFIX SPANISH	WORD EXAMPLES
-tion	action addition nation	-ción	acción adición nación
-al	additional national	-al	adicional nacional
-ist	artist tourist	-ista	artista tourista
-ble	double possible	-ble	doble posible
-nce	tolerance independence	-ncia	tolerancia independencia

Model how to use a word cognate to figure out the meaning of affixes and roots. For example, the word *predict* in Spanish is *predecir*. Circle the prefix in each word and have students notice similarities. Underline the root in each word and have students discuss what *dict*/*decir* might mean. Spanish speakers have an advantage figuring out the root meaning as *decir* is a common word in Spanish meaning "to say." See page 124 for more on teaching cognates.

MODEL READING USING AFFIXES AND ROOTS TO FIGURE OUT WORD MEANING

1. Begin with an unfamiliar word containing a common prefix your students understand (e.g., *unjust*).

2. Model annotating a word to circle the prefix, underline a root, and/or highlight a suffix.

3. Model using the meaning of the prefix to figure out the word meaning. Think aloud, "I know the prefix *un-* means 'not,' so I think the word *unjust* must mean 'not just, or not fair.'"

4. Model identifying the suffix in a word and using the suffix to figure out the meaning or part of speech of a word. Think aloud, "I know *-ing* is a verb ending, so I think the word *retreating* might be a verb. *Retreat* is something you do. Now, let me look at the rest of the word, or context clues p. 216, to figure out the meaning."

DIFFERENTIATION TIP: For an easier first lesson, begin by only focusing on the prefix. When students are successful, repeat the same routine using the suffix. Finally, build to an integrated routine of analyzing both prefix and suffix in the word.

SCAFFOLD LANGUAGE DURING A TASK

All of the scaffolds in this section are to help students collaborate in conversation to identify affixes and roots in a word and use them to figure out word meaning.

CONVERSATION PROMPTS AND LINGUISTIC FRAME EXAMPLES

	CONVERSATION PROMPTS	LINGUISTIC FRAMES
Identify Affixes and Roots	Is there a prefix? What's the prefix? Is there a root word? What's the root? Is there a suffix? What's the suffix?	I circled the prefix _____. I think the prefix is _____. I think this prefix means _____. I underlined the root _____. I think the root _____ means _____. I highlighted the suffix _____. This suffix tells me the word is a _____ (part of speech).
Use Affixes and Roots to Figure Out Word Meaning	Which clues within the word can help us figure it out? Word bank of clues: *root, prefix, suffix* What do you think the word means, and why? Justify your thinking with evidence from the word (*root, prefix, suffix*).	I don't know what _____ means. Let's look for clues in the word to figure it out. I think the word _____ means _____ because _____. The prefix _____ means _____. The root _____ means _____. That makes me think the word could mean _____.

CATEGORIZE PREFIXES IN A GRAPHIC ORGANIZER

For the highest scaffold, pre-teach the prefixes students will use to figure out the word meaning in your lesson task. Post them in a digital or print chart students can reference easily during the task. See pages 231–232 for charts of the most common prefixes and suffixes.

PREFIX	MEANING	WORD EXAMPLES
dis-	not, opposite	disagree distaste dislike
pre-	before	prefix predict prepare

ROOT WORD TREE

When you want students to use roots to figure out the meaning of words, pre-teach common roots by engaging students in creating root word trees such as the following. Post student-created word trees as linguistic scaffolds for the task of using roots to figure out the meaning of a new word.

TEACH LANGUAGE BEYOND A TASK

In addition to providing linguistic scaffolds *during* a task, it is valuable to provide designated language lessons that help students advance their use of academic English. Such designated ELD lessons are most powerful when they intentionally connect to the language students need to thrive in core literacy.

TEACH THE MOST COMMON ENGLISH PREFIXES

Use a chart to teach the most common English prefixes. Complete the first examples as a model and guide students in using the prefix and meaning to figure out the meanings of word examples.

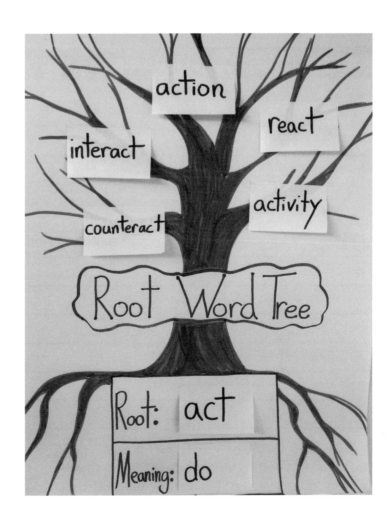

Chart Completed by Teacher

PREFIX	MEANING	WORD EXAMPLES
dis-	not, opposite	disagree distaste dislike
in-, im-, ir-, ill-	not, opposite of	inactive impossible illogical irresponsible

Once students understand the concept and how to use the chart, assign each pair or table group a prefix to research using dictionaries or digital sources. Have the students collaborate to find the meaning of the prefix and three to four words using the prefix that students are likely to understand.

Chart for the Collaborative Activity

PREFIX	MEANING	WORD EXAMPLES
dis-	not, opposite	disagree distaste dislike
in-, im-, ir-, ill-	not, opposite of	inactive impossible illogical irresponsible
pre-		
re-		
un-		
en-, em-		
non-		
over-		

Have students enter their findings on a class chart (e.g., digital shared document, Google Form, or chart posted on the wall). Schedule each group to teach their prefix to the class (e.g., one per day or two per week) in your classroom routine.

Completed Chart Example

PREFIX	MEANING	WORD EXAMPLES
dis-	not, opposite	disagree distaste dislike
in-, im-, ir-, ill-	not, opposite of	inactive impossible illogical irresponsible
pre-	before	prefix predict prepare
re-	again	return reread
un-	not	unsafe unkind unafraid
en-, em-	cause to	empower enjoy
non-	not, opposite of	nonfiction nonessential
over-	too much, above	overgrown overconfident overcome
sub-	under, lower	submarine subpar

TEACH THE MOST COMMON ENGLISH SUFFIXES

Use the same lesson sequence as above to have students learn and teach one another the most common English suffixes. Note that an online search is an easier way to look up words with a specific suffix than a print dictionary.

SUFFIX	MEANING	WORD EXAMPLES
-s, -es	plurals	chairs foxes
-ed	past-tense verbs	walked opened
-ing	present participle verb	walking opening
-ly	characteristic of	happily slowly
-er, -or	person	painter writer
-ion, -tion, -ation, -ition	process	exploration revolution
-ible, -able	can be done	agreeable
-er	comparison	smaller hotter
-ful	full of	joyful stressful

QUESTIONS TO REFLECT AND ADAPT TEACHING

Watch students each time they use affixes and roots to figure out word meanings, and reflect:

- What are my goals for student learning (p. 222)? Which aspects of these goals can students now understand and do? Which are goals for growth?

- How do the scaffolds I use impact student engagement and learning? Do they advance or hinder student participation? Advance or hinder learning? Advance or hinder critical thinking? Advance or hinder language use?

- What shifts will I make in my teaching and scaffolds to build on the strengths I see in my students and to help them thrive with rigorous expectations?

Adjust scaffolds and supports continuously to build on strengths and help students realize increasing levels of self-direction and success.

QUICK GUIDE TO ADAPT SUPPORTS ACCORDING TO NEED

If . . .	Then . . .
Students struggle unproductively or are off task	⮝ Increase supports
Some students don't participate	⮝ Increase supports
Students struggle with a specific aspect of a task	⮝ Increase supports
Students actively engage in learning through challenge	*Keep this sweet spot!*
Students (above emerging EL) only copy your model	⮟ Decrease supports
Student responses are predictable or canned	⮟ Decrease supports
Students don't get to struggle, think, or problem-solve	⮟ Decrease supports
You want to assess how students approach a task	⮟ Decrease supports

NOTES

_____

_____

_____

_____

_____

_____

_____

_____

_____

iStock.com/asiseeit

CHAPTER 11

READ TO ANALYZE AND INFER

"Children want to understand—they're hardwired to understand—and they love to be surprised and challenged by the depth and quality of their own and others' insights. We need to remember to ask the questions that lead to deeper understanding and then stand back! Their insights await us all."

—Ellin Oliver Keene (2011, p. 33)

WHAT AND WHY?

After reading for gist, reread the text with a specific focus that will engage students in thinking critically about the text or text content. Choose a specific comprehension emphasis according to your purpose for reading and instructional goals. Inference and analysis are students' opportunity to engage in the higher-level thinking and communication tasks of making and justifying claims with text evidence.

Reading to analyze and infer is the third step of the close reading routine.

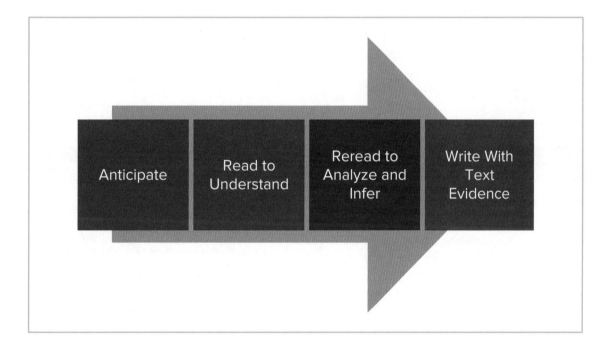

Anticipate → Read to Understand → Reread to Analyze and Infer → Write With Text Evidence

READ TO ANALYZE AND INFER GOALS IN THIS CHAPTER

11.1 Make Claims About Texts

11.2 Justify Claims With Text Evidence

11.3 Make Inferences About Characters

11.4 Make Claims About Theme and Author's Message

11.5 Compare and Contrast

11.1 MAKE CLAIMS ABOUT TEXTS

PURPOSE: I make claims to express my own opinions, interpretations, and conclusions about the texts I read. I communicate claims clearly in speaking and writing to strengthen the power of my voice in the world.

EXPECT

What students will know and be able to do:

	LITERACY GOALS	LANGUAGE FOR SUCCESS
Claim	I can make a claim about an academic topic or text.	I can express a claim about an academic topic or text in conversations with peers, and we can negotiate ideas together in extended conversations.
	I can write a topic sentence or thesis statement that makes a claim about a text.	I can write a topic sentence that communicates a claim using language appropriate for audience and purpose.
	For more nuanced goals by reading standard, see pages 256, 266, and 274 in this chapter.	For more nuanced goals by reading standard, see pages 256, 266, and 274 in this chapter.

ENGAGE

What students do to learn and demonstrate current understandings about making a claim: Typically, when students make claims about a text, the task is very specific (e.g., "What is the theme? What can you infer about the characters? What is the author's bias?"). For specific tasks and supports related to each, see each section in this chapter:

a. Characters (p. 256)

b. Theme (p. 266)

c. Comparisons Across Texts (p. 274)

The core routine for *any* specific focus is as follows:

1. **READ:** Read or reread a text or section of text with a specific comprehension focus (e.g., "What is the theme?").

2. **ANNOTATE:** Write "off the page" thoughts or interpretations in the margins of the text. Underline text evidence that supports your thinking.

3. **DISCUSS:** What inferences did you make? What "off the page" thoughts did you notice as you read (e.g., "What is the theme? How do you know?")?

When a text cannot be annotated, choose a favorite alternate option and make it routine. Alternate options include the following:

- Have students use a self-stick note to mark evidence in a text and reference (or read) the evidence when explaining the inference to peers.

- Use a double-entry journal (p. 79). Have students write their "off the page" thought/inference/conclusion on one side and text evidence to support it on the other.

- Have students write their inference in a graphic organizer (p. 290) and write each piece of text evidence on a self-stick note that will fit in the organizer.

Find scaffolds for this task on pages 238–241. When your primary goal is assessment, use the minimum scaffolds needed to ensure students understand and can actively engage in the task. Then, as you repeat this routine with new texts, adjust based on what you observe to strategically support and challenge all students.

OBSERVE

What teachers watch and listen for as students engage:

Literacy goals:

- Do students make claims that go beyond what is literally stated in the text? Do they add their own interpretation/insight/conclusion or just summarize what the text already says?

- Are students' claims logical based on the text and their own prior experience? (Remember to ask for explanation and listen to understand, as what seems illogical from your perspective may actually be a creative, high-level interpretation from a student's unique point of view.)

Language use:

- Do students express claims about higher-order thinking tasks clearly in speaking and writing?

- Do students use informal or formal language when making claims?

- What word choices do you hear? What vocabulary might students need to have strong word choice with this task?

- What grammatical choices do you hear? What types of grammatical structures do students need to effectively communicate with this task?

Collaborative conversations:

- Do students each just make a claim and stop talking, or do they engage in an extended conversation to build up ideas together?

SUPPORT

Use what you learned from observing students to prioritize what you will teach and support to help them thrive with making claims about texts and expressing their text-based ideas in speaking and writing.

PERSONALIZATION CHART

IF STUDENTS' INFERENTIAL CLAIMS	THEN
Are invisible: • Students are silent in peer conversations. • Students leave the page blank. • Students are focused on something else during the task. • Responses demonstrate confusion.	Use "build background" strategies to connect to students' prior knowledge and experiences, teach concept vocabulary, and model making claims. Use "scaffold language" strategies, as appropriate, to engage learners at the optimal level of challenge and support.
Are illogical: • The inference doesn't make sense based on the clues and student experiences.	Reflect: • Is the inference logical from the students' point of view and cultural frames of reference? Structure a peer conversation using linguistic frames that encourage students to justify their thinking. Listen to understand diverse perspectives, not a specific inference you consider "correct." If the student's response demonstrates confusion with the concept, use the strategies listed above.
Are formulaic, or always follow the same pattern	Don't provide linguistic frames, or provide increased variety in the frames you use to scaffold language. Teach the "Four Tiers for Making a Claim" language mini-lesson on page 241 in this chapter.

CHOOSE SUPPORTS STRATEGICALLY

This section offers you a menu of support options to *choose* or *lose* based on your students' ever-evolving needs. There are *way* too many options here to put into one lesson. Be strategic in choosing the supports that are most relevant to what your students need right now to build on what they already can do to excel in new ways.

To find the optimal level of supports, reflect critically on each option. For example, ask yourself, "Will this support help my students extend beyond what they can do on their own, or stagnate their growth or self-direction?"

Remember, differentiation is messy. Don't wait for perfection! Choose the supports you anticipate are the best fit right now, and then watch and listen to students as they engage to reflect and adapt your approach.

Use the headings in this section to choose supports based on why and when you use them before, during, or beyond engaging students in reading closely to analyze tasks to make a claim and discuss claims in conversations with peers:

Build Background

Scaffold Language During a Task

Teach Language Beyond a Task

These headings share titles with Chapters 5, 6, and 7, respectively—a reminder that strategies here are examples of strategies introduced in those prior chapters now applied to this very specific context of helping students make claims about texts in collaborative conversations or writing.

BUILD BACKGROUND

Use the "Frayer Model" strategy (5.2, p. 114) or "Direct Instruction Vocabulary Routine" (5.4, p. 120) to teach concept words: *claim* and *inference*.

BUILD BACKGROUND FROM FAMILIAR TO ACADEMIC CONTEXT

Build on students' natural ability to express opinions by having them make claims on a familiar topic, relevant to your class. For example, one middle school teacher on a committee for a school assembly asks her students to make claims about which music should be used to start and conclude the assembly. First, she structures think-pair-share to have students express their ideas and options and justify their thinking. Next, students engage in a whole-class discussion to share their opinions and negotiate ideas to reach an agreement on the songs to use. As students engage in discussing and negotiating for this relevant purpose, the teacher takes notes on how students make claims. For speedy note-taking, she omits the content and often just writes frames of what they say:

I think _____ should _____.

_____ is the best because _____.

_____ is inspirational. _____ is _____ (adjective).

The teacher posts these frames on the board and uses them to teach students the concept of making a claim. The next day, she builds on this background knowledge to have students make claims in an academic context. Students read a short text on pollution, then engage in think-pair-share to discuss the author's claims about pollution.

If helpful to advance participation and language use, update the frames from the previous day to relate to this task. For example, post these frames:

The author thinks _____ is important because _____.

Pollution is _____ (adjective).

BUILDING BACKGROUND FROM MULTIMEDIA TO TEXT

Build on students' natural ability to make inferences by having them first make inferences from a photo or video clip on a familiar topic. Then have them apply that knowledge to do a similar task to make an inference based on a text on a familiar topic. Use the same visuals and linguistic supports in both lessons to explicitly connect the two tasks.

COMPARE EXEMPLARS

Project the following four claims on the board:

1. I think carrots are the best snack.

2. You should eat carrots.

3. Carrots are healthy and delicious.

4. Carrots benefit our health.

Flip-to Tip: Flip to 5.8 (p. 130) to learn more about the strategy for comparing exemplars.

COLLABORATIVE CONVERSATION: Engage students in discussing with partners or table groups one or more of the following tasks:

COMPARE: Are these all claims? How are they similar? How are they different?

EVALUATE BASED ON AUDIENCE: Which claim would seem most natural for one friend to say to another friend after school? Why? Which claim would be the most effective topic sentence for an academic essay? Why?

TEACH LANGUAGE: Use the language mini-lesson "Four Tiers for Making a Claim" (p. 241) for explicitly teaching academic language for four different approaches to making claims.

ANALYZE CLAIMS IN MENTOR TEXTS

Engage students in analyzing claims in mentor texts such as letters to the editor, academic essays, TED Talk transcripts, or any other text that models effective communication of an opinion or claim. Have students first identify sentences that make a claim, then collaborate to evaluate their impact.

- Is the claim effective for this audience and purpose? Why or why not?

- What language choices does the author make? How do language choices affect the impact of this claim?

- Have students gather many different claims from text and compare them for language choices. How are these similar? How are they different? Which go together? How will we categorize these? Why? (Build background for this task by teaching the language mini-lesson "Four Tiers for Making a Claim.")

SCAFFOLD LANGUAGE DURING A TASK

The best linguistic scaffolds for making claims vary based on the task, topic, and audience. For specific tasks and linguistic supports related to making claims about main idea, characters, theme, and more, see each section of this chapter that follows such as the scaffolds for claims about characters on page 258. In the meantime, let's unpack the language structures of making claims that cut across any topic or context with a lesson to build language beyond the task. For each of the four tiers of making a claim, I embed word banks and response frames you can also use to scaffold language during a task.

TEACH LANGUAGE BEYOND A TASK

FOUR TIERS FOR MAKING A CLAIM

By analyzing hundreds of mentor texts, I identified four common approaches to making a claim. These are not the *only* ways to make claims but are a powerful first focus area for teachers helping academic English learners (ELs) speak and write with persuasion.

Use these four tiers as a learning progression first to help you identify the kinds of claims students are making, and then to help students expand their repertoire of language choices to be persuasive across diverse contexts.

1. **Explicitly state opinion using *I* as the subject and a thinking/feeling verb.**

    Example: <u>I think</u> bullying is the most pressing problem teens face today.

    Verb Bank: *think, believe, feel*

    Sample Response Frames: I think _____. I feel _____.
    I believe _____.

This tier is especially valuable in contexts where teachers want students to be explicit about the fact that they are expressing opinions.

This is the best place to start when helping students be aware that they are making claims, especially in primary grades and with students new to English. Students at all levels benefit from exploring these questions:

- When is it most appropriate and effective to use "I" statements to express opinions? When is it least effective?

2. **Explicitly state opinion using *should* or *should not* as a modal auxiliary verb.**

> Examples: Teens should not be allowed to use credit cards.
>
> Schools should encourage the use of mobile devices in daily lessons.
>
> Auxiliary Verb Bank: *should, should not, must, must not*
>
> Sample Response Frame: _____ should/should not _____.

3. **Implicitly state opinion using an adjective to show bias.**

> Example: It is inhumane to keep wild animals locked up in zoos.
>
> Adjective Word Bank: *kind, cruel, inhumane, humane*
>
> Sample Response Frame: It is _____ to _____.

Flip-to Tip: Flip to 6.4 (p. 148) to learn more about the "Sentence Chart" strategy.

This third tier is a specific way to show students how to express an opinion without using *I* as the subject or even using *should*. Instead of saying "Standardized testing should be banned," we say "Standardized testing is harmful."

4. **Implicitly state opinion using a verb to show positive/negative influence.**

> Example: Zoos harm the lives of innocent wild animals.
>
> Verb Bank: *harm, help, benefit, enhance*

Sample Sentence Chart to scaffold task to make claims about the effects of standardized testing:

SUBJECT	VERB	WHAT? WHEN? WHY?
Standardized testing	harms	
	hinders	
	helps	
	benefits	
	enhances	

Notice these four tiers of claims build from personal to academic, and from explicit to implicit. In academic contexts, where arguments are often more subtle and impersonal, the third and fourth tiers of making claims are often the most effective. This is not to say that these are always superior. In some contexts, telling it like it is with "I" statements is most effective, and other times using *should* or *should not* is the best way to communicate a value statement directly.

Always consider audience and purpose when determining which approach will be most effective to have an impact.

Differentiate Linguistic Supports: One Example

BRIDGING Light or No Support	Have students discuss claims via think-write-pair-share without linguistic scaffolds. Engage partners in analyzing the linguistic choices they made and revising claims to have a greater impact for this audience and purpose. COLLABORATIVE CONVERSATION PROMPT: How can we revise the claims we write to have the best impact on our audience?
EXPANDING Moderate Support	Build on students' successes with expressing opinions in the first person to have them speak and write claims without using "I" statements. Use the Tier III and IV examples and linguistic frames to teach these language structures. Engage students in collaborative conversation to practice using these language structures orally before applying them to academic writing. Collaborate with students to build word banks of persuasive adjectives and verbs relevant to the topic and task.
EMERGING Substantial Support	Emphasize first-person claims first. Use the Tier I examples and frames (e.g., "I think _____ is _____") to model and guide students in expressing opinions about familiar topics and texts. Provide word banks specific to the task. Use total physical response, choral response, and/or acting out to ensure students understand and fully engage in using the new language.

QUESTIONS TO REFLECT AND ADAPT TEACHING

Watch students each time they annotate and discuss. Reflect:

- What are my goals for student learning (p. 236)? Which aspects of these goals can students now understand and do? Which are goals for growth?

- How do the scaffolds I use impact student engagement and learning? Do they advance or hinder student participation? Advance or hinder learning? Advance or hinder critical thinking? Advance or hinder language use?

- What shifts will I make in my teaching and scaffolds to build on the strengths I see in my students and help them thrive with rigorous expectations?

Adjust scaffolds and supports continuously to build on strengths and help students realize increasing levels of self-direction and success.

QUICK GUIDE TO ADAPT SUPPORTS ACCORDING TO NEED

If . . .	Then . . .
Students struggle unproductively or are off task	⯅ Increase supports
Some students don't participate	⯅ Increase supports
Students struggle with a specific aspect of a task	⯅ Increase supports
Students actively engage in learning through challenge	*Keep this sweet spot!*
Students (above emerging EL) only copy your model	⯆ Decrease supports
Student responses are predictable or canned	⯆ Decrease supports
Students don't get to struggle, think, or problem-solve	⯆ Decrease supports
You want to assess how students approach a task	⯆ Decrease supports

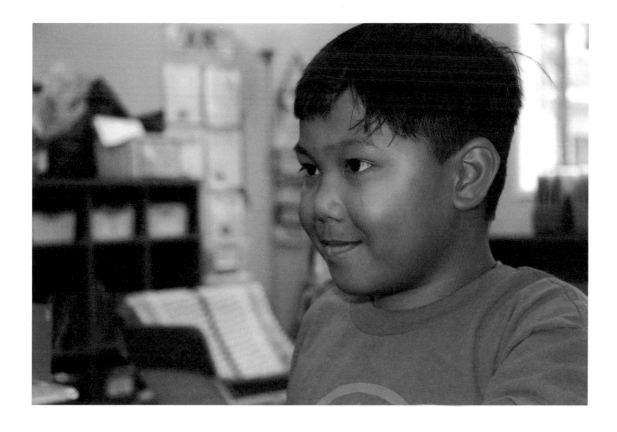

NOTES

_____

_____

_____

_____

_____

_____

_____

_____

_____

_____

11.2 JUSTIFY CLAIMS WITH TEXT EVIDENCE

PURPOSE: I support my claims with evidence to strengthen the power of my voice and help others understand my perspective. Justifying claims with evidence is a skill that helps me speak and write with influence in and beyond school.

EXPECT

What students will know and be able to do:

	LITERACY GOALS	LANGUAGE FOR SUCCESS
Support	I can **support** my thinking with evidence and explanation. I can quote or paraphrase relevant **text evidence**. I can **explain** how the text evidence supports my inference.	I can explain my ideas in conversations with peers and also ask questions to encourage peers to justify their ideas (e.g., "How do you know?"). I can write with expository organization to support my claims with evidence and explanation. I can use transitions and referents to connect ideas across sentences.

ENGAGE

What students do to learn and demonstrate current understandings about justifying a claim: Use this routine every time students reread a text to make inferences, draw conclusions, or respond to any open-ended task that requires students to make and justify claims. Watch students during these tasks as a formative assessment before, during, and beyond teaching the skill.

Use a three-step task to engage students:

1. *REREAD:* After reading a text (or excerpt) for literal comprehension, students reread it to make inferences or draw conclusions. This can be a broad task (e.g., making an inference) or a focused task guided by a specific question (e.g., "What is the theme?").

2. *ANNOTATE:* Write inferences in the margin or on a self-stick note. Underline clues in the text that support the ideas.

3. *COLLABORATE IN CONVERSATION:* Collaborate to make claims about the text, and justify thinking with text evidence and explanation.

4. *WRITE A SHORT RESPONSE (OPTIONAL):* When students demonstrate success with the first three steps and you have instructional time to bring the conversation to writing, have students write a paragraph of three or more sentences in which they write their claim and support their idea with text evidence and explanation. (See the next section for specific strategies and scaffolds for this step.)

Find scaffolds for this task on pages 248–253. When your primary goal is assessment, use the minimum scaffolds needed to ensure students understand and can actively engage in the task. Then, as you repeat this routine with new texts, adjust based on what you observe to strategically support and challenge all students.

OBSERVE

What teachers watch and listen for as students engage:

Literacy goals:

- Do students **support** their thinking with text evidence? When students reference text evidence, do they quote it or paraphrase in effective ways?

- Do students **explain** how the text evidence supports their inferences?

Language use:

- What language choices do students make when speaking and writing about inferences? What do these reveal about their strengths and needs with language essential for success with the task?

- In writing, do students connect ideas coherently within and across sentences in a paragraph? Notice, for example, their use of transitions (e.g., "*For example* . . .") or referents (e.g., "*This* shows . . .") to connect ideas across sentences.

Collaborative conversations:

- Are students contributing to the conversation and listening?

- Do students justify their thinking in conversations with peers? Do they prompt one another for evidence, as appropriate (e.g., "How do you know? What did you read that gave you that idea?").

SUPPORT

Use what you learned from observing students to prioritize what you will teach and support to help them thrive with justifying claims about texts in collaborative conversations and writing.

PERSONALIZATION CHART

IF STUDENTS	THEN
Don't yet demonstrate that they understand the concept of supporting a claim	Use "build background" strategies in this chapter to connect to students' prior knowledge and experiences, teach concept vocabulary, and model the concept of supporting a claim. Use "scaffold language" strategies, as appropriate, to engage learners at the optimal level of challenge and support.
Use text evidence that is irrelevant or random	Type or cut out examples of text evidence that are relevant and irrelevant to the task. Don't label the difference, but give the mixed-up examples to partners and have them collaborate to organize the evidence according to relevance. Use the fishbowl strategy on page 60 to model a conversation in which students negotiate the relevance of evidence, building up ideas together.
Use relevant text evidence but don't explain how the evidence supports the inference	Use the "Model Expectations With an Exemplar" strategy and example (5.7, p. 128). Use the "Collaborate to Contrast Exemplars" strategy (5.8, p. 130) to have students compare two exemplars, one with explanation and one without. Have students discuss, "Which is stronger, and why?"
Write their claim and support but you notice the argument seems choppy or lacks cohesion	Use the language mini-lesson example in 7.2 (p. 162) to teach language for cohesion. Create banks of phrases students might use to introduce text evidence and to explain text evidence.

CHOOSE SUPPORTS STRATEGICALLY

This section offers you a menu of support options to *choose* or *lose* based on your students' ever-evolving needs. There are *way* too many options here to put into one lesson. Be strategic in choosing the supports that are most relevant to what your students need right now to build on what they already can do to excel in new ways.

To find the optimal level of supports, reflect critically on each option. For example, ask yourself, "Will this support help my students extend beyond what they can do on their own, or stagnate their growth or self-direction?"

Remember, differentiation is messy. Don't wait for perfection! Choose the supports you anticipate are the best fit right now, and then watch and listen to students as they engage to reflect and adapt your approach.

Use the headings in this section to choose supports based on why and when you use them before, during, or beyond engaging students in reading closely to find evidence to justify claims and in effectively justifying their thinking in conversations and writing:

> Build Background
>
> Scaffold Language During a Task
>
> Teach Language Beyond a Task

These headings share titles with Chapters 5, 6, and 7, respectively—a reminder that strategies here are examples of strategies introduced in those prior chapters now applied to this very specific context of helping students justify claims with text evidence.

BUILD BACKGROUND

TEACH CONCEPT WORDS

Teach students the concept words *support*, *justify*, *text evidence*, and *explanation*. If students know most of the words and you only want to teach one in depth, use the "Frayer Model" strategy (5.2, p. 114). When teaching many, use the "Direct Instruction Vocabulary Routine" (5.4, p. 120). In tandem with teaching the words, build background in the concepts using other strategies in this section. To deepen word knowledge, use the "Teach Word Relationships" strategies (7.4, p. 166) with the same words throughout the week.

TEACH THE CONCEPT WITH TOTAL PHYSICAL RESPONSE

Hold your palm out horizontally like the top of a table. Say, "This is the claim." Have students create the same action with their hand and repeat, "Claim." Ask, "If I make this the top of a table but don't give it legs, what will happen?" Many may say it will fall down. Now use your other hand to create table legs to hold your top hand securely (I spread out my fingers and curve them up so the tips each support part of the table). Say, "This is the support." Have students make the same hand motions and repeat the concept words with you.

As you talk about claims or supports from this point forward, use the hand signals with your words. This helps build connections across the many different contexts in which you talk about support and claims.

TEACH *JUSTIFY* WITH THE COGNATE

If you have ELs with expertise in Spanish, French, Italian, Catalan, or Romanian, use the cognate from that language to teach *justify*. For example, write the Spanish cognate *justificar* under the word *justify*. Ask students to compare the words and notice the similarities and differences. Underline *justi* in both words and have students discuss what the meaning might be. Flip to p. 124 for more on using cognates.

BUILD BACKGROUND IN A FAMILIAR CONTEXT

Connect to students' prior knowledge for supporting claims with evidence by engaging them in making and justifying claims about a photo. For example, before having students make inferential claims about characters, I show them a photo of my friend Giovanny. I say,

I'm going to show you a picture of my friend Giovanny. I won't tell you anything about him. As soon as you see the picture, your mind will start making inferences. Be prepared to tell your partner what you infer about Giovanny and how you know.

Flip-to Tip: Flip to 5.7 on p. 128 for a routine and lesson specific to the goal of making and justifying claims with evidence.

CONVERSATION PROMPT: "What can you infer about Giovanny? How do you know? What evidence do you see in the picture to support your thinking?"

Encourage partners to listen to one another and ask for evidence. As an additional scaffold, write questions they might ask such as "How do you know?" and "What's your evidence?"

After students discuss with partners, use an equitable approach to call on individuals to share with the class. As they share, reinforce the concepts of "claim" and "support" with their examples and the concept hand signals (from the total physical response strategy above). Prompt for support, when needed.

Build from this background knowledge to engage students in making and justifying inferences about a text. Reread a section of a familiar text that focuses on a character or situation. Use the same conversation prompt: "What can you infer about _____? How do you know? What evidence do you see in the text to support your thinking?"

MODEL EXPECTATIONS WITH AN EXEMPLAR

Flip to 5.6 pages 128–129 for a routine and lesson specific to the goal of making and justifying claims with evidence.

SCAFFOLD LANGUAGE DURING A TASK

BE STRATEGIC: Listen first to student conversations to notice how they build on ideas together. Listen for language use.

If your goal is to extend students' academic language use, then create frames from the effective structures students use. Then add one or more frames, as appropriate, to help stretch students to use more precise vocabulary and more sentence complexity or variety as appropriate to the task.

If your goal is to help students negotiate and build up ideas together, then model these conversation skills and provide prompts and frames initially to help students use the skills in their discussions.

FOCUS	CONVERSATION PROMPTS	POSSIBLE LINGUISTIC FRAMES
Support With Text Evidence	How do you know? What evidence supports your idea? What clues gave you that idea?	One clue that shows me this is _____. I know this because I read _____. One detail that **shows** this is _____. The author **demonstrates this point** when (paraphrase text evidence).
Explain Your Thinking	What do you mean by that? Please explain how that evidence supports your idea.	This quote shows that _____. This means that _____. The quote "_____" **illustrates** that _____. It is **evident** that (repeat claim) when (describe a specific event or detail in text).

WORD BANKS

Nouns to Reference a Text

text   poem

passage   stanza

story   line

paragraph

SCAFFOLD EXTENDED CONVERSATIONS

To foster extended conversations and make supporting ideas central to your task, post questions partners can ask one another to elicit more information, such as "How do you know?" and "Tell me more." Flip to "Linguistic Frames for Conversations" (3.8, p. 70) for many examples of prompts and questions students can ask. Read these chorally with students and encourage them to use these in their conversations to ask one another for evidence and explanation to support their ideas.

GRAPHIC ORGANIZER

Use the graphic organizer "Claim and Justify With Text Evidence" on page 290 of the Appendix in tandem with close reading to annotate evidence to support claims. Model using the organizer to write a claim, gather evidence during close reading, and organize evidence to prepare for discussion or writing. Before you have students write, model using the organizer to write a short paragraph including the claim, evidence, and explanation.

CLAIM:
SUPPORT:
SUPPORT:
SUPPORT:

Write the theme in the claim section and specific evidence from the text to support this idea in each box below. You can use small self-stick notes to write evidence while reading, then transfer those notes to this organizer to prepare to write a short paragraph.

TEACH LANGUAGE BEYOND A TASK

In addition to providing linguistic scaffolds *during* a task, it is valuable to provide designated language lessons that help students advance their use of academic English. Such designated English language development (ELD) lessons are most powerful when they intentionally connect to the language students need to thrive in core literacy.

TEACH LANGUAGE FROM A TEXT: EMBEDDED TEXT EVIDENCE IN A SENTENCE

Use the "Teach Language From a Text" strategy (7.2, p. 162) to teach specific aspects of language relevant to this task. Use the example on page 162 for a lesson most students need to build cohesion when writing arguments. Or use the same mini-lesson routine to teach other relevant language goals such as the following:

TEXT-LEVEL LANGUAGE: Teach to organize claim, support, and evidence in a logical flow. Use the exemplar on page 128 to model expectations.

SENTENCE-LEVEL LANGUAGE: Teach how to embed a quote from the text within a sentence such as the following:

> The narrator shows her father's fear in the second stanza "that words might cut in two his daughter's heart (el corazón) and lock the alien part."

WORD-LEVEL LANGUAGE: Highlight the words in an academic argument that reference the text specifically (e.g., *text, stanza, line, poem*) and teach students to use precision and variety when referencing a text.

COLOR-CODED COLLABORATION

Pair students and give each pair two markers (different colors) and a sentence strip (or strip of paper long enough to write on one line). Have students collaborate to write a short paragraph in response to a text-dependent task (e.g., "What is the theme?") that includes a claim, text evidence, and an explanation. For shared accountability, each student uses a different-color marker, and both colors must be part of the final product. Post all paragraphs and have students do a gallery walk (p. 80) to look for specific examples of success criteria in each paragraph.

EXPAND CONCEPT VOCABULARY

Use modeling, the "Direct Instruction Vocabulary Routine" (5.4, p. 120), and "Teach Word Relationships" (7.4, p. 166) to teach additional concept vocabulary for making and justifying claims. Choose vocabulary that is most relevant to your local curriculum, tasks, and assessments. Words to consider include the following:

Counterclaim

Counter

Refute

Defend

Rationalize/rationale

Validate/valid

Oppose/opposite

Disclaim

These are great words for building consciousness about word roots and affixes! Create a word family chart with different forms of these words (see 7.4, p. 167, for the "Word Families" strategy) and analyze patterns to learn more about prefixes and suffixes (see 10.3, p. 222, for more on prefixes and suffixes).

QUESTIONS TO REFLECT AND ADAPT TEACHING

Watch students each time they annotate and discuss. Reflect:

- What are my goals for student learning (p. 246)? Which aspects of these goals can students now understand and do? Which are goals for growth?

- How do the scaffolds I use impact student engagement and learning? Do they advance or hinder student participation? Advance or hinder learning? Advance or hinder critical thinking? Advance or hinder language use?

- What shifts will I make in my teaching and scaffolds to build on the strengths I see in my students and help them thrive with rigorous expectations?

Adjust scaffolds and supports continuously to build on strengths and help students realize increasing levels of self-direction and success.

QUICK GUIDE TO ADAPT SUPPORTS ACCORDING TO NEED

If . . .	Then . . .
Students struggle unproductively or are off task	⤊ Increase supports
Some students don't participate	⤊ Increase supports
Students struggle with a specific aspect of a task	⤊ Increase supports
Students actively engage in learning through challenge	*Keep this sweet spot!*
Students (above emerging EL) only copy your model	⤋ Decrease supports
Student responses are predictable or canned	⤋ Decrease supports
Students don't get to struggle, think, or problem-solve	⤋ Decrease supports
You want to assess how students approach a task	⤋ Decrease supports

NOTES

_____

_____

_____

_____

_____

_____

_____

_____

_____

_____

_____

_____

11.3 MAKE INFERENCES ABOUT CHARACTERS

PURPOSE: I make inferences to make meaning from what I read. I support my inferences with evidence to strengthen the power of my voice and help others understand my perspective.

EXPECT

What students will know and be able to do:

	LITERACY GOALS	LANGUAGE FOR SUCCESS
Infer	I can make logical **inferences** about the characters. I can name the text and author in my claim.	I can discuss inferences about characters with peers using precise adjectives (e.g., to describe emotions or character traits) and evidence from the text. I can express my claim in writing using a complex sentence structure to include the title of the text and author's name with my claim.
Support	I can **support** my thinking with evidence and explanation. I can quote or paraphrase relevant **text evidence**. I can **explain** how the text evidence supports my inference.	I can express academic ideas in writing using expository organization to effectively state and support my claims. I can use transitions to connect ideas across sentences.

ENGAGE

What students do to learn and demonstrate current understandings about making an inference: Plan these tasks into your routine every time students read a text to make and justify inferences about characters. Watch students during these tasks as a formative assessment before, during, and after teaching self-monitoring and context clues.

Use a three-step task to engage students:

1. **READ:** Reread a story or section of a story to reflect on the emotions or personality traits of a character.

2. **ANNOTATE:** Underline clues that reveal character. Write ideas in the margin or on a self-stick note.

3. **DISCUSS:** "What can you infer about (character name)? How do you know?"

4. **WRITE A SHORT RESPONSE (OPTIONAL):** When students demonstrate success with the first three steps and you have instructional time to bring the conversation to writing, have students write a paragraph of three or more sentences in which they write a claim about a character and support their idea with text evidence and explanation. (See the next section for specific strategies and scaffolds for this step.)

When a text cannot be annotated, choose a favorite alternate option and make it routine. Alternate options include the following:

- Have students use a self-stick note to mark evidence in a text and reference (or read) the text evidence when explaining the inference to peers.

- Use a double-entry journal by drawing a line down the center of a page and writing inferences on one side and related text evidence on the other. Model and have students use this strategy.

- Have students write their inference in a graphic organizer (p. 290) and write each piece of text evidence on a self-stick note that will fit in the organizer.

Find scaffolds for this task on pages 258–265. When your primary goal is assessment, use the minimum scaffolds needed to ensure students understand and can actively engage in the task. Then, as you repeat this routine with new texts, adjust based on what you observe to strategically support and challenge all students.

OBSERVE

What teachers watch and listen for as students engage:

Literacy goals:

- Do students make logical inferences about the character? Are the inferences about emotions, character traits, or how a character changes in the text?

- Do students support their thinking with relevant text evidence? (Notice what they underline and what they say.)

- What aspects of the success criteria are goals for growth?

Language use:

- Do students engage in an extended conversation, building up ideas together?
- What word choices do you hear? What vocabulary might students need to have strong word choice with this task?
- What grammatical choices do you hear? What types of grammatical structures do students need to effectively communicate with this task?

Collaborative conversations:

- Are students contributing to the conversation and listening?
- Are students each saying one idea, or are they building up ideas together in an extended conversation?

SUPPORT

Use what you learned from observing students to prioritize what you will teach and support to help them thrive with making and justifying claims about characters in collaborative conversations and writing.

PERSONALIZATION CHART

IF STUDENT INFERENCES ABOUT CHARACTER	THEN
Are invisible: - Students are silent in peer conversations. - Students leave the page blank. - Students are focused on something else during the task. - Responses demonstrate confusion.	Use "build background" strategies to connect to students' prior knowledge and experiences, teach concept vocabulary, and model making claims. Use "scaffold language" strategies, as appropriate, to engage learners at the optimal level of challenge and support.
Are illogical: - The inference doesn't make sense based on the clues and student experiences.	Reflect: - Is the inference logical from the students' point of view and cultural frames of reference? Structure a peer conversation using linguistic frames that encourage students to justify their thinking. Listen to understand diverse perspectives, not a specific inference you consider "correct." If the student's response demonstrates confusion with the concept, use the strategies listed above.

IF STUDENT INFERENCES ABOUT CHARACTER	THEN
Show limited use of vocabulary in making inferences about characters (e.g., basic emotion words like *sad*, *happy*)	Use the "Word Banks" strategy (6.2, p. 144) to help students use more precise words during the task. See sample word banks in this chapter. Teach new vocabulary for character traits or emotions using the "Direct Instruction Vocabulary Routine" (5.4, p. 120).
Are logical inferences about individual characters	Increase rigor of text or tasks and/or remove scaffolds to foster increasing levels of academic achievement and student-directed learning. EXTEND LEARNING WITH A CRITICAL ANALYSIS OF CHARACTERS IN TEXTS: Engage students in a critical, comparative inquiry about how characters of different genders or ethnic or cultural backgrounds are portrayed in texts. Compare, for example, character traits of male and female characters in fairy tales. What trends do you observe? Compare portrayal of white and non-white people and populations in your history book or classroom literature. Do these texts reinforce negative or surface stereotypes or foster more nuanced understandings of deep culture and humanity?

CHOOSE SUPPORTS STRATEGICALLY

This section offers you a menu of support options to *choose* or *lose* based on your students' ever-evolving needs. There are *way* too many options here to put into one lesson. Be strategic in choosing the supports that are most relevant to what your students need right now to build on what they already can do to excel in new ways.

To find the optimal level of supports, reflect critically on each option. For example, ask yourself, "Will this support help my students extend beyond what they can do on their own, or stagnate their growth or self-direction?"

Remember, differentiation is messy. Don't wait for perfection! Choose the supports you anticipate are the best fit right now, and then watch and listen to students as they engage to reflect and adapt your approach.

Use the headings in this section to choose supports based on why and when you use them before, during, or beyond engaging students in discussing and writing inferences about characters in texts:

> Build Background
>
> Scaffold Language During a Task
>
> Teach Language Beyond a Task

These headings share titles with Chapters 5, 6, and 7, respectively—a reminder that strategies here are examples of strategies introduced in those prior chapters now applied to this very specific context of helping students make and justify inferences about characters in texts.

BUILD BACKGROUND

TEACH CONCEPT WORDS

Teach the concept words *character*, *trait*, and *emotion*. If students know most of the words and you only want to teach one in depth, use the "Frayer Model" strategy (5.2, p. 114). When teaching many, use the "Direct Instruction Vocabulary Routine" (5.4, p. 120). In tandem with teaching the words, build background in the concepts using other strategies in this section.

CONNECT TO STUDENTS' LIFE EXPERIENCES

Structure a think-write-pair-share task to have students share a character trait that describes them and evidence from their life that shows the trait. For example, "People may think I'm energetic when they see me salsa dancing." For additional support, provide a response frame: "People may think I'm _____ when they see me _____." Build from this to have students write a short paragraph describing something they say and/or do that shows a specific character trait. Be clear you want students not to write the trait adjective in the paragraph but to "show, not tell," via description. Collect all the paragraphs and then use these as classroom texts to have students make inferences and justify with text evidence. Tech tip: if you use Google Docs, have students submit their writing digitally so you can easily copy-paste-print their texts or share them digitally if all students have devices.

BUILD BACKGROUND FROM PICTURES TO TEXT

Build on students' natural ability to make inferences about characters by having them make an inference about a photo and justify it with evidence from the photo. Build from this success to have students make inferences about a character described in a short section of text. Use the same conversation prompts and scaffolds in both tasks to make the connection explicit between them.

MODEL READING CLOSELY
TO MAKE A CLAIM ABOUT A CHARACTER

FAMILIAR TO ACADEMIC: Begin teaching students to infer and justify with texts on familiar topics that connect to students' background knowledge and expertise beyond school. Build from these successes to have students make inferences about texts that introduce new topics and ideas to students.

PRIMARY LANGUAGE TO ENGLISH: The cognitive skill of making and justifying inferences transfers across languages. If emerging English speakers in your classroom are fluent in their home language and have at least one peer who speaks that language, it is valuable to have them explaining and justifying inferences in their primary language. Then, build from what students understand about inferences in their primary language to retell in English. Even if you don't speak the primary language, giving students time to process and discuss in the primary language before communicating in English is helpful.

FOCUSED QUESTIONS TO BROAD, OPEN-ENDED TASKS: Choose a task that is as broad as possible for every student to clearly understand what to do and engage with productive struggle or success. If students are new to inferring, annotating, discussing, and justifying with evidence, begin with a specific task. Move toward broad as students learn to increase the challenge *and* opportunity for diverse thinking and approaches.

Specific	How does (character name) feel in this moment? How do you know? What details in the text show you that (character name) feels this way?
	Would (character name) make a good friend? Why or why not?
	What can you infer about (character name)'s personality? Support your inference with evidence from the text.
	How did (character name) change in the story? Support your inference with evidence from the text.
	What can you infer about (character name)? Support your inference with evidence from the text.
Broad	What conclusion can be drawn about the characters of _____? Support your analysis with details from the text.

Notice that from specific to broad the prompts increase in challenge (from describing emotion to describing character change or conclusions) and in breadth of options (from one character in one moment to any character in the text). As students demonstrate success, build from specific tasks to broad prompts to empower students to thrive with more challenging, open-ended, and varied tasks.

SCAFFOLD LANGUAGE DURING A TASK

Be Strategic: Listen to their conversations to notice how students build on ideas together. Listen for language use. Only provide linguistic scaffolds that build on what students can do to help them use language in new or more effective ways for this task.

CONVERSATION PROMPTS AND LINGUISTIC FRAME EXAMPLES

FOCUS	CONVERSATION PROMPTS	POSSIBLE LINGUISTIC SUPPORTS
Character Feelings	How does _____ feel? Support your analysis with details from the text.	(Character name) feels _____. I infer (character name) feels _____ because _____. I infer _____. The author shows this with the clue _____.
Character Traits	What can you infer about _____ as a character? Would _____ make a good friend? Why or why not? What conclusion can be drawn about the narrator? Support your analysis with details from the text.	(Character name) is _____. I can infer (character name) is _____ because _____. Adjective bank for character trait words (e.g., *caring, uncaring, wise, foolish, courageous, fearful*)
Character Change	What does (character name) learn in the story? How is (character name) different by the end of the story?	In the book (title), (character name) learns _____. Verb bank for character growth (e.g., *learns, discovers, finds, grows, becomes*)
General Conclusion	What conclusion can be drawn about the characters of _____? Support your analysis with details from the text.	Students use any frames from above as appropriate to support the type of conclusion they draw.

LINGUISTIC FRAMES

Be strategic: Listen for the sentence structures students use in the first conversation and create frames from successful structures. Provide at least one additional frame as an option to increase complexity or add variety to language use.

The following frames are examples of tiered supports for this task that increase in complexity or challenge:

I think (character name) feels _____.

I infer _____ feels _____.

I infer _____ feels _____ because _____.

I infer _____. The author shows this with the clue _____.

WORD BANK

Be strategic: Listen for the emotion words students use in their first conversations. Write these to begin a word bank. Teach additional precise words and add them to the word bank. Continue to grow the bank across multiple texts and conversations as students learn new words.

Word Bank Examples

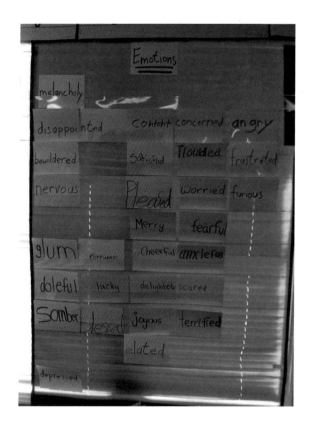

Adjectives to Describe Emotions	
depressed	joyful
afraid	confident
angry	pleased
nervous	calm

Adjectives to Describe Character Traits	
caring	uncaring
wise	foolish
generous	selfish
kind	mean

WORD WHEEL

Create a word wheel with eight to ten precise adjectives students can use.

GRAPHIC ORGANIZER

Use the graphic organizer "Claim and Justify With Text Evidence" on page 290 of the Appendix in tandem with close reading to annotate and make claims about characters. Model using the organizer to write a claim, gather evidence during close reading, and organize evidence to prepare for discussion or writing. Before you have students write, model using the organizer to write a short paragraph including the claim, evidence, and an explanation.

TEACH LANGUAGE BEYOND A TASK

In addition to providing linguistic scaffolds *during* a task, it is valuable to provide designated language lessons that help students advance their use of academic English. Such designated ELD lessons are most powerful when they intentionally connect to the language students need to thrive in core literacy.

TEACH WORD RELATIONSHIPS

Making claims about characters requires deep vocabulary knowledge for talking about traits, emotions, and change in a story. Beyond providing word banks, engage students in learning how the words relate to one another. Use the "Compare and Contrast" strategy (7.4, p. 166) to have students compare words for nuances in meaning (e.g., *disappointed* vs. *sad*) or the "Organize Words by Meaning" strategy (7.4, p. 166) to have students analyze connections across many related words (e.g., *selfish*, *generous*, *giving*, *altruistic*).

COLOR-CODED COLLABORATION

Pair students and give each pair two markers (different colors) and a sentence strip (or strip of paper long enough to write on one line). Have students collaborate to write a three-sentence paragraph about a character including a claim with support, text evidence, and an explanation. For shared accountability, each student uses a different-color marker, and both colors must be part of the final product.

SYNTAX SURGERY

Cut up a short three-sentence paragraph including a claim with support and explanation, such as the ones students wrote in the previous activity, into separate words. Have partners collaborate to reconstruct the paragraphs.

QUESTIONS TO REFLECT AND ADAPT TEACHING

Watch students each time they annotate and discuss characters. Reflect:

- What are my goals for student learning (p. 256)? Which aspects of these goals can students now understand and do? Which are goals for growth?

- How do the scaffolds I use impact student engagement and learning? Do they advance or hinder student participation? Advance or hinder learning? Advance or hinder critical thinking? Advance or hinder language use?

- What shifts will I make in my teaching and scaffolds to build on the strengths I see in my students and help them thrive with rigorous expectations?

Adjust scaffolds and supports continuously to build on strengths and help students realize increasing levels of self-direction and success.

QUICK GUIDE TO ADAPT SUPPORTS ACCORDING TO NEED

If . . .	Then . . .
Students struggle unproductively or are off task	⤊ Increase supports
Some students don't participate	⤊ Increase supports
Students struggle with a specific aspect of a task	⤊ Increase supports
Students actively engage in learning through challenge	*Keep this sweet spot!*
Students (above emerging EL) only copy your model	⤋ Decrease supports
Student responses are predictable or canned	⤋ Decrease supports
Students don't get to struggle, think, or problem-solve	⤋ Decrease supports
You want to assess how students approach a task	⤋ Decrease supports

---

11.4 MAKE AND JUSTIFY CLAIMS ABOUT THEME AND AUTHOR'S MESSAGE

PURPOSE: We talk and write about theme to deepen our understanding of literature. We learn to make claims and justify thinking with evidence to strengthen the power of our voices in and beyond the classroom.

EXPECT

What students will know and be able to do:

	LITERACY GOALS	LANGUAGE FOR SUCCESS
Make Claims About Theme	I can make logical **inferences** about the theme and author's message. I can cite the text and author in my claim.	I can communicate my inferences effectively in speaking and writing using precise vocabulary (e.g., general nouns to describe theme). I can express my claim in writing using a complex sentence structure to include the title of the text and author's name with my inference about theme.
Support	I can **support** my thinking with evidence and explanation. I can quote or paraphrase relevant **text evidence**. I can **explain** how the text evidence supports my inference.	I can express ideas in writing using expository organization to support my claims with evidence and explanation. I can use transitions and referents to connect ideas across sentences.

ENGAGE

What students do to learn and demonstrate current understandings about making and justifying a claim about theme: Plan these tasks into your routine every time students read closely to make and justify claims about theme. Watch students during these tasks as a formative assessment before, during, and after teaching self-monitoring and context clues.

Use a three-step task to engage students:

1. *READ:* Reread a text to identify theme or author's message.

2. *ANNOTATE:* As students read, have students underline clues related to theme or message. Students also write ideas about theme or message in the margins or on self-stick notes.

3. *COLLABORATE IN CONVERSATION:* Have peers discuss, "What is the theme of this text? What is the author's message? How do you know? What evidence supports your idea?"

4. *WRITE A SHORT RESPONSE (OPTIONAL):* When students demonstrate success with the first three steps and you have instructional time to bring the conversation to writing, have students write a paragraph of three or more sentences in which they state the theme of the story and support their idea with text evidence and explanation. (See the next section for specific strategies and scaffolds for this step.)

Find scaffolds for this task on 268–273. When your primary goal is assessment, use the minimum scaffolds needed to ensure students understand and can actively engage in the task. Then, as you repeat this routine with new texts, adjust based on what you observe to strategically support and challenge all students.

OBSERVE

What teachers watch and listen for as students engage:

Literacy goals:

- Do students make logical inferences?
- Do they use relevant text evidence?
- Do they explain their thinking?

Language use:

- Do students communicate theme in a way that their peers understand?
- What language choices do students make? What do these reveal about their strengths and needs with language essential for success with this task?
- If there are errors, do they interfere with communication?

Conversation:

- Do students deepen their thinking about theme through the conversation, or just each say one prepared idea and stop talking?
- Do students reference the text in conversation to support their ideas?

SUPPORT

Use what you learned from observing students to prioritize what you will teach and support to help them thrive with making and justifying claims about the theme of different texts in collaborative conversations and writing.

PERSONALIZATION CHART

IF STUDENT CLAIMS ABOUT THEME	THEN
Are invisible: • Students are silent in peer conversations. • Students leave the page blank. • Students are focused on something else during the task. • Responses demonstrate confusion.	Use "build background" strategies to connect to students' prior knowledge and experiences, teach concept vocabulary, and model making claims. Use "scaffold language" strategies, as appropriate, to engage learners at the optimal level of challenge and support.
Are illogical: • The inference doesn't make sense based on the clues and student experiences.	Reflect: • Is the inference logical from the students' point of view and cultural frames of reference? Structure a peer conversation using linguistic frames that encourage students to justify their thinking. Listen to understand diverse perspectives, not a specific inference you consider "correct." If the student response demonstrates confusion with the concept, use the strategies listed above.
Demonstrate vague or general word choice	Use the "Word Banks" strategy (6.2, p. 144) to help students use more precise words during the task. See sample word banks on pages 270–272 in this chapter. Teach concept nouns for communicating theme (e.g., *generosity, honesty, justice*) by modeling theme with each story you read and/or teaching words via direct instruction (5.4, p. 120).

CHOOSE SUPPORTS STRATEGICALLY

This section offers you a menu of support options to *choose* or *lose* based on your students' ever-evolving needs. There are *way* too many options here to put into one lesson. Be strategic in choosing the supports that are most relevant to what your students need right now to build on what they already can do to excel in new ways.

To find the optimal level of supports, reflect critically on each option. For example, ask yourself, "Will this support help my students extend beyond what they can do on their own, or stagnate their growth or self-direction?"

Remember, differentiation is messy. Don't wait for perfection! Choose the supports you anticipate are the best fit right now, and then watch and listen to students as they engage to reflect and adapt your approach.

Use the headings in this section to choose supports based on why and when you use them before, during, or beyond engaging students in reading closely for theme and collaborating to discuss or write about theme:

> Build Background
>
> Scaffold Language During a Task
>
> Teach Language Beyond a Task

These headings share titles with Chapters 5, 6, and 7, respectively—a reminder that strategies here are examples of strategies introduced in those prior chapters now applied to this very specific context of helping students collaborate to read for theme and communicate ideas about theme in speaking and writing.

BUILD BACKGROUND IN CONCEPTS

TEACH CONCEPT VOCABULARY WITH THE FRAYER MODEL

Student-Friendly Definition: The lesson or message the author communicates through a text	Characteristics: • A big idea • Something you interpret after reading the whole text • What the author wants you to learn or value
THEME NOUN	
Examples: The theme of the story is • Justice • Honesty • Courage • Determination The theme/message of this story is • Be yourself • Be kind to others • If you fail, try again	Nonexamples: The story is about • A bull • A bull who doesn't want to fight A theme is *not* a specific detail from the story. A theme is *not* stated in the text.

Flip-to Tip:
Flip to page 114 to learn more about the "Frayer Model" strategy.

TEACH THEME WITH THE COGNATE

If any students speak a language with a cognate for theme (*tema* in Spanish or Italian, *thème* in French), use the cognate and cognate routine on page 124 to teach the word. Flip to page 124 to learn the cognate strategy.

MODEL READING FOR THEME

Use think-aloud (p. 126) to model reading and reflecting to make inferences about theme of a story. Explain your idea for theme with evidence from the text. Many stories only have one or two really obvious themes. For this reason, model theme with one or two stories before having students discuss their own idea of theme with a *new* story.

Model explaining theme with a sentence. For example: "The story teaches us that it is important to treat people fairly."

Write other possible phrases for expressing theme (ideally that connect to stories the class has recently shared). Examples include the following:

- Courage is important.
- It is important to remember your family.
- Being kind is more important than being rich.

For higher levels of language use, model expressing theme with a general noun. For example, "Louis Sachar's novel *Holes* is a story about **justice**."

Post a word bank of other general nouns to describe theme such as the following:

justice	honesty	fairness
courage	friendship	determination
remembrance	discovery	acceptance
finding faith	loss of innocence	accepting love
understanding	overcoming prejudice	

ANALYZE EXEMPLARS TO IDENTIFY SUCCESS CRITERIA

Have students analyze an exemplar of a paragraph or short essay that includes a claim about theme and justification with text evidence and explanation to mark examples of the success criteria in that example. Marking tasks might include underlining the inference about theme, checking each example of text evidence, and highlighting phrases or sentences that explain the evidence.

EVALUATE AND COMPARE EXEMPLARS

Have peers **collaborate to compare two exemplars** including one that meets criteria and one that is missing some elements. Have them identify which is stronger and why.

SCAFFOLD LANGUAGE DURING A TASK

Be Strategic: Listen to their conversations to notice how students build on ideas together
Listen for language use.

FOCUS	CONVERSATION PROMPTS	POSSIBLE LINGUISTIC FRAME
Theme	What is the author's message? Support your analysis with details from the text. What does the author most want the reader to learn from this story? What is the author's **message**? What is the theme of _____?	The author's message in _____ is _____. _____ is a story about _____. The poem (title) communicates the idea that _____. _____ is about the importance of _____.

USE WORD BANKS TO ENHANCE WORD CHOICE ABOUT THEME

BE STRATEGIC: Listen to the word choices students make to talk about theme. Begin a word bank (including word phrases) with their effective choices. Add new words to the bank and teach them to students, and encourage students to use these words as they talk and write about theme.

Verbs and Verb Phrases to Express What a Text Communicates		
shows	expresses	reveals
communicates	helps readers understand that . . .	

For example, "The poem 'Bilingual/Bilingüe' <u>communicates</u> the power of knowing two languages."

General Nouns to Describe Theme		
justice	honesty	fairness
courage	friendship	determination
remembrance	discovery	acceptance
finding faith	loss of innocence	accepting love
understanding	overcoming prejudice	generosity

For example, "*The Giving Tree* is a story about generosity."

Nouns to Reference a Text

text   poem

passage   stanza

story   line

paragraph

Phrase Bank for Explaining Evidence

This shows that _____.

One example is _____.

GRAPHIC ORGANIZER

Use the graphic organizer "Claim and Justify With Text Evidence" on page 290 of the Appendix in tandem with close reading to annotate and make claims about theme and author's message. Model using the organizer to write a claim, gather evidence during close reading, and organize evidence to prepare for discussion or writing. Before you have students write, model using the organizer to write a short paragraph including the claim, evidence, and an explanation.

Vary Supports to Differentiate Theme: One Example

BRIDGING Light or No Support	Have students reread a text and annotate it with their thoughts about the theme or message. Have them write ideas in the margins and underline evidence that supports their thinking.
	Next structure peer discussions (group or partner) to have students share, negotiate, and build up ideas together about the message in the text.
	After students discuss, have them each write a short paragraph about theme.
EXPANDING Moderate Support	Assign the same task as above but chunk the task into parts and structure it with more modeling and scaffolds:
	First, annotate and discuss ideas for theme with a partner. Write a theme on a shared graphic organizer.
	Next, reread to find text evidence to support this idea. Write the evidence on small self-stick notes.
	Finally, organize the evidence in the graphic organizer and collaborate to write a justification of the theme that incorporates text evidence and explanation.
	Provide modeling, linguistic frames, and word banks when needed at each step.

<table>
<tr><td>EMERGING
Substantial Support</td><td>Begin with a familiar movie or text students have read in their primary language. Provide one linguistic frame (e.g., "The theme of this story is _____ ") and a bank of phrases that explain theme to complete the sentence. Teach the meaning of new vocabulary with action, illustrations, and/or cognates (e.g., *tema* is *theme* in Spanish). Guide choral repetition of options and have students choose from the options. Connect from this lesson to identify theme in other familiar stories or texts. Build and connect to the concept of theme in primary language when possible.</td></tr>
</table>

QUESTIONS TO REFLECT AND ADAPT TEACHING

Watch students each time they annotate and discuss theme, and reflect:

- What are my goals for student learning (p. 266)? Which aspects of these goals can students now understand and do? Which are goals for growth?

- How do the scaffolds I use impact student engagement and learning? Do they advance or hinder student participation? Advance or hinder learning? Advance or hinder critical thinking? Advance or hinder language use?

- What shifts will I make in my teaching and scaffolds to build on the strengths I see in my students and help them thrive with rigorous expectations?

Adjust scaffolds and supports continuously to build on strengths and help students realize increasing levels of self-direction and success.

QUICK GUIDE TO ADAPT SUPPORTS ACCORDING TO NEED

If . . .	Then . . .
Students struggle unproductively or are off task	⌃ Increase supports
Some students don't participate	⌃ Increase supports
Students struggle with a specific aspect of a task	⌃ Increase supports
Students actively engage in learning through challenge	*Keep this sweet spot!*
Students (above emerging EL) only copy your model	⌄ Decrease supports
Student responses are predictable or canned	⌄ Decrease supports
Students don't get to struggle, think, or problem-solve	⌄ Decrease supports
You want to assess how students approach a task	⌄ Decrease supports

---

11.5 COMPARE AND CONTRAST

PURPOSE: I compare and contrast ideas to make sense of what I read and connect ideas within and across texts. Making comparisons helps me think creatively and deeply about what I read and learn. I learn to communicate comparisons to share my unique insights with others.

EXPECT

What students will know and be able to do:

	LITERACY GOALS	LANGUAGE FOR SUCCESS
Compare Within Texts	I can compare and contrast ideas within an informational text. I can compare and contrast characters within a narrative.	I can read to both comprehend literal details and think about how ideas or characters are similar or different in texts. I can understand and use language to compare (e.g., *both*) and contrast (e.g., *however*) in conversations with peers.
Compare Across Texts	I can compare ideas, characters, or events across texts. I can compare how two different texts and authors present the same information. I can make text-to-text connections to deepen my understanding of what I read.	I can read closely to compare concrete topics (e.g., characters) and abstract ideas (e.g., text organization) across more than one text. I can communicate and understand comparisons about multiple texts in peer conversations.

ENGAGE

What students do to learn and demonstrate current understandings about comparing and contrasting: Tasks to compare and contrast vary by context and focus. Some everyday comparison tasks include the following:

EVERYDAY TASKS WITH COMPARE AND CONTRAST

Talk and Write About Reading

- Compare characters or events within or across stories.
- Compare texts.

Write for Audience and Purpose

- Write an informational text that involves a comparison.
- Compare two mentor texts (for organization, language use, or other aspects of craft). How are they similar or different?

Deep Learning

- Creative analogies: How is (a newly learned concept) like (a specific, unrelated object)? For example, after teaching photosynthesis, ask students to discuss, "How is photosynthesis like a power cord?"

Use a three-step task to engage students:

1. *READ/OBSERVE:* Gather information about similarities and differences. Optional: write notes on a Venn diagram.
2. *COLLABORATE IN CONVERSATION:* Have peers collaborate to compare. Discussion questions include "How are these similar?" and "How are they different?" Optional: collaborate to create (or revise) a Venn diagram to show your findings.
3. *COLLABORATE TO WRITE (OPTIONAL):* When instructional time allows, have students take their conversation to writing and collaborate to write a paragraph or short essay that synthesizes what they discussed.

Find scaffolds for this task on pages 276–282. When your primary goal is assessment, use the minimum scaffolds needed to ensure students understand and can actively engage in the task. Then, as you repeat this routine with new texts, adjust based on what you observe to strategically support and challenge all students.

OBSERVE

What teachers watch and listen for as students engage:

Compare and contrast:

- Do students identify and explain similarities?
- Do students identify and explain differences?
- Do students compare details/ideas/concepts within a text or across texts?
- Do students compare physical details and/or abstract ideas?

Language use:

- Do students use language of comparison (e.g., *both, and*) when comparing similarities in conversation and writing?
- Do students use language of contrast (e.g., *but, however, yet, bigger/smaller*) when contrasting differences in conversations and writing?

- When writing a paragraph or essay, do students organize the text effectively to compare or contrast ideas? What effective language choices do they make? What do these reveal about their strengths and needs with language essential for success in comparing and contrasting ideas in writing?

Collaborative conversations:

- Are students contributing to the conversation and listening?
- Are students each saying one idea or building up ideas together in an extended conversation?

SUPPORT

Use what you learned from observing students to prioritize what you will teach and support to help them thrive with making comparisons about ideas within or across texts in speaking and writing.

PERSONALIZATION CHART

IF STUDENT COMPARISONS	THEN
Are invisible: • Students are silent in peer conversations. • Students leave the page blank. • Students are focused on something else during the task.	Reflect: • Is the text I'm using engaging for this task? • Do students understand *why* it is valuable to learn this skill? • Do they understand *how* to do the task (in any language)? • Do they have the language to communicate their thinking with this task? Use "build background" and "scaffold language" strategies as appropriate to help all learners engage at the optimal level of challenge and support. Use engagement strategies from Chapter 2, as needed, to foster accountable participation.
Demonstrate confusion about the concept of comparing and contrasting	Use "build background" strategies in this chapter to connect to students' prior knowledge, teach concept vocabulary, and model how to compare and contrast.
Communicate ideas in phrases or simple sentences	Use linguistic frames and word banks on pages 279–281 of this chapter to scaffold language during the task. Teach language mini-lessons in comparison language on pages 281–282 of this chapter.
Don't show comparison language in writing	Use the "Teach Language From a Text" language mini-lesson (7.2, p. 162) to model how authors use comparison language in a text and help students apply their learning to writing and revising.

CHOOSE SUPPORTS STRATEGICALLY

This section offers you a menu of support options to *choose or lose* based on your students' ever-evolving needs. There are *way* too many options here to put into one lesson. Be strategic in choosing the supports that are most relevant to what your students need right now to build on what they already can do to excel in new ways.

To find the optimal level of supports, reflect critically on each option. For example, ask yourself, "Will this support help my students extend beyond what they can do on their own, or stagnate their growth or self-direction?"

Remember, differentiation is messy. Don't wait for perfection! Choose the supports you anticipate are the best fit right now, and then watch and listen to students as they engage to reflect and adapt your approach.

Use the headings in this section to choose supports based on why and when you use them before, during, or beyond engaging students in reading closely to compare ideas and in communicating their thinking in conversations and writing:

> Build Background
> Scaffold Language During a Task
> Teach Language Beyond a Task

These headings share titles with Chapters 5, 6, and 7, respectively—a reminder that strategies here are examples of strategies introduced in those prior chapters now applied to this very specific context of helping students compare and contrast ideas within and beyond texts in conversations and writing.

BUILD BACKGROUND

TEACH CONCEPT WORDS

Teach the concept words *compare, similar, alike, contrast,* and *different.* If students know most of the words and you only want to teach one in depth, use the "Frayer Model" strategy (5.2, p. 114). When teaching many, use the "Direct Instruction Vocabulary Routine" (5.4, p. 120). In tandem with teaching the words, build background in the concepts and build the words into task directions and linguistic frames. To deepen word knowledge, also use the "Teach Word Relationships" strategies (7.4, p. 166) with the same words throughout the week.

TEACH COMPARISON VOCABULARY WITH COGNATES

If you have ELs with expertise in Spanish, French, Italian, Catalan, or Romanian, use the cognate strategy on p. 124 to teach the words *compare, similar,* and *different.* For example, the Spanish cognates are as follows:

ENGLISH	SPANISH
compare	comparar
similar	similar
different	differente

BUILD BACKGROUND FROM LIFE EXPERIENCE TO TEXT

Build on students' natural ability to compare and contrast by having them first compare and contrast any two things relevant to their interests and background knowledge (e.g., two popular songs you can play in class, two sports kids play or watch, two foods). Build from this experience to have students compare two ideas or topics from a text or content learning. Use the same visuals (e.g., Venn diagram) and linguistic supports in both lessons to explicitly connect the two tasks. Remind students that even when we change the topic, the sentence structures and concept vocabulary we use to talk about similarities and differences are similar.

BUILD FROM STUDENTS' LANGUAGE CHOICES

Begin by engaging students in comparing two objects or concepts and listen for the comparison language they naturally use. Create response frames from their effective language choices (e.g., "_____, but _____"). Then build on these successes by teaching one or more sentence structures (e.g., "While _____, _____") they can use to compare ideas in new ways. Have them practice using the new language with peers in conversation and/or writing.

MODEL CLOSE READING TO COMPARE

Model rereading to compare ideas or concepts in a text. Model think-aloud and writing ideas into a Venn diagram ("I do"), engage students in collaborating to reread and add ideas to the diagram ("We do"), and check for understanding and give immediate feedback as needed to ensure all understand.

MODEL WRITING TO COMPARE

Model using the Venn diagram from the previous activity to write a paragraph that compares the ideas. Model writing the first part of the paragraph ("I do"), then have students collaborate to write the next part together as you check for understanding and give feedback ("We do").

ANALYZE EXEMPLARS TO IDENTIFY SUCCESS CRITERIA

Have students analyze an exemplar to mark examples of comparison language in the exemplar. Marking tasks might include highlighting sentences that compare or contrast two ideas within the sentence or underlining the words or punctuation in that sentence that tell the reader this is a comparison.

EVALUATE AND COMPARE EXEMPLARS

Have peers **collaborate to compare two exemplars** including one that effectively compares ideas and one that includes different ideas in different sentences without showing any connections between the ideas. Have them identify which is stronger and why.

SCAFFOLD LANGUAGE DURING A TASK

BE STRATEGIC: Listen first to student conversations to notice how they build on ideas together. Listen for language use.

CONVERSATION PROMPTS AND LINGUISTIC FRAME EXAMPLES

FOCUS	CONVERSATION PROMPTS	POSSIBLE LINGUISTIC FRAMES
Compare Similarities	Compare _____ and _____. How are _____ and _____ **alike**? How is _____ like _____? How are _____ and _____ **similar**? What characteristics do _____ and _____ have in **common**?	_____ have/are _____. Both _____ and _____ have/are _____. One similarity is _____, and _____ both _____. _____ and _____ are similar in that they both _____.
Contrast Differences	Contrast _____ and _____. How are they different? How is/are _____ **different from** _____?	_____ have _____, but _____ have _____. _____ are _____, **yet** _____ are _____. _____. Yet _____. _____. However, _____. _____. On the other hand, _____. _____. On the contrary, _____. _____ is different from _____ in that _____. While_____, _____. Although_____, _____. Even though_____, _____. Unlike_____, _____. Whereas_____, _____.

USE A VENN DIAGRAM

Use a **graphic organizer** to make the concept of comparison visual and to clearly differentiate the difference between similarities and differences.

Venn Diagram

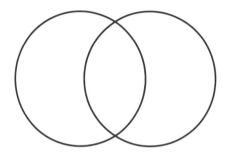

USE A MATRIX TO GENERATE AND ORGANIZE A TASK-SPECIFIC WORD BANK

A comparison matrix is especially valuable for comparing more than two things or for building specific categories of vocabulary for the comparison. For example, the following comparison matrix helps a class collaborate to generate adjectives about what they are comparing in four different categories. Use pair-share to have students generate ideas for the chart, and post what they share into one class chart that will also serve as a word bank when students compare these two items in speaking and writing.

		CHARACTERISTICS			
		FLAVOR	TEXTURE	SHAPE	COLOR
Items to be compared	Hot Cheetos				
	Doritos				
	Pretzels				

Use a **graphic organizer** to make the concept of comparison visual, and to clearly differentiate the difference between similarities and differences.

WORD BANKS

Be strategic: Listen to the language choices students make as they compare similarities and contrast differences. Begin a word bank using their effective choices. Build on student language to teach new words and add them to the bank. Post the word banks when students compare and contrast, and encourage students to use the words that best help them communicate their ideas.

Compare Similarities		
share	have in common	
similar	alike	like
both	same	equal

Contrast Differences		
different	difference	unlike
but	however	yet
on the contrary	while	

TEACH LANGUAGE BEYOND A TASK

In addition to providing linguistic scaffolds *during* a task, it is valuable to provide designated language lessons that help students advance their use of academic English. Such designated ELD lessons are most powerful when they intentionally connect to the language students need to thrive in core literacy.

TEACH COMPARATIVES AND SUPERLATIVES

Key Words and Phrases			
least	less	more	most
fewest	fewer		
smallest	smaller	bigger	biggest
quietest	more quiet	louder	loudest
earliest	earlier	later	latest

Sentences: *Lupe arrives to class **earlier than** any other student.*

*Ms. Jones is **the tallest** teacher in the school.*

TEACH WORD RELATIONSHIPS

Use the "Word Families" strategy (see 7.4, p. 167) to engage students in using the chart to deepen word learning with concept words. The following example emphasizes some of the word families related to comparisons.

Word Family Chart Example

VERB	NOUN	ADJECTIVE
compare	comparison	comparable
	similarity	similar
	difference	different

SYNTAX SURGERY

Use the Syntax (or Paragraph) Surgery strategy (7.3, p. 164) with a short paragraph that includes language to compare or contrast. Give each table group a copy of a paragraph scrambled into separate words or phrases, and have each team reconstruct the paragraph together.

QUESTIONS TO REFLECT AND ADAPT TEACHING

Watch students each time they annotate and discuss comparisons, and reflect:

- What are my goals for student learning (p. 274)? Which aspects of these goals can students now understand and do? Which are goals for growth?

- How do the scaffolds I use impact student engagement and learning? Do they advance or hinder student participation? Advance or hinder learning? Advance or hinder critical thinking? Advance or hinder language use?

- What shifts will I make in my teaching and scaffolds to build on the strengths I see in my students and help them thrive with rigorous expectations?

Adjust scaffolds and supports continuously to build on strengths and help students realize increasing levels of self-direction and success.

QUICK GUIDE TO ADAPT SUPPORTS ACCORDING TO NEED

If . . .	Then . . .
Students struggle unproductively or are off task	⌃ Increase supports
Some students don't participate	⌃ Increase supports
Students struggle with a specific aspect of a task	⌃ Increase supports
Students actively engage in learning through challenge	*Keep this sweet spot!*
Students (above emerging EL) only copy your model	⌄ Decrease supports
Student responses are predictable or canned	⌄ Decrease supports
Students don't get to struggle, think, or problem-solve	⌄ Decrease supports
You want to assess how students approach a task	⌄ Decrease supports

NOTES

_____

_____

_____

_____

_____

_____

_____

_____

_____

APPENDIX

GRAPHIC ORGANIZERS

CONVERSATIONS

- Collaborative Brainstorm

SUPPORTS

- Frayer Model
- Direct Vocabulary Instruction
- Word Family Chart
- Organize Cause and Effect
- Claim and Justify With Text Evidence

COLLABORATIVE BRAINSTORM

FRAYER MODEL

Student-Friendly Definition:	Characteristics:

Word:

Part of Speech:

Examples:	Nonexamples:

Use the word in a sentence:

DIRECT VOCABULARY INSTRUCTION

WORD	PART OF SPEECH	EXPLAIN	EXAMPLE(S)

Use the Word

WORD	PART OF SPEECH	EXPLAIN	EXAMPLE(S)

Use the Word

WORD FAMILY CHART

NOUN	VERB	ADJECTIVE	ADVERB

CAUSES

EFFECTS

CLAIM:

SUPPORT:

SUPPORT:

SUPPORT:

REFERENCES

Arreaga-Mayer, C., & Perdomo-Rivera, C. (1996). Ecobehavioral analysis of instruction for at-risk language-minority students. *Elementary School Journal, 96*, 245–258.

August, D., Carlo, M., Dressler, C., & Snow, C. (2005). The critical role of vocabulary development for English language learners. *Learning Disabilities Research and Practice, 20*(1), 50–57. http://doi.org/10.1111/j.1540-5826.2005.00120.x

August, D., & Shanahan, T. (Eds). (2006). *Developing literacy in second-language learners: Report of the national literacy panel on language-minority children and youth: Report of the national literacy panel on language-minority children and youth.* Mahwah, NJ: Erlbaum.

Beck, I., McKeown, M., & Kucan, L. (2002). *Bringing words to life: Robust vocabulary instruction.* New York, NY: Guilford Press.

Beers, K., & Probst, R. E. (2013). *Notice and note: Strategies for close reading.* Portsmouth, NY: Heinemann.

Bravo, M. A., Hiebert, E. H., & Pearson, P. D. (2007). Tapping the linguistic resources of Spanish/English bilinguals: The role of cognates in science. In R. K. Wagner, A. Muse, & K. Tannenbaum (Eds.), *Vocabulary development and its implications on reading comprehension* (pp. 140–156). New York, NY: Guilford Press.

Brophy, J. E. (1983). Research on the self-fulfilling prophecy and teacher expectations. *Journal of Educational Psychology, 75*(5), 631–661.

Calderón, M. (2007). *Teaching reading to English language learners, grades 6–12: A framework for improving achievement in the content areas.* Thousand Oaks, CA: Corwin.

California State Board of Education. (2012). *California English Language Development Standards Grades K–12.* Retrieved from http://www.cde.ca.gov/sp/el/er/documents/eldstndspublication14.pdf

Californians Together. (2015). *States report data on long-term English learners and students at risk of becoming long-term English learners.* Retrieved from https://www.californianstogether.org/tate-reports-data-on-long-term-english-learners-and-students-at-risk-of-becoming-long-term-english-learners/

Carrasquillo, A., & Rodríguez, V. (2002). *Language minority children in the mainstream classroom.* Clevedon, UK: Multilingual Matters.

Chenoweth, K., & Noguera, P. (2009). *How it's being done: Urgent lessons from unexpected schools.* Boston, MA: Harvard Education Press.

Cheuk, T. (2013). *Relationships and convergences among the mathematics, science, and ELA practices.* Refined version of diagram created by the Understanding Language Initiative for ELP Standards. Palo Alto, CA: Stanford University.

Cisneros, S. (1991). *The house on Mango Street.* New York, NY: Vintage.

Crawford, M., & Zwiers, J. (2011). *Academic conversations: Classroom talk that fosters critical thinking and content understandings.* Portland, ME: Stenhouse.

Darling-Hammond, L., & Schon, E. (1996). Who teaches and why: Dilemmas for building a profession for twenty-first century schools. In J. Silkula, T. Buttery, & E. Guyton (Eds.), *Handbook of research on teacher education* (pp. 67–101). New York, NY: Macmillan.

Duke, N. K., & Pearson, P. D. (2008). Effective practices for developing reading comprehension. *The Journal of Education, 189*(1/2), 107–122.

Emdin, C. (2016). *For white folks who teach in the hood . . . and the rest of y'all too: Reality pedagogy and urban education.* Boston, MA: Beacon Press.

Fang, Z., Schleppegrell, M., & Cox, B. (2006). Understanding the language demands of schooling: Nouns in academic registers. *Journal of Literacy Research, 38*(3), 247–273. http://doi.org/10.1207/s15548430jlr3803_1

Ferlazzo, L. (2016, September 9). "Why we teach now": An interview with Sonia Nieto. *Education Week.* Retrieved from http://blogs.edweek.org/teachers/classroom_qa_with_larry_ferlazzo/2016/09/why_we_teach_now_an_interview_with_sonia_nieto.html

Fisher, D., & Frey, N. (2013a). *Rigorous reading: 5 access points for comprehending complex texts.* Thousand Oaks, CA: Corwin.

Fisher, D., & Frey, N. (2013b). *Text-dependent questions: Pathways to close and critical reading.* Thousand Oaks, CA: Corwin.

Fisher, D., Frey, N., & Hattie, J. (2016). *Visible learning for literacy: Implementing the practices that work best to accelerate student learning.* Thousand Oaks, CA: Corwin.

Francis, D., Lesaux, N., & August, D. (2006). Language of instruction. In D. August & T. Shanahan (Eds.), *Developing literacy in second-language learners: Report of the National Literacy Panel on language-minority children and youth* (pp. 365–413). Mahwah, NJ: Erlbaum.

Gershenson, S., Holt, S. B., & Papageorge, N. W. (2015). *Who believes in me: The effect of student-teacher demographic on teacher expectations.* Kalamazoo, MI: Upjohn Institute for Employment Research.

Gersten, R., Baker, S., Shanahan, T., Linan-Thompson, S., Collins, P., & Scarcella, R. (2007). *Effective literacy and English language instruction for English learners in the elementary grades: A practice guide.* Washington, DC: U.S. Department of Education.

Gibbons, P. (2002). *Scaffolding language, scaffolding learning: Teaching second language learners in the mainstream classroom.* Portsmouth, NH: Heinemann.

Gibbons, P. (2009). *English learners, academic literacy, and thinking: Learning in the challenge zone.* Portsmouth, NH: Heinemann.

Goldenberg, C., & Coleman, R. (2010). *Promoting academic achievement among English learners: A guide to the research.* Thousand Oaks, CA: Corwin.

Goodenow, C. (1993). Classroom belonging among early adolescent students. *The Journal of Early Adolescence, 13*(1), 21–43. http://doi.org/10.1177/0272431693013001002

Hammond, Z. (2015). *Culturally responsive teaching and the brain: Promoting authentic engagement and rigor among culturally and linguistically diverse students.* Thousand Oaks, CA: Corwin.

Harvey, S. (2011). Comprehension to what end? In H. S. Daniels (Ed.), *Comprehension going forward: Where we are/what's next edited* (pp. 111–127). Porstmouth, NH: Heinemann.

Hattie, J. (2012). *Visible learning for teachers: Maximizing impact on learning.* New York, NY: Routledge.

Heritage, B. M. (2007). Formative assessment: What do teachers need to know and do? *Phi Delta Kappa, 89*(2), 140–145.

Hofstede, G., Hofstede, G. J., & Minkov, M. (2010). *Cultures and organizations: Software of the mind.* New York, NY: McGraw-Hill.

Holmes, J., & Guerra Ramos, R. (1995). False friends and reckless guessers: Observing cognate recognition strategies. In T. Huskin, M. Haunes, & J. Coady (Eds.), *Second language reading and vocabulary learning.* Norwood, NJ: Ablex.

Honigsfeld, A., & Dove, M. (2010). *Collaboration and co-teaching: Strategies for English learners.* Thousand Oaks, CA: Corwin.

Keene, E. O. (2011). Comprehension instruction grows up. In H. S. Daniels (Ed.), *Comprehension going forward: Where we are/what's next edited* (pp. 111–127). Portsmouth, NH: Heinemann.

Kinsella, K., & Singer, T. (2010). *Longman elementary dictionary and thesaurus: Pedagogical guide.* Essex, England: Pearson Education.

Lapp, D., Fisher, D., & Frey, N. (2012, September). Background knowledge: The instructional starting line begins with what students already know. *Voices From the Middle, 20*(1), 7–9.

Lauber, P. (1996). *Hurricanes: Earth's mightiest storms.* New York, NY: Scholastic.

LeMoine, N. (2007). *Meeting the needs of Standard English learning: Scaffolding access to core instructional curricula* (A concept paper). Los Angeles, CA: Los Angeles Unified School District.

LeMoine, N., & Soto, I. (2017). *Academic language mastery: Culture in context.* Thousand Oaks, CA: Corwin.

Marzano, R. (2004). *Building background knowledge for academic achievement.* Alexandria, VA: ASCD.

Maslow, A. H. (1943). A theory of human motivation. *Psychological Review, 50(4),* 370–396.

National Center for Education Statistics. (2013–2014). *First Look report.* Retrieved from https://nces .ed.gov/pubs2015/2015151/index.asp

National Governors Association Center for Best Practices & Council of Chief State School Officers. (2010). *Common Core State Standards.* Washington, DC: Author.

Noguera, P., Darling-Hammond, L., & Friedlaender, D. (2015, October). Equal opportunity for deeper learning. Deeper Learning Research Series. *Jobs for the Future.*

Noguera, P., & Wing, J. Y. (2006). *Unfinished business: Closing the racial achievement gap in our schools.* San Francisco, CA: Jossey-Bass.

Nuri-Robins, K., Lindsey, D. B., Lindsey, R. B., & Terrell, R. D. (2011). *Culturally proficient instruction* (3rd ed.). Thousand Oaks, CA: Corwin.

Oláh, L. N. (2008, October). Every teacher a language teacher. *GSE News.* Retrieved from http://www .gse.upenn.edu/review/feature/olah

Oxford Living Dictionaries. (2017). *Standard and non-standard English.* Retrieved from https:// en.oxforddictionaries.com/explore/standard-and-non-standard-dialects

Pearson, P. D. (1985). Changing the face of reading comprehension instruction. *The Reading Teacher,* 38(8), 724–738.

Pollock, T. (2012). Unpacking everyday "teacher talk" about students and families of color: Implications for teacher and school leader development. *Urban Education, 48*(6), 863–894.

Pullman, G. (1999). AAVE is not Standard English with mistakes. In R. Wheeler (Ed.), *The workings of language* (pp. 39–58). Westport, CT: Praeger.

Quezada, R. L., Lindsey, R. B., & Lindsey, R. B. (2012). *Culturally proficient practice: Supporting educators of English learning students.* Thousand Oaks, CA: Corwin.

Quinn, H. (2011). *Language demands and opportunities in relation to Next Generation Science Standards for ELLs: What teachers need to know.* Palo Alto, CA: Stanford Graduate School of Education. Retrieved from http://ell.stanford.edu/publication/language-demands-and- opportunities-relation-next-generation-science-standards-ells

Rosenthal, R., & Jacobsen, L. (1968). *Pygmalion in the classroom.* New York, NY: Rinehart & Winston.

Sachar, L. (2000). *Holes.* New York, NY: Dell Yearling.

Santos, M., Darling-Hammond, L., & Cheuk, T. (n.d.). *Teacher development to appropriate to support ELLs.* Palo Alto, CA: Stanford Graduate School of Education. Retrieved from http://ell.stanford .edu/publication/teacher-development-appropriate-support-ells

Saphier, J. (2017). *High-expectations teaching.* Thousand Oaks, CA: Corwin.

Schmitt, N., Jiang, X., & Grabe, W. (2011). The percentage of words known in a text and reading comprehension. *Modern Language Journal, 95*(1), 26–43. http://doi.org/10.1111/j.1540-4781.2011 .01146.x

Scieszka, J., & Smith, L. *The true story of the three little pigs.* New York: Viking Kestrel.

Serravallo, J. (2015). *The reading strategies book: Your everything guide to developing skilled readers.* Portsmouth, NH: Heinemann.

Singer, T. W. (2015). *Opening doors to equity: A practical guide to observation-based teacher learning.* Thousand Oaks, CA: Corwin.

Singer, T., & Zwiers, J. (2016, April). What conversations can capture. *Education Leadership. 73*(7). Retrieved from http://www.ascd.org/publications/educational-leadership/apr16/vol73/num07/ What-Conversations-Can-Capture.aspx

Staats, C., Capatosto, K., Wright, R. A., & Jackson, V. W. (2016). *State of the science: Implicit bias review.* Retrieved from http://kirwaninstitute.osu.edu/my-product/2016-state-of-the-science-implicit-bias-review/

Tatum, A. W. (2009). *Reading for their life: (Re)building the textual lineages of African American adolescent males.* Portsmouth, NH: Heinemann.

Taylor, H. (1991). *Standard English, Black English, and bidialectalism: A controversy.* New York, NY: Lang.

Thomas, W. P., & Collier, V. (2002). *A national study of school effectiveness for language minority students' long-term academic achievement.* National Association for Language Development in the Curriculum. Retrieved from https://www.naldic.org.uk/research-and-information/ research+summaries/collier-thomas.html

Valdés, G., Kibler, A., & Walqui, A. (2014, March). *Changes in the expertise of ESL professionals: Knowledge and action in an era of new standards.* Alexandria, VA: TESOL International Association.

Van Allsburg, C. (1984). *The mysteries of Harris Burdick.* Boston, MA: Houghton Mifflin.

van Lier, L. (2007). Action-based teaching, autonomy and identity. *Innovation in Language Learning and Teaching, 1*(1), 46–65. http://doi.org/10.2167/illt42.0

van Lier, L., & Walqui, A. (2012). *Language and the Common Core State Standards.* Palo Alto, CA: Stanford Graduate School of Education. Retrieved from http://ell.stanford.edu/publication/ language-and-common-core-state-standards

Vygotsky, L. S. (1978). *Mind in society: The development of higher psychological processes.* Cambridge, MA: Harvard University Press.

Walqui, A., & Heritage, M. (2012). *Instruction for diverse groups of ELLs.* Palo Alto, CA: Stanford Graduate School of Education. Retrieved from http://ell.stanford.edu/publication/instruction-diverse-groups-ells

Walton, G. M., & Cohen, G. L. (2007). A question of belonging: Race, social fit and achievement. *Journal of Personality and Social Psychology, 92*(1), 82–96.

Washburn, K. (2010). *The architecture of learning: Designing instruction for the learning brain.* Pelham, AL: Clerestory Press.

WIDA. (2012). *Amplification of the English Language Development Standards, Kindergarten–Grade 12*. Retrieved from https://www.wida.us/standards/eld.aspx

Williams, T., Perry, M., Oregón, I., Brazil, N., Hakuta, K., Haertel, E., . . . Levin, J. (2007). *Similar English learner students, different results: Why do some schools do better? A follow-up analysis, based on a large-scale survey of California elementary schools serving low-income and EL students.* Mountain View, CA: EdSource.

Zwiers, J. (2008). *Building academic language: Essential practices for content classrooms.* San Francisco, CA: Jossey-Bass.

Zwiers, J., O'Hara, S., & Pritchard, R. (2013, December). *Eight essential shifts for teaching Common Core standards to academic English learners.* Davis, CA: Academic Language Development Network. Retrieved from https://ncwpsummer2015.wikispaces.com/file/view/8%20Shifts%20 for%20Teaching%20CC%20to%20AELs%20-%20PDF%20(1).pdf/555035691/8%20Shifts%20 for%20Teaching%20CC%20to%20AELs%20-%20PDF%20(1).pdf

Zwiers, J., O'Hara, S., & Pritchard, R. (Eds.). (2014). *Common Core standards in diverse classrooms: Essential practices for developing academic language and disciplinary literacy.* Portland, ME: Stenhouse.

Zwiers, J., & Soto, I. (2017). *Academic language mastery: Conversational discourse in context.* Thousand Oaks, CA: Corwin.

INDEX

word bank tables, 147 (box)
See also Differentiation; Teaching, adapting
Syntax surgery, 148, 164–165, 202, 265, 282
Synthesis, 13–14

Talking Chips, 57
Tatum, Alfred, 27
Taylor, H., 27
Teachable moments, fishbowl and, 61
Teacher teams, 31. *See also* Colleagues,
    collaboration with
Teaching, adapting, 34–35
    for character inferences, 265
    for collaborative conversations, 69
    for compare and contrast, 282
    for identifying main ideas, 215
    for making claims, 243
    for self-monitoring/context clues, 221
    to struggle, 37, 38
    for supporting claims, 253
    for teaching affixes/roots, 232
    for theme, 273
    See also Supports, personalizing
Teaching, reflective, 12
    actions for, 36–37
    anticipation, 182–203
    close reading routine and, 178
    cycle for, 11 (figure), 33–38
    for ELs, 89
    reflection on, 36
    resources for, 39
    for supports, 95–98
Teaching language beyond a task, 190–191, 201–202
    for affixes/roots, 229–231
    approaches to making claims, 241–243
    for character inferences, 264–265
    for compare and contrast, 281–282
    linguistic scaffolds for making claims, 161
    for supporting claims, 252–253
Texts, choosing, 27–28
Theme, 30 (table), 266–273
Think-aloud, 126–127
Think-pair-share, 52
Think-pair-write-share, 54
Think-write, 67
Think-write-pair-share, 54, 194
Thomas, W. P., 8
Thumb Vote, 76–77
Tier II vocabulary, 120–122, 157 (figure)
Time, concept of, 23
Total physical response (TPR), 74, 76–77, 249
Tracking, 29–30
Traveling 4-by-4, 59
True Story of the Three Little Pigs, The (Scieszka), 148
Turn taking, for collaborative conversations, 67

Understanding, checking for, 73

Value, 10, 11
    of errors, 26, 140–141
    of nonstandard English dialects, 25
Valued, feeling, 20

Values, cultural, 22
Van Lier, Leo, 89, 176
Variety, routine and, 176–177
Venn diagram, 280
Visuals, 73
Vocabulary, 120
    direct instruction note-taking scaffold, 121 (figure)
    direct vocabulary instruction organizer, 120 (figure)
    direct vocabulary instruction routine, 120–122
    Frayer Model, 114–117, 118–119, 187, 269 (box), 286
    limitations of teaching, 157
    preteaching, 73, 114–117
    reflections on, 134
    teaching using cognates, 124–125
    TPR and, 76
    See also Academic language
Vocabulary, concept, 209–211
Vote With Your Feet, 77
Vygotsky, L. S., 94

Walqui, A., 89
Walton, G. M., 20
Washburn, K., 37, 112
What's in the Bag? 202
Word banks, 74–75, 89, 93, 99–100, 136, 139, 141,
    143 (box), 144 (box), 144–147, 145 (box), 146 (box),
    147 (box), 196, 200 (box)
    for character inferences, 259, 263, 263 (box)
    for collaborative conversations, 67–68, 144, 144 (box)
    for compare and contrast, 280–281, 281 (box)
    for details, 212 (box)
    differentiating using, 145 (box)
    for main idea, 212, 212 (box), 213
    for making claims, 242
    for making predictions, 188–189, 189 (box)
    question words, 198, 198 (box), 200 (box)
    for supporting claims, 251 (box)
    for theme, 268 (box), 270 (box), 271, 271 (box)
    See also Linguistic scaffolds
Word bank table, 146–147
Word choice, 144, 149, 213
Word families, 167
    graphic organizer, 288
Word relationships
    for character inferences, 264
    for compare and contrast, 282
Word wheel, 264
Wright, R. A., 19
Writing
    accountability in, 81
    collaboration for, 80–81
    digital vs. paper, 81
    and insights into proficiency, 98–99
    word banks for, 144
Writing, color-coded, 80, 118, 150, 177, 194
Writing online together, 81

"Yes, and," 25

Zone of proximal development (ZPD), 94
Zwiers, Jeff, 23, 37, 89

A SAGE Publishing Company

CORWIN HAS ONE MISSION: to enhance education through intentional professional learning.

We build long-term relationships with our authors, educators, clients, and associations who partner with us to develop and continuously improve the best evidence-based practices that establish and support lifelong learning.

THE PROFESSIONAL LEARNING ASSOCIATION

Learning Forward is a nonprofit, international membership association of learning educators committed to one vision in K–12 education: Excellent teaching and learning every day. To realize that vision, Learning Forward pursues its mission to build the capacity of leaders to establish and sustain highly effective professional learning. Information about membership, services, and products is available from www.learningforward.org.